More Advance Acclaim for *Lean Impact*

"Ann Mei Chang understands what it takes to create social impact on a massive scale. In this book, she lays out a clear course for developing more effective solutions to our greatest human challenges, including the persistence of extreme poverty, and most importantly ensuring they are able to reach millions."

—Sir Fazle Hasan Abed, Founder and Chairperson, BRAC

"Run, don't walk, to buy this book if you are interested in innovation or simply in finding solutions to our world's current problems. *Lean Impact* is smart and thoughtful, a mix of head and heart, practical and yet full of hope. Ann Mei Chang's wisdom will provide a useful guide for how to think, and more important, how to act."

—Jacqueline Novogratz, CEO, Acumen

"*Lean Impact* helps us all see a brighter future in fighting global poverty – by bringing lessons from innovation successes in the tech, NGO, and business worlds to bear on the world's biggest problems. It's a book anyone who cares about making change in the world should read and take to heart. I believe innovation and learning fast from mistakes is what will ultimately save the lives of at least 10 million children in the next decade and hopefully more."

—Carolyn Miles, President and CEO, Save the Children

"*Innovation* and *scale* are two of the hottest topics in the social sector today – yet that attention has not yet led to nearly enough breakthrough ideas achieving widespread impact. Ann Mei Chang's book *Lean Impact* explains why current approaches limit our impact and what we can do to fix that. Based on deep work across sectors, Chang offers fresh insights into how leaders can chart a path from innovation to impact at scale. An important read for all those seeking change – in the United States and around the world."

—Jeffrey L. Bradach, Managing Partner
and Cofounder, Bridgespan Group

"Ann Mei Chang's new book *Lean Impact* is a must-read for development professionals, policy-makers, and indeed anyone interested in ensuring more effective programs to lift people out of poverty. Chang brings a 'disruptive' sensibility garnered from her many years in Silicon Valley to the challenges of international development and poverty alleviation more generally. The development field has long needed fresh breezes of radically creative ideas. Chang delivers them in this immensely readable and practical volume."

—David Gordon, Senior Advisor and former Chairman,
Eurasia Group and former Director of Policy Planning,
US Department of State

"The most successful social enterprises continually iterate in pursuit of transformational change. *Lean Impact* demystifies the process of social innovation and makes it accessible to entrepreneurs and grant makers alike."

—Christy Chin, Managing Partner,
Draper Richards Kaplan Foundation

"*Lean Impact* distills the essence of social innovation into an accessible book, packed with practical examples. These approaches to design, test, iterate, and scale will accelerate our collective ability to bring breakthrough solutions to those who need them most."

—Michelle Nunn, President and CEO, CARE USA

"*Lean Impact* is indispensable. Ann Mei Chang challenges us to ask ourselves hard questions: Do you know how well your efforts are working? What improvements have you made in response to feedback? As the urgency for transformational impact grows for our planet and people, today's social entrepreneurs, nonprofits, philanthropies, and governments must embrace user-focused, hypothesis-driven experimentation. Ann Mei does a masterful job of sharing compelling and inspiring stories of what we can achieve when we put aside our biases and assumptions to design solutions that meet real needs."

—Victor Reinoso, COO, Independent Sector

"*Lean Impact* is going to be an essential reference for this generation of development workers. The book's many case studies provide both inspiring examples and cautionary tales that help explain in clear, actionable language how the independent sector can adapt Silicon Valley's playbook for growing and scaling innovation to build agile twenty-first-century social enterprises dedicated to creating more just, inclusive, and prosperous communities."

—Patrick Fine, CEO, FHI 360

"To tackle the intractable problems that our world faces today, we need effective methodologies for innovation. *Lean Impact* provides compelling tools and techniques for developing solutions with positive social impact that are highly complementary to human-centered design."

—Jocelyn Wyatt, CEO, IDEO.org

"From Silicon Valley to bureaucratic Washington DC to the poverty-stricken villages of the developing world, Ann Mei Chang chronicles an adventurous journey as she attempts to apply the innovative techniques learned in the high-tech world to the challenges of development cooperation. This book is a must-read for aspiring development professionals and any citizen who cares about the effort to support those trying to escape the shackles of poverty."

—Brian Atwood, Senior Fellow, Watson Institute, Brown University and former Administrator, USAID

"This book is a must-read for anyone seeking to have real impact in their communities and the world. It provides practical advice on how to define outcomes, measure impact, and demonstrate change. Ann Mei inspires leaders to deliver outcomes."

—Sonal Shah, Executive Director, Beeck Center for Social Impact & Innovation at Georgetown University

"For years innovation has lagged in the social change sector. This is starting to change but not nearly fast enough. *Lean Impact* is a timely wake-up call and a practical approach for social entrepreneurs and change makers everywhere. It should be required reading for funders and practitioners who are committed to bigger, better impact and smart solutions for our toughest challenges."

—Neal Keny-Guyer, CEO, Mercy Corps

"Innovation and smart risk-taking are the norm in Silicon Valley, but less so in the social sector. That's because of how we fund, account for costs, and tell stories. Ann Mei Chang, with a foot in both of these worlds, has given us a blueprint for how to do things differently. The result is required reading for philanthropists and leaders of nonprofits and a recipe for better conversations all around."

—Alix Zwane, CEO, Global Innovation Fund

LEAN
IMPACT

LEAN IMPACT

How to Innovate for Radically
Greater Social Good

ANN MEI CHANG

WILEY

Published by John Wiley & Sons, Inc., Hoboken, New Jersey.
Published simultaneously in Canada.

For general information on our other products and services or for technical support, please contact our
Customer Care Department within the United States at (800) 762-2974, outside the United States at
(317) 572-3993 or fax (317) 572-4002.

Wiley publishes in a variety of print and electronic formats and by print-on-demand. Some material
included with standard print versions of this book may not be included in e-books or in print-on-demand.
If this book refers to media such as a CD or DVD that is not included in the version you purchased, you
may download this material at http://booksupport.wiley.com. For more information about Wiley
products, visit www.wiley.com.

Library of Congress Cataloging-in-Publication Data:

Names: Chang, Ann Mei, author.
Title: Lean impact : how to innovate for radically greater social good / Ann Mei Chang.
Description: Hoboken, New Jersey : John Wiley & Sons, Inc., [2019] | Includes index. |
Identifiers: LCCN 2018031109 (print) | LCCN 2018033310 (ebook) | ISBN 9781119506645 (ePub) |
   ISBN 9781119506591 (Adobe PDF) | ISBN 9781119506607 (hardcover)
Subjects: LCSH: Social entrepreneurship. | Social responsibility of business.
Classification: LCC HD60 (ebook) | LCC HD60 .C4429 2019 (print) | DDC 658.4/063–dc23
LC record available at https://lccn.loc.gov/2018031109

Cover image: © lmnoom / Getty Images
Cover design: Wiley

Printed in the United States of America

V10004447_091218

*For the women who have been
my role models, mentors, and inspiration on this journey*

Florence, Elizabeth, Anne-Marie, Melanne, Sonal, Henrietta, Lona

Contents

Foreword

As the twenty-first century winds up its second decade, it's become more and more obvious – nearly to the point of becoming that rarely achieved thing, utter clarity – that innovation is no longer just a Silicon Valley buzzword. It's not even just a technology buzzword any more. Organizations of all kinds – business, political, educational, cultural, charitable – know the choice they face is to innovate or to die out. Groups that have social good at the center of their missions, which do so much critical work in the world and are always striving to do more, and do it better, have also realized that this kind of evolution is the key to fulfilling their goals. I've spoken to countless organizations of this kind over the years that are eager and ready to embrace innovation. They know it will make their urgent work more focused, efficient, and better directed towards problems that truly need solving. They also know that following a Lean Startup–style process of experimentation will lead them to uncover areas of concern that they might otherwise not discover – an invaluable tool when we're talking about poverty, hunger, health, safety, and so many other issues that need serious attention. There's no shortage of good to be done in the world, and no one knows that better than the people who are invested in making social impact.

What they haven't known, for the most part, is how to start innovating. That's why *Lean Impact* is such an important book. Most writing on innovation is aimed at the business world, in which different rules and politics are at play. *Lean Impact* dives headfirst into the work of social good and walks through its challenges and opportunities to explain how to innovate within them. It's comprehensive, totally straightforward, and illustrated with great stories about people who are already working in this way. Ann Mei Chang, whom I've known for many years, is the perfect person to write such a book. She learned all about innovation in Silicon Valley over the course of a twenty-year career and then made a truly inspiring pivot into non-profits and government. As the chief innovation officer and executive director of the US Global Development Lab at USAID, she had the awesome job of overseeing the Lab's work identifying the kinds of breakthrough innovations that have meaningful impact on peoples' lives, and also bringing in modern approaches and tools, including technology, to help transform the way development work is done around the world. As she says, she knew she had a lot to learn when she made the switch. She learned it well, and now, she's sharing that knowledge and experience with everyone who picks up this book.

Lean Impact is full of inspiring stories of organizations pivoting to meet the true needs of the people they serve. They're set all over the world – Indonesia, Liberia, Uganda, Kenya, El Salvador, India, Bangladesh, the United Kingdom, and right here in the United States. They range from a company that helps immigrants learn English based on data from customers about what they really wanted, to one that has so far provided 12 million solar lights to 62 countries and is aiming for more. There's a story about how a passion for pro-tecting orangutans led to the building of a local health clinic in Indonesia – a solution that would never have been arrived at without using Lean Impact techniques to discover that the real problem was a lack of local medical services. The list goes on and on: an innova-tion story that begins with something as simple as a soccer game; the evolution of a company that was founded to provide free eyeglasses into a force for political advocacy and policy change; a story about combating youth unemployment in South Africa; one about easier access to food stamps in California; and another about a housing and services network for the chronically homeless.

Along with all these real-life examples comes a ton of practical information about methods for working in the current system, new funding models, and even ways to start encouraging change from within. *Lean Impact* discusses the ways organizations can serve their two very different, but equally important, customers – funders and users – a crucial skill set for success in the world of social good. It also pays close attention to funders themselves – foundations, government agencies, philanthropists, impact investors, and donors – offering tools that will help them direct their aid in ways that best support the projects they're involved in. A book that explains this clearly and compellingly is a hugely important contribution.

I've had many conversations with funders who want to know how they can be more useful. More often than not, when I tell them they need to change the way they give grants and donations by funding actual outcomes rather than giving groups a large sum of money and waiting to see what happens at the end of a year (or two years, or more) they rarely call me again. Until now, this idea, and change of any kind, has simply seemed too radical a departure from the way things have always been done. *Lean Impact* will make it seem not only possible, but preferable. I'm thrilled to see the ideas in *The Lean Startup* used in these new, incredibly valuable ways, and to see how Ann Mei has developed and customized them to meet the particular needs of social innovation. Value and growth are the main dimensions of Lean Startup, and now a third one has been added: impact.

Impact is a critically important concept when it comes to social innovation, generally used in the context of measuring whether social interventions do or don't work. But conceptually, it's very similar to the problem of measuring success in a business before you have profits. That's why lean methods are so perfectly suited to this kind of work. The only real difference is that instead of talking about maximizing shareholder value, *Lean Impact* talks about maximizing social impact. An advance party of pioneers, some of whom you'll read about here, is already doing this, but we need more. This book is a way to help add to their numbers.

Lean Impact is not only transformational for the social sector, though. My hope is that people in other kinds of businesses and organizations will also pick it up and, after reading about the dedicated people and clear strategies whose stories Ann Mei has gathered, think about how the products and institutions they build affect the world. All of us have more to learn about how we make impact so we can move together into this new era.

—Eric Ries, author of *The Lean Startup* and *The Startup Way*

Introduction

As I lie on the roof of a small boat puttering down the Ywe River, drifting past lush vegetation punctuated by the occasional flash of bright gold from the stupa of a Buddhist shrine, my mind turns over a jumble of insights from an eye-opening day. I had arrived in the Irrawaddy Delta region of Myanmar the night before, after flying halfway around the world and bumping along for eight hours on largely unpaved roads. Following a restless night in the best local guesthouse listening to my neighbor's hacking cough through thin walls that rose a foot short of the ceiling, I had eagerly embarked on one of my first field visits to witness the noble work being done to fight global poverty.

Myanmar was at a critical juncture. Life was gradually returning to normal after the 2008 devastation of Cyclone Nargis, which had killed almost 100,000 people. Hope for a brighter future was swelling, following the release of pro-democracy leader Aung San Suu Kyi from house arrest and the first open parliamentary elections in decades. Yet, many people remained desperately poor, toiled on small family farms, and eked out an average income of less than two dollars a day. The program I was here to visit worked with some of these

Lean Impact: How to Innovate for Radically Greater Social Good, First Edition. Ann Mei Chang. © 2019 Ann Mei Chang. Published 2019 by John Wiley & Sons, Inc.

smallholder farmers in the delta region to improve their agricultural yields, and thereby their incomes.

My day started with an early three-hour boat ride to one of these villages. As I walked among the thatched huts and surrounding fields, the women and men proudly showed me their thriving crops of rice and vegetables. I also visited the cramped shack where local staff slept during the week so they could provide training on modern farming techniques, supply improved seeds, and help form farming collectives to achieve better economies of scale. The dedication of both the farmers and the staff was inspiring. Everyone was working tirelessly to make life better.

Back in town, the leadership team explained how the program was managed. On one wall of the office hung a large chalkboard, with a grid listing each of the villages down one side and all the planned activities, along with their associated targets, across the top. At the end of each week, the local staff would convene to review progress and tally the number of people that had been reached. It was a well-oiled machine.

But, breaking the cycle of poverty is incredibly complex, and we are far from having all the answers. So, I asked, how well were these efforts working? What improvements had been made to the program during the first two years? And, how could we help many more farmers? I got back a lot of blank stares.

I quickly learned that this isn't how it works. As with many global development programs, the entire design had been laid out years before in the original grant proposal, largely by staff at headquarters back in the United States. The job of the staff working in the delta was to execute on this plan and hit their quarterly targets, not to learn and improve. To make matters worse, the total number of farmers being reached by the multimillion-dollar program – perhaps several thousand – was tiny in a region of over six million people, roughly a third of whom were living below the poverty line.[1] Was

---

[1] "Ayeyarwaddy Region: A Snapshot of Child Wellbeing," UNICEF, n.d., accessed April 25, 2018, https://www.unicef.org/myanmar/Ayeyarwaddy_Region_Profile_Final.pdf.

it possible to do better? After the allotted four years, the program was slated to end whether it was working or not. Never mind if more help was needed there or in a neighboring area. The team could keep their fingers crossed for a new grant or another donor to take interest. Otherwise, it would be time to pack up and go home.

Back on the boat, as I soaked in the warm January sunshine, I thought that there had to be a better way. People are working so hard to make a difference, and yet their hands are tied. Executing a rigid, one-off program is no way to deliver the most impact for the most people. We could do so much more. Over the course of my subsequent travels to countries as far afield as Liberia, Uganda, Zimbabwe, Guatemala, India, and Mongolia, I saw a similar scenario repeated over and over again.

I decided to devote the second half of my career to understanding these perverse dynamics and finding a way to improve the system.

TWO WORLDS COLLIDE

This may seem like an unusual reaction. Most people return from field visits with a burning passion to help the people or habitats they have seen, not grapple with the bureaucratic processes and management philosophy behind the work. But, I'm an engineer.

Seven years ago, after over 20 years in the tech industry, I made a long-planned transition to spend the second half of my career trying to make the world a better place. That may sound trite, but it really was that simple. As much as I loved the challenges of building software, I knew I wanted to do something more meaningful in my life. The question was what. I certainly wasn't an expert in poverty alleviation, healthcare, education, conservation, human rights, or anything else that seemed to matter. And, having long ago moved from software engineering into management roles, I wasn't even particularly qualified to write code. Nevertheless, I plunged in with the sincere hope of finding a worthwhile way to contribute beyond merely stuffing envelopes.

This visit to Myanmar was one of the early steps in my learning process. If I would have any hope of making a difference, I knew I first had to understand the work being done on the front lines. I have been fortunate to have the opportunity to learn from some of the industry's best through my work in US government, at a top international nonprofit, and with the numerous partners of both.

Coming off eight years at Google, some of the Silicon Valley hubris had certainly rubbed off on me, for better or worse. Anything seemed possible. While I was leading the mobile engineering team in the late 2000s, turn-by-turn navigation was the number one feature request of mobile users of Google Maps. However, our path to market was stymied by a duopoly of map-data providers, who offered licenses for a flat fee but required an annual per user charge for navigation services. Not something we could afford for a free product. When we brought this dilemma to Google's cofounders, Larry and Sergey, they authorized an extraordinary effort: to drive all the streets in the world to build our own mapping database. The satnav industry, accustomed to charging users $5–10 a month for its services, was turned on its head.

Not only did I learn to think big, I also grew to appreciate the value of experimentation. Despite being an industry leader, Google doesn't rest on its laurels. Each day it runs hundreds of experiments to test both major and minor enhancements to its services. Although Google didn't invent web search, it out-innovated its competitors by testing, learning, and iterating faster. As a result, Google products are appreciably better today than they were last year or the year before.

It was this perspective that I brought with me to the Irrawaddy Delta. I couldn't help but ask, Is this working? Can we do better? Can we reach more people? And, is it possible to permanently transform the system?

Okay, I admit I was a bit naive. My boundless enthusiasm soon crashed squarely into cold reality. I quickly learned that social innovation – the development of better solutions to social and environmental challenges – is much harder than tech innovation. Funding constraints can severely limit experimentation. The needs of beneficiaries and the priorities of donors don't always align. Short-term wins are rewarded over long-term growth. Measuring social outcomes is much harder than counting clicks. And, taking risks has far greater implications when it involves real lives.

Yet I firmly believe that the same techniques for innovation that have fueled dramatic progress in Silicon Valley can be the basis for creating radically greater social good. Since my trip to Myanmar, I have found more and more pioneering organizations that are taking this approach and showing compelling results. Innovation doesn't have to be time consuming or expensive. In fact, by recognizing problems early we can *save* time and money.

Just as companies have a responsibility to maximize shareholder value, mission-driven organizations have a responsibility to maximize social benefit to society. After living in both spheres, I was inspired to write *Lean Impact* to share my belief that innovation can transform the world in the ways that truly matter.

THE LEAN STARTUP MOVEMENT

In almost every industry, companies have sought to emulate the dynamism of Silicon Valley that has made it a hotbed of innovation. Not only have technology advances upended almost every aspect of our lives, but year after year solutions to problems both large and small improve by leaps and bounds. Emblematic of this unrelenting pace of progress is Moore's law, which for more than 50 years has accurately predicted that the number of transistors on a chip would double every two years, delivering exponentially greater computing power. Why shouldn't we seek the same pace of progress when it comes to the world's toughest problems?

A burst of innovation in the software sector was unleashed in part by the transition from shipping software in shrink-wrapped boxes to releasing in the cloud. Time between updates has gone from a year or more to days or even hours. And, by virtue of being online, companies can immediately see how users respond. Software development has been transformed. Eric Ries popularized this new approach to continuous innovation in his 2011 bestselling book, *The Lean Startup*.[2]

Eric's goal was "to improve the success rate of new innovative products worldwide." With *The Lean Startup*, he succeeded in launching a global movement. Today, thousands converge at related conferences and summits, an industry of consulting and training services has arisen, and self-organized Meetups provide peer support and learning around the world. Eric's second book, *The Startup Way*,[3] squarely addressed the growing recognition that larger corporations must become more entrepreneurial or fall behind. And, increasingly, mission-driven organizations are being drawn to these same best practices to further their work.

INNOVATING FOR GOOD

Perhaps not surprisingly, a number of barriers make it more difficult to innovate for purpose rather than for profit. But if anything, accelerating our ability to deliver solutions that work better and faster, and reach scale, is even more important when it comes to social challenges. We're talking about improving and saving lives, not just releasing another app or making more bucks. It's time for us to reinvent our approach to social good for the twenty-first century.

What will people want and embrace? Can we make a more transformative impact? Is it possible to reach the scale of the enormous need? While we certainly don't have all the answers today, we have a responsibility do everything in our power to find them. To maximize our chance of success amid such complex challenges, we need a methodology to manage risk and accelerate learning.

---

[2] Eric Ries, *The Lean Startup: How Today's Entrepreneurs Use Continuous Innovation to Create Radically Successful Businesses* (New York: Crown Business, 2011).
[3] Eric Ries, *The Startup Way: How Modern Companies Use Entrepreneurial Management to Transform Culture & Drive Long-Term Growth* (New York: Currency, 2017).

The demand for social innovation is real. In a 2017 survey of 145 nonprofit leaders, the Bridgespan Group found that 80% considered innovation to be an "urgent imperative," but that only 40% believed that their organizations were set up for it.[4]

Lean Impact will challenge you to think bigger, by expanding your vision of the potential for change. Perhaps counterintuitively, it will also encourage you to start smaller and to accelerate learning by validating your assumptions before making larger investments. Above all, it will urge you to keep a laser focus on your mission, which may lead you beyond your initial solution or even institution. I hope you'll join me on this journey to blaze a path to greater impact and scale.

HOW THIS BOOK IS ORGANIZED

This book is divided into three parts: "Inspire," "Validate," and "Transform."

Part I, "Inspire," makes the case that audacious goals and a relentless drive to maximize impact are as important as, if not more important than, altruism in our pursuit of social change. When our current interventions fall well short of the problems we aim to tackle, we must look further for better solutions. New paths inevitably entail greater uncertainty, thus a scientific approach to iterative learning is needed to reduce risk and help us determine what works. We have a responsibility to society to do more.

Part II, "Validate," dives into the core of the Lean Impact methodology, detailing the process of continuous validation through a social innovation lens. Real-life examples from around the world will demonstrate how to increase the value you deliver to beneficiaries, identify engines that can accelerate growth, and maximize

---

[4] Nidhi Sahni, Laura Lanzerotti, Amira Bliss, and Daniel Pike, "Is Your Nonprofit Built for Sustained Innovation?" *Stanford Social Innovation Review*, August 1, 2017, https://ssir.org/articles/entry/is_your_nonprofit_built_for_sustained_innovation.

your resulting social impact. We'll also explore techniques to test assumptions and speed up your feedback loop using minimum viable products (MVPs).

Part III, "Transform," tackles the broader ecosystem that must be engaged for social good. Many intractable problems require a systems approach to address market and policy failures. One of the biggest barriers to social innovation is the nature of funding, which has the power to facilitate, but more often undermines, experimentation. And, for Lean Impact to take hold, organizations need a culture that embraces risk and rewards ambition. The book ends by considering how social purpose has become increasingly interwoven into business practices, investment options, career choices, and consumer purchasing. More and more real solutions will cross conventional boundaries.

WHO SHOULD READ THIS BOOK?

Whether you are a funder, service provider, entrepreneur, policy maker, academic, or champion of social good, you are here because you care about long-term sustainable impact. At the same time, we all face enormous pressure to help people who are suffering today, to generate immediate results and positive stories, or to simply keep the lights on. We are running so fast with so little that it's hard to imagine how we can possibly do more. Yet we must.

No meaningful social change happens in isolation. We work in complex systems that extend far beyond any one organization. In order for impact to stick, we must deploy interventions, raise funds, engage communities, reshape markets, change policies, and more. Thus, this book is intended for the full spectrum of people who seek to deliver greater social good through their professions, time, or money. Note that innovation is not just for startups. While we often associate the term innovation with scrappy social enterprises and disruptive technologies, it is equally essential for the continuous renewal and enhanced performance of existing programs and larger institutions.

Lean Impact will help those working to build and scale social interventions – from nonprofit staff to social entrepreneurs to corporate project managers – deliver dramatically better results. It will help those funding social good – from foundations to government agencies to philanthropists to impact investors – create the incentives that enable social innovation to thrive. It will help local, state, national, and international governments support measured risk taking and adopt more effective interventions for public good. And, amidst a rising tide of citizens inspired to contribute to society through their time, work, and money, it will help the broader public recognize the pathways that can maximize their own impact.

I don't claim to have all the answers. Rather, I hope to help us all ask the crucial questions that will steer us towards a more promising path forward. This book draws on my interviews and visits with over 200 organizations across the United States and around the world, with diverse roles and structures, tackling a wide range of social challenges. I have learned from and been inspired by their practical experiences, successes, and failures, and hope you will be as well.

For this journey, all you need is genuine curiosity and a readiness to take action. Even small steps can make a huge difference. If you're not sure where to start, turn to the next page.

Part I
Inspire

Chapter One

Innovation Is the Path, Impact Is the Destination

"Innovation" may be the most overused buzzword in the world today. As the pace of change continues to accelerate and our challenges grow ever more complex, we know we need to do something different just to keep up, let alone get ahead. Finding better ways to tackle the most pressing problems facing people and the planet is no exception. Over the past few years, the notion of innovation for social good has caught on like wildfire, with the term popping up in mission statements, messaging, job descriptions, and initiatives. This quest for social innovation has led to a proliferation of contests, hackathons, and pilots that may make a big splash, but has yielded limited tangible results.

So we should start by asking, What is innovation?

One unfortunate consequence of the hype has been that, in common parlance, innovation has often become conflated with invention. While invention is the spark of a new idea, innovation is the process of deploying that initial breakthrough to a constructive use. Thomas Edison's famous quote, "Genius is 1% inspiration, 99% perspiration," puts this in perspective. In other words, innovation is

Lean Impact: How to Innovate for Radically Greater Social Good, First Edition. Ann Mei Chang.
© 2019 Ann Mei Chang. Published 2019 by John Wiley & Sons, Inc.

the long, hard slog that is required to take a promising invention (the 1%) and transform it into, in our case, meaningful social impact. Social innovation involves iterative testing and improvement, refining business models, influencing partners and policy, fine-tuning logistics, and many other practicalities. Not as sexy as a big idea, but ultimately more important.

My colleague Peter Singer, CEO of Grand Challenges Canada, sums this up nicely when he observes, "Innovation is the path, impact is the destination." This reminds us to stay focused on the ultimate change we seek to make in the world – whether it's to alleviate suffering, end an injustice, or protect the environment. Innovation should be in service to that goal.

DELIVERING RESULTS

When a friend or charity asks you to donate to a cause, what is the pitch you typically hear? Perhaps a story about children who are suffering and need your help, or a terrible injustice that has to be set right? The organization is committed to addressing this devastating issue, so you dig deep into your pockets and give. The world praises both you and the charity for doing good. But, this is only the first step.

We should rightfully celebrate the commitment of mission-driven nonprofits, the generosity of philanthropists, and the sacrifices of dedicated staff and volunteers. And, we should applaud the social enterprises, impact investors, and triple bottom line companies who meld profit with purpose. But, we can't stop there. Results matter. We have a responsibility to deliver the most we possibly can, both for those who need our assistance and for those who entrust us with their time or money. True impact comes from engaging with both our hearts and our heads.

Lean Impact takes an uncompromising attitude towards maximizing social good, drawing inspiration from *The Lean Startup* and other modern innovation practices. At its core are the basic tenets of the scientific method – hypothesis-driven experiments that reduce risk and increase the pace of learning. By applying these techniques to validate perceived customer value, an engine for growth, and the ensuing societal benefit of our interventions, we can achieve greater impact at greater scale.

Despite its scientific basis, Lean Impact is not rocket science. It simply accepts that no solution is likely to be designed perfectly at the outset, particularly considering the innate uncertainty of working on complex problems in dynamic environments. Thus, rather than crafting an intricate plan in advance, a more adaptive and learning-oriented approach can achieve better results. By recognizing when the best path forward remains unclear, we can avoid deploying solutions that aren't wanted, don't work, or can't scale.

Even Silicon Valley doesn't always get this right. Prior to joining Google, I was the VP of engineering at an exciting, venture-backed startup. After years building an elaborate, beautifully polished online experience, we launched with great fanfare. Alas, it wasn't quite the instant hit we'd hoped. While a number of passionate users loved the product and some features showed real promise, major gaps in both the product design and the business model were quickly exposed. Unfortunately, we had spent almost all our capital to get to this point and were running out of cash. Soon I was laid off, along with half my team and most of the other executives. An interesting coda to this woeful tale is that Eric Ries, author of *The Lean Startup*, was among the engineers at the company. The experience proved to be formative for both of us.

The lessons from that failed startup are equally applicable to mission-driven work. In a similar way, we have a tendency to devise elaborate plans and expect them to succeed. The all-too-common nature of project-based funding encourages, and in some cases requires, a model of advanced planning within defined constraints. To apply for grants, organizations are typically expected to articulate compelling answers in detailed proposals that imply more confidence than is warranted. Of course, too often, that plan doesn't play out exactly as anticipated, sometimes leading to suboptimal results, outright failure, or, even worse, damaging unintended consequences.

Furthermore, these programs are usually confined to a predetermined timeframe and budget, rather than being designed to persist and expand over time. Even when they do succeed within their original parameters, they rarely lead to transformative impact.

Consider two possible ways to design a fictional car, as shown in Figure 1.1. The traditional plan–execute approach involves lengthy planning by engineers, product designers, industrial designers, and

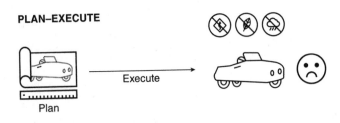

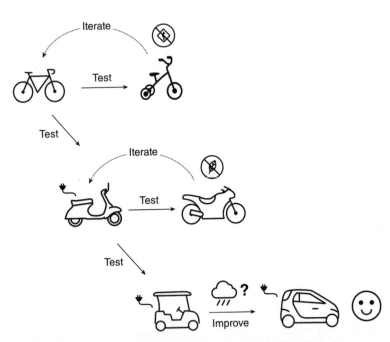

Figure 1.1   The plan–execute versus the test–iterate approach to design.

marketers, followed by an expensive manufacturing and production process. By the time the car ships years later, environmental standards may have changed or we may discover too late that customers find an open-air car too impractical. This is essentially what happened at my startup.

Instead, a test–iterate approach starts with the simplest possible prototype to see how users respond under real-world conditions. We could discover early that a three-wheeled design doesn't handle turns well or that environmentally sensitive customers won't buy a gas-guzzler, and iterate to take a different tack. Addressing other lessons, such as the need for protection from the elements, might only require an enhancement rather than an entirely new direction. Once we confirm we're on the right track, we can prudently take the next step and make a bigger investment to build a more sophisticated version. By identifying any mismatches early, we avoid wasting time and money and gain a higher confidence that the final product will be well received.

It is important to clarify that "lean" does not mean cheap. Rather, think of "lean" as cutting out the fat, or waste. Providing a tool is a waste if people don't use it for the intended purpose. Implementing a 10-part intervention is a waste when a 5-part version yields similar benefits. Deploying a one-off program for a thousand people is a waste if there could be a way to reach millions. The aim of Lean Impact is to find the most efficient path to deliver the greatest social benefit at the largest possible scale.

Okay, maybe that sounds good in the abstract, but what would this look like in reality?

LEARNING WHILE LEARNING

Testing and iterating to improve social outcomes may look some-what different from optimizing an online business, but it is based on the same underlying principles. Let's take a look at an education nonprofit, and how it made its transition to Lean Impact.

In the year 2000, hundreds of parents and community members in the San Francisco Bay Area came together in search of a better approach to high school education. They sought a replicable model to provide high-quality education to every child, regardless of background. Based on these discussions, Summit Public Schools opened its first school, Summit Preparatory Charter High School, in 2003. Founder and CEO Diane Tavenner had been a public school teacher herself and was passionate about preparing all students for future success. She set her sights high, with a goal of seeing 100% of her students graduate from college.

Eight years later, as Summit Prep's first cohort completed college, the results were impressive and significantly better than the national average, but fell short of Diane's goal. Many students needed more intensive academic preparation, and success in college often hinged on skills, such as persevering in the face of obstacles, that Summit's high-support environment didn't foster.

While she felt pressure to keep scaling based on this initial success, Diane saw the results as an opportunity to rethink Summit's educational model. But waiting for years to see the results of each high school cohort would be way too slow. She realized that she had to change the culture, tools, and processes to enable a faster iteration cycle if she was going to make the kind of shift she needed. So, rather than deciding on a particular set of interventions up front, she focused on embedding a culture and process for constant feedback and improvement. Diane and her team reviewed learning best practices and reflected on the skills, knowledge, and habits that lead to a fulfilling life. They also read *The Lean Startup*.

Over the course of 57 week-long variations with 400 students for two hours a day, Summit iterated on the duration, frequency, sequence, and structure of class elements, balancing a mix of teacher-led lessons, Khan Academy online content and exercises, one-on-one tutoring, and small-group interactive projects. Each week, the team collected learning assessments, student satisfaction surveys, and reports from focus groups. These were combined with contextual data on how students and teachers spent their time, the resources they used, and the order in which they used them. Together, this data revealed a rich picture of the classroom and which approaches showed promise or should be dropped. Through these rapid-cycle prototypes, Summit's transformative approach to personalized learning began to take shape. Modifications ranged from small tweaks in curriculum to a complete reconfiguration of the school day.

By finding a way to speed up its feedback loop in a domain in which ultimate success takes years to measure and iteration is traditionally slow, Summit was able to dramatically accelerate its own learning, progress, and impact. In 2017, 99% of the seniors who graduated from one of Summit's five Bay Area high schools were accepted into college. Once enrolled in college, Summit alumni are twice as likely to complete college compared to their peers. The Summit Public Schools model has been nationally recognized and adopted in over 300 public schools across the United States.

THE NEED

In many ways, the world has never been better. The average human is richer and healthier than ever before. Since 1990, global poverty, maternal and child mortality, and the number of children not enrolled in primary school have all been cut roughly in half.

Yet new challenges are fast emerging. Although income inequality across countries has declined, it has been increasing within countries.[1] And while interstate conflict has been reduced, civil wars and terrorism are on the rise. At the end of 2016, over 65 million people were displaced from their homes due to conflict or persecution, the

[1] Jos Verbeek and Israel Osorio Rodarte, "Increasingly, Inequality Within, not Across, Countries Is Rising," World Bank *Let's Talk Development* blog, October 2, 2015, https://blogs.worldbank.org/developmenttalk/increasingly-inequality-within-not-across-countries-rising.

most since the Second World War.[2] The number and intensity of climate-related natural disasters has risen. And in 2015, the Ebola epidemic reminded us of how rapidly a dangerous virus can spread around the world.

Here in the United States, the forces of globalization and automation are causing anxiety as the economy transforms more quickly than ever, leaving many behind. The American dream has been shattered with the decline in social mobility. Racial tension and anti-immigrant sentiment have flourished, the opioid crisis has made drug overdoses the leading cause of death for Americans under 50, and trust in government and political parties has eroded to near all-time lows.

To tackle both long-standing social ills and new challenges, 193 of the world's leaders came together at the United Nations in 2015 to adopt a shared vision – the Sustainable Development Goals (SDGs), which aim to end poverty, protect the planet, and promote prosperity and well-being for all. Unfortunately, experts estimate that for developing countries alone less than half of the required funding exists, leaving an annual shortfall of two to three trillion dollars.

This is a common story. We never have enough money to tackle the problems we face. And yet, the status quo is not acceptable. Certainly, we need to continue to advocate for more funding. We also need to recognize that our current interventions are insufficient. The path forward must include better solutions that will deliver far greater bang for buck and reach many more people over time.

BARRIERS TO SOCIAL INNOVATION

Let's be real. Innovation for social good is harder than innovation for business. Period. It took me some time to realize this. Like many practitioners of Lean Startup, the techniques seemed so universal

---

[2] Adrian Edwards, "Forced Displacement Worldwide at Its Highest in Decades," UNHCR, June 19, 2017, http://www.unhcr.org/afr/news/stories/2017/6/5941561f4/forced-displacement-worldwide-its-highest-decades.html.

that it was hard for me to imagine a domain in which they wouldn't apply. Then I tried. I shared the Lean Startup methodology with a nonprofit. At first, reactions were positive, even enthusiastic. Most people recognized the innate uncertainty of their work and welcomed ideas for being more nimble, managing risk, and accelerating progress towards their mission. But then, nothing changed.

When people returned to their desks, they found a grant proposal to write or previously funded activities to execute. I discovered that traditional grants require that a detailed design be laid out in a proposal – down to discrete activities, budgets, and staffing – and that implementation must faithfully adhere to that plan. I came to call this the *enforced waterfall* model, in reference to the outdated process for building shrink-wrapped software when the need to manufacture and distribute floppy disks or CDs meant infrequent, high-stakes releases. Each stage of designing, building, testing, and shipping was planned in advance and performed sequentially. The advent of the Web and cloud-based computing freed software development from these strictures and unleashed a wave of innovation.

Unfortunately, breaking out of this mode is not a simple matter of convincing your manager. Even the CEO may have little say. Control often sits with the donors who hold the purse strings. Imagine if software engineers had to beseech a venture capitalist (VC) for permission before trying any new idea for a feature. That would certainly slow down innovation. Entrepreneurs do exist everywhere, but if they are grant funded, their arms may be tied behind their backs.

Those mission-driven organizations that are fortunate enough to have access to more flexible funding may still find difficulty in satisfying their two entirely different types of customers: beneficiaries and funders. Even individual donors and impact investors frequently focus on defined geographies or sectors – be that health, education, poverty, climate, or otherwise. What if you're funded to reduce malaria, but you discover that what is most needed are primary healthcare clinics? What if you're funded to reduce rural poverty through agriculture, but people prefer to migrate to the city? What if you're funded to improve girls' education, but you realize what would make the biggest difference is sanitary pads? In the private sector, satisfying your user will increase profits and delight investors. But in the social sector, what people want, what will make the greatest impact, and what funders will pay for are not always the same.

The barriers to innovation don't end there. Our instincts may lead us astray when working with populations whose experiences are quite different from our own. We work at the treacherous intersection of failed markets and failed policies. Metrics tend to be geared towards compliance and accountability, rather than decision-making and learning. Measuring social impact is far more complicated than measuring e-commerce transactions. And, taking risks implies a potential for failure that could jeopardize funding streams or make things worse for vulnerable people who are already living on the edge.

If you've found it difficult to adopt concepts from *The Lean Startup* and other innovation toolkits, you're not alone. But, despite the added complexities, many mission-oriented organizations have found it not only possible, but transformative. They are better serving their customers, accelerating their growth, and magnifying their impact.

PRINCIPLES OF LEAN IMPACT

Lean Impact is an approach to maximizing social benefit in the face of the complex challenges in our society. It builds upon the best practices for innovation from the Lean Startup and beyond, while introducing new techniques tailored to the unique nature of the mission-driven arena. By combining scientific rigor with entrepreneurial agility, we can dramatically increase both the depth and breadth of our impact.

The essence of Lean Impact is captured by three core guiding principles. Throughout this book, I'll demonstrate the power of this new mindset and how to translate it into practical action to fuel social innovation.

- *Think big.* Be audacious in the difference you aspire to make, basing your goals on the size of the real need in the world rather than what seems incrementally achievable.
- *Start small.* Between a desire to help people who are suffering today and pressure from funders to hit delivery targets, interventions often scale too soon. Starting small and staying small makes it far easier to learn and adapt – setting you on a path to greater impact over time.
- *Relentlessly seek impact.* Whether due to excitement, attachment, or the requirements imposed by a funder, we can become wedded to our intervention, technology, or institution. To make the biggest impact, fall in love with the problem, not your solution.

A NONLINEAR PROCESS

While *The Lean Startup* concentrates on the process of testing and validation, *Lean Impact*, by necessity, incorporates a broader perspective to bring these tools to the realm of social innovation. Tech startups have no trouble thinking big, and are encouraged to do so by the ecosystem of heady VCs who support them. They approach challenges with an abundance mentality. On the other hand, social and environmental interventions are often planned within tight constraints – of existing budget, limited staff, or the time window and dollar amount of a particular grant opportunity. Thus, the journey to massive impact at scale must begin earlier.

In Chapter Five, we'll explore the techniques for validated learning pioneered by *The Lean Startup*. But before we get there, Chapter Two sets the stage by setting an audacious goal for social impact that breaks out of a mindset of scarcity and moves into a mindset of transformation. In Chapter Three, we begin to work towards that goal by investing in a deep understanding of our

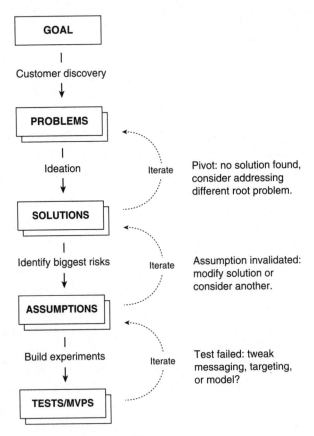

Figure 1.2   The Lean Impact workflow.

customers, stakeholders, and the underlying problems that impede change. Many social innovations falter because they haven't established this critical foundation and leap too hastily into a solution. With a clear goal, customer, and problem, we think outside the box in Chapter Four to identify solutions that have the potential to address these unmet needs.

Lean Impact is not a linear process. As shown in Figure 1.2, your goal is a relatively fixed destination. But to achieve it, you may choose to tackle one or more problems standing in the way. Based on that problem, you could consider multiple potential solutions. The success of each solution, in turn, depends on a number of assumptions.

By running experiments, you can validate or invalidate those assumptions to determine if there is a viable path forward.

Of course, a lot can go wrong. If a test fails, you may need to iterate by tweaking your model, trying an alternative solution, or perhaps making a more significant pivot by tackling a different problem altogether. On the other hand, if validation succeeds, you can have the confidence to move forward and increase your fidelity or scale, likely revealing a whole new layer of assumptions to be tested. The best social entrepreneurs approach this journey with humility, flexibility, and grit.

THE GROWING MOVEMENT

Despite the obstacles to innovation, nonprofits, social enterprises, companies, foundations, philanthropists, governments, and impact investors are beginning to chart a new path that embraces many of the concepts from *The Lean Startup* to solve the pressing social and environmental issues of our time. They are starting small, listening to their customers, rapidly iterating on solutions, and designing business models that can scale sustainably. *Lean Impact* shares the successes of these early pioneers, and serves as a guide for anyone working to achieve radically greater social good.

Let's take a look at how.

Chapter Two
What Is Your Audacious Goal?

In the year 2000, 191 of the world's leaders gathered at the Millennium Summit in New York City to adopt the Millennium Development Goals (MDGs), a bold set of eight goals for tackling the most crucial challenges in global development by the year 2015. This was the first time that quantifiable development measures had been endorsed on the world stage, presaging a move towards more data driven strategies. Goal 2 was to "achieve universal primary education." Over the next 15 years, net enrollment increased dramatically, from 83% to 91%. Though it fell short of universal enrollment, this represented an impressive (nearly 50%) decrease in the number of children out of school globally.

Goals do focus minds, but not always on the right priorities. While more kids attended school, in many countries the quality of education actually declined. And as of 2015, over a hundred million youth still lacked basic literacy. Learning from the MDGs and mindful of new challenges in the twenty-first century, the next-generation SDGs for 2030 focus on the *quality* of education, with Goal 4 to "ensure inclusive and quality education for all and promote lifelong learning."

Lean Impact: How to Innovate for Radically Greater Social Good, First Edition. Ann Mei Chang. © 2019 Ann Mei Chang. Published 2019 by John Wiley & Sons, Inc.

Establishing a goal seems as if it should be straightforward. After all, in business the goal is typically to increase profits. Wouldn't the analog for a mission-driven organization be to increase social benefit? Yes, but it doesn't turn out to be quite so easy.

When I started leading the mobile engineering team at Google, our goal was clear: to build a billion-dollar business. At the time, the iPhone had just launched, and our revenue was only $50 million annually. We had a long way to go. Nevertheless, this stretch goal galvanized the team. Engineers dreamed up features to increase usage, business development sought partnerships that would drive traffic, and sales found new customers to buy ads. At each weekly leadership meeting, we reviewed our metrics. If there was an unexpected uptick or downturn, we'd track down the cause. With a significant boost from the popularity of both iPhone and Android, we hit our billion-dollar target in only three years, increasing revenues by a factor of 20.

In contrast, mission-oriented goals tend to be vaguely worded, along the lines of "reduce poverty," "tackle injustice," or "fight climate change." These are all worthy aspirations, but in the absence of a clear timeframe or measure of success, how do we know if we're making enough progress? Are we setting our ambitions high enough? What level of risk is appropriate? At Google, our billion-dollar target focused minds far more than if we had simply agreed to increase revenues.

Upon joining the US Agency for International Development (USAID) as the first executive director of the Global Development Lab (the Lab), I encountered this tendency firsthand. The Lab had recently been established as a new bureau to accelerate our progress in fighting global poverty through science, technology, innovation, and partnerships. Yet, when I asked how we would measure our success, I was simply told, "Identify breakthrough innovations." After a bit of encouragement, my team eventually agreed on a goal of identifying 10 breakthrough innovations in five years that each would improve the lives of at least a million people, demonstrate evidence of substantial impact, and have a financially sustainable path forward. The implications quickly became apparent. The Lab had sourced many promising early-stage innovations, but few had reached this stage of maturity. With the new clarity, we shifted our priorities and invested more to help the most successful candidates in our portfolio get to scale.

The birth of innovation begins with a clear, aspirational goal. This is the top-down vision of the change you seek to create, rather than the bottom-up calculation of what appears achievable with foreseeable improvements on your current trajectory. Ask yourself, What does success look like? Take a walk outside the office to reflect on the world you hope to bring about. Talk to your mentors and role models. Remember why you got into this work in the first place. Your goal is your North Star that is crystallized by an ambitious target.

I have come to believe that unclear and conservative goals are one of the root causes of inertia in the social sector. Given the degree to which reputation can influence funding from both individuals and institutions, the fear of setting a quantifiable stretch goal, then being punished for failing to reach it, is understandable. Yet without a long-term aspirational goal, day-to-day pressures can cause us to focus on short-term wins rather than searching for better solutions that will make a bigger difference.

THINK BIG

In some ways the social sector is incredibly audacious. In others, it is not nearly audacious enough. We dive in fearlessly to tackle the long-standing, entrenched, and intractable ills of our society with passion and commitment. At the same time, the real pressures of funding and operations often limit the size and scope of our ambitions, so that they fall far short of the real need. This is why one of the core principles of Lean Impact is to think big.

Take Ben Mangan, the cofounder and former CEO of EARN, a nonprofit that helps low-income Americans meet their financial goals by developing a habit of saving. After 10 years, EARN had grown to become one of the largest microsavings providers in the United States and was being feted for its success. While opening 7000 goal-based savings accounts placed it near the top of its sector, one day Ben stepped back and realized that EARN was barely making a dent in the 50–70 million Americans in need of greater financial security.

So, he pivoted. At an awards dinner in 2012, Ben surprised the audience by announcing an ambitious goal to help a million people save a total of a billion dollars by 2022. To do so required an entirely different approach. EARN would never reach that degree of scale with its existing model, which included in-person visits and a dollar-for-dollar financial match. Instead, EARN pivoted its strategy and built a technology platform to support a lighter weight, self-service model. In the first year of its new SaverLife program it reached 85,000 new users, more than 10 times as many as the total number reached over its prior 15 years.

Ben's realization is one that doesn't happen often enough. When we focus on short-term deliverables, we can lose sight of the big picture. The nature of grant proposals and tight budgets in the social sector encourage a model of planning within constraints – by determining the best use of available resources – rather than strategizing relative to needs – by finding a viable solution, then seeking out the resources that will be required.

It's important to take a step back and ask the question, Are we trying to empty the ocean with a spoon? In other words, if the size of our problem is in the tens or hundreds of millions, do we have a plausible path to reach a substantial proportion of that audience given our cost structure, funding sources, and degree of complexity? If not, shouldn't we direct at least *some* of our investment towards finding a solution that could go farther?

HOCKEY STICK GROWTH

In the tech startup world, companies aspire to achieve hockey stick growth (see Figure 2.1). On a graph, the projected audience hits an inflection point and shifts from slow, linear growth (the blade) to surging, exponential growth (the shaft). When seeking funding for

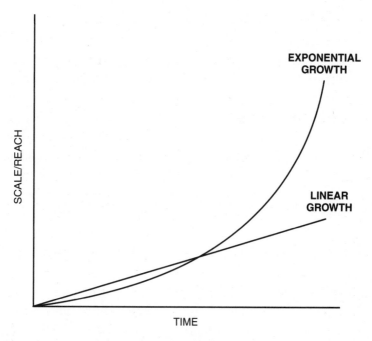

Figure 2.1   Exponential, or hockey stick, growth.

their business ideas from VCs, startups proudly display such hockey stick charts and make the case for how and why they can achieve these ambitious targets.

We don't see a lot of projections of such exponential growth for social impact. Why not? Even many of the most successful mission-driven organizations seem to be, at best, on a perpetual linear growth path. True, they are scaling, but slowly, and are unlikely to reach the size of the need in our generation. If we don't aim to make a massive impact, it is unlikely we will.

One problem is that most social-sector organizations are conditioned to live on a shoestring. For every dollar raised, a deliverable is expected. If you receive a grant for $1 million for workforce development and it costs $100 to provide services for each person, you are expected to train 10,000 people. Each dollar buys you exactly one dollar of value – the very definition of linear growth. Precious little wiggle room exists to fund the research and experimentation that might bend the curve with a disruptive solution or creative business model.

Scaling social solutions requires a mindset shift from the linear growth path of service delivery to the exponential growth path of transformation. This starts with an audacious vision for change based on an assessment of the size of the need rather than a projection of anticipated progress. Such a goal forces us to think beyond the confines of a single program or institution to seek the business, policy, or replication models that can massively accelerate growth over time. We'll explore these and other paths to scale in Chapter Eight.

Contrary to the business world, scaling an individual entity is not always the best way to deliver on an ambitious social mission. In many cases, what is needed is to heal the market and policy failures in a broken ecosystem through collective action. Chapter Ten will delve beyond the enterprise into the realm of systems change.

To maximize social good, we must think beyond ourselves and beyond our current organizations, to embrace a bold vision for the world we want, then relentlessly pursue ways to make it a reality.

A STRATEGY FOR UNCERTAINTY

There is often a mismatch between our strategy and the nature of the problem. Consider the difference between opening a local dry cleaning shop versus starting a company like Amazon. For a dry cleaner, the customer need, solution, and business model are all well understood. If a particular community is underserved, it's straightforward to open a business and fill the niche. On the other hand, Amazon started with the aspiration to become the "Earth's Biggest Bookstore" based on what was at the time the highly speculative proposition of selling books online. Amazon had to experiment on many levels – from product mix to online experience to cost efficiencies – before landing on a promising path.

The difference between these two ventures lies in both certainty and scope. In the social sector we're creating a lot of dry cleaners, while the problems we are tackling (think generational cycles of poverty, social justice, and environmental degradation) have a level of uncertainty and scale more like Amazon's. If both your problem and solution are well understood, you can simply execute on a defined plan. On the other hand, when the solution is unclear and the needs are vastly underserved, we must take greater risk, set higher ambitions, and test multiple alternatives. Had Amazon operated like a dry cleaner, it never would have stretched to achieve the success it has today.

You might wonder whether there is a place for small, locally focused nonprofits. Absolutely. But it is also worth considering a few questions. In your geographical area, are you reaching everyone who could stand to benefit? Would it be possible to deliver greater value or cost savings with economies of scale, either through growth or by merging with another entity? Are you delivering the best possible outcomes per dollar spent? If so, could other organizations, communities, or geographies benefit from your solution, either by expanding operations, franchising, promoting replication, or advocating for policy change?

YOUR NORTH STAR

If your goal is the distant North Star, towards which you constantly steer, then it must be clearly articulated so that everyone involved can row in the same direction. The magnitude of social impact is based on a combination of breadth and depth – how far we reach and to what degree we improve on the status quo. Such choices will inevitably affect direction, priorities, success criteria, and decision-making. If we don't know what success looks like, how will we rally others to achieve it?

As Astro Teller, head of X, Google's moonshot factory, points out, there is a significant difference between trying to increase the fuel efficiency of a car by 10% versus by 10 times. Counterintuitively, he claims that in some cases a 10-fold improvement could turn out to be easier, as far more people have already sought to squeeze out incremental improvements and largely exhausted the possibilities.[1] While both scenarios seek fuel efficiency, this quantifiable goal has dramatic implications for the appropriate approach and degree of risk to take.

One common argument I hear against setting measurable objectives is, What if we miss our target? The fear is typically of reputational damage or losing donor support. But there is an important distinction between committed activities and aspirational goals. Delivering on your commitments is important to build trust and credibility, and these should not be taken lightly. On the other hand, the purpose of aspirational goals is to stretch thinking and inspire. Articulating the difference clearly with stakeholders can separate the accountability associated with management objectives from the vision you want to rally everyone towards.

A well-defined goal should minimally answer the basic questions of *how many*, to *what extent*, and by *when*: that is, the date by which you aim to achieve the desired depth and breadth of impact. As an example, the social enterprise myAgro aims "to increase the income of a million smallholder farmers by $1.50 per day by 2025." The clarity of its ambition drives the team to continually seek ways to simplify their model and cut costs, as they recognize that financial sustainability is the only way to reach that degree of scale.

For an entire organization or initiative, I recommend considering a timeframe of at least ten years to keep the focus on your long-term ambition. Think big. Work down from the size of the need that exists in the world, rather than working up from what seems achievable based on what you know today. Ask if reaching your target will move the needle appreciably. The best approach to helping a thousand people in a single community may be quite different from one helping ten million across the country, even assuming you will want

---

[1] Astro Teller, "Google X Head on Moonshots: 10X Is Easier Than 10 Percent," *Wired*, February 11, 2013, https://www.wired.com/2013/02/moonshots-matter-heres-how-to-make-them-happen.

to start small in either case. Later, when we turn to *validated learning* in Chapter Five, we'll discuss the *innovation metrics* that can be used to measure interim progress toward this goal.

Your goal should be measurable so it can serve as a benchmark for tradeoffs. This means cold hard numbers for both impact and scale. Are you targeting a 10% or a 10-fold improvement? Do you hope to reach all people or animals, or only certain demographics, species, or geographies? These choices will have implications for how you understand the problems and needs, the design of your solution, and potential paths to scale.

While some impact indicators may be slow and expensive to measure, in Chapter Nine we'll discuss proxies that can enable faster feedback loops. Avoid the temptation to focus on tactical metrics, such as the dollars raised or number of people reached through trainings, services, or other interventions. These only reflect activity and don't equate with having made a substantive difference. If your organization works across multiple problem spaces, consider setting separate goals for each rather than aggregating them into one vague and meaningless target.

ENDS VERSUS MEANS

One pitfall that is all too common in mission-driven work is conflating our ends and our means. We can become so immersed in designing and deploying an intervention that we lose perspective on our ultimate goal and fail to recognize when our solution may be insufficient. I encountered this phenomenon while leading a workshop on Lean Impact at TEDGlobal 2017. As most of the participants didn't know each other, I thought a good way to break the ice would be to have each table introduce themselves, share a problem they were passionate about, and agree on a goal for the purposes of the exercise. It didn't turn out the way I expected.

Many of the groups immediately began discussing potential solutions. One became immersed in planning an anti–wildlife trafficking media campaign. Another debated technologies for an electronic fence that could zap disease-transmitting mosquitoes. I found myself running back and forth between tables to prod each team to step back from its solution and focus on how the world would be better if it was successful. Eventually, the goals started to emerge. The first team wanted to protect increasingly endangered jaguars by eliminating poaching (a single jaguar's fangs, claws, pelt, and genitalia sell for $20,000 in Asia[2]). The second team wanted to reduce mosquito borne diseases in Africa by 50%. I had underestimated the gravitational pull of a compelling solution.

There's a tendency to describe goals in terms of progress in deploying an intervention, rather than focusing on the purpose of the work. That is, the claim "10,000 people will be trained in better farming techniques" describes an activity that may or may not be effective, whereas the statement "10,000 farmers will have increased their incomes by 50%" describes the desired outcome. The latter keeps us focused on the change we hope to effect and forces us to consider the possibility that our initial approach may not turn out to be the best path.

Why is this conflation common in the social sector? To start with, there is no easy metric, such as business profitability, to focus minds. But I expect that the need for a core differentiator is a larger factor. An organization constantly pitches its "solution" to donors, promotes it in its marketing, and works to deliver it. That solution becomes what the organization is known and sought out for. And, even isolated stories of success can create an emotional attachment that makes it difficult to let go of a marginal intervention. Instead we should try to hold lightly onto any solution and use evidence rather than conviction to determine whether it works.

Sam Goldman discovered this on his path to starting one of the most successful early social enterprises, d.light. While serving as a Peace Corps volunteer in Benin, Sam's 15-year-old neighbor was

[2] "Asia's Appetite for Endangered Species Is Relentless," *The Economist*, April 19, 2018.

badly burned in a kerosene accident. Sam became inspired to find a way to provide the 1.6 billion people who live without electricity access to safer, affordable light. As part of the Design for Extreme Affordability class at Stanford University in 2006, his team researched how energy needs were being met in Myanmar and Cambodia. They discovered an existing system of kids who shuttled lead acid batteries every few days to recharge them at generators. Based on this informal activity, the team's first design, the Forever-Bright, was a low-cost LED light run off batteries that could be recharged by a diesel generator.

Sam soon cofounded d.light and started to delve into other markets, including India. There, he discovered that generators were not as readily available as in those initial countries. The original solution wouldn't work, and it was time to pivot. When he tested solar lanterns as an alternative, he discovered they were a far better solution to the problem. Solar was magical and blew people's minds. For the first time, people could have free light day after day. Demand grew. Following many more pivots, d.light has now sold close to 20 million solar light and power products in 62 countries.

One of the core principles for Lean Impact is to relentlessly seek impact. A clearly defined goal reminds us how high to aim and offers a benchmark against which to measure our progress. Is our solution moving the needle appreciably? Is it doing so quickly enough? Can it reach sufficient numbers? Will it reach those most in need? A goal helps us determine if we are getting close, have an aspect that needs some improvement, or are way off the mark.

Chapter Three
Love the Problem, Not Your Solution

When Proximity Designs decided to work with smallholder farmers in Myanmar, the husband and wife cofounders, Jim Taylor and Debbie Aung Din, packed up their lives and moved there. They believed that poverty is so complicated that you need to be close to the problem – proximate – to understand its dynamics, have empathy for the people affected, and gain deep knowledge of the local realities.

In 2004, Jim and Debbie took aim at the problem of irrigation with a goal of improving crop production and relieving the back-breaking work of hauling water daily from distant sources. As existing alternatives were too expensive for their target customers, they set out to design a portable, lightweight, and affordable treadle pump – a foot-powered suction pump to draw groundwater to the surface. Being local meant they could involve their users in every stage of the design process. It also allowed them to solicit rapid feedback from farmers on each iteration of their prototypes, sometimes on a daily basis.

Proximity believes in treating people as customers, giving them choice and dignity. Distributing goods for free implies deciding who

Lean Impact: How to Innovate for Radically Greater Social Good, First Edition. Ann Mei Chang. © 2019 Ann Mei Chang. Published 2019 by John Wiley & Sons, Inc.

receives them – putting people in the position of being supplicants and potentially creating divisive dynamics in a village. Instead, they decided to sell their treadle pumps. A farmer's decision to buy or not sends a clear signal about their perceived value, reveals important consumer insight, and keeps Proximity accountable to their customers. Charging for the pumps also opened the path towards a financially sustainable venture, along with the potential for far greater reach and scale.

After Cyclone Nargis devastated the country in 2008, Proximity responded immediately. It worked to understand what communities most needed and as a result designed simple shelters, water storage tanks, and a package of supplies to get farms up and running again. International aid agencies and nonprofits arrived later, with preprogrammed packages that were often not relevant for the local conditions.

Nine years later, Proximity is the largest social enterprise in Myanmar and has reached 80% of the farming population, increasing their incomes by an average of $250 a year. It has made an economic impact estimated at over half a billion dollars in the past five years.

BEING PROXIMATE

Now that Chapter Two has helped us establish a clear, audacious goal, the obvious question is how to achieve it. To do so, we have to start by understanding the people involved and the problems they face.

Mission-driven work tends to serve disadvantaged populations whose needs, priorities, cultures, and experiences may be nothing like those who are seeking to help. Thus, our instincts and interpretation of priorities can be misleading. Geography, language, or even different neighborhoods or vernacular can create further barriers to understanding. On top of that, we often seek to intervene in the middle of complex systems, at points of market, government, and policy failure. Unintended consequences are a legitimate risk.

Let's get real. Good solutions are unlikely to come from within the comforts of a fancy glass office, far removed from the problem at hand. Such efforts tend to produce inappropriate or impractical proposals, such as building an app for people who don't even have smartphones.

Instead, the best social entrepreneurs start by deeply understanding their customers. How do they live their lives? What are their challenges, needs, and desires? Are their experiences relatively uniform or do they vary across different demographics? Beyond the direct beneficiary, what are the motivations of others who may be affected by your work, such as community members, government, donors, existing providers, and other stakeholders? The less like you your intended customers are, the more you'll need to invest in building trust and understanding. This means being proximate, a dose of humility, and lots of listening.

Today, before creating a new product or service, Proximity Designs spends six weeks doing a deep dive. Teams get as close as possible to the people they hope to serve by setting up a pop-up studio in or near a typical community. The space is tailored to the problem at hand and left open 24/7 to create a casual social environment that welcomes serendipity. By being immersed in a community, the team can live and breathe their experiences and get to know people more intimately. The studio also serves as an inspiring workspace where creative juices can flow and ideas start to emerge.

Being proximate matters even when working with populations near your home turf. When Dr. Sarah Schulman, a founder of social design firm InWithForward, was asked by the British Colombian government in Canada to address the social isolation of adults living with cognitive disability, she and her team moved into a public housing complex in Burnaby to live alongside their customers. From there, they undertook 50 ethnographic studies and discovered people felt bored, stuck, and isolated by the same old "special education" programs.

The conversations in group homes and day programs gave rise to Kudoz, a diverse catalog of experiences offered by volunteer individuals and businesses. Think Uber for social services, but free. Options have included How's a City Built? Learn About Vancouver's Architecture, Get Outside and Play Pokemon Go, and Practical First Aid. Kudoz became a new platform for learning and exchange. Participants were empowered to explore new interests, and hosts could give back while sharing their own passions.

Parachuting into a new environment for a few days or weeks may yield valuable insights but is often insufficient. Understanding your users shouldn't be a one-time investment. Of course, this is easiest if you are based in or near your customers and integrate community members among your staff. With ongoing channels for rapid formal and informal feedback, users can participate in the design process and continue to provide unexpected insights.

Making the effort to listen doesn't necessarily mean people will always be willing to share. After taking several online Acumen courses, including Human-centered Design, Professor Kevin Schneider at Oral Roberts University integrated multidisciplinary approaches into his curriculum as a way to better understand poverty. On one project, his students sought to improve the quality of life in Carrilho, a remote village on the east coast of Brazil. Yet, when they arrived to conduct an initial needs assessment, no one was willing to speak with these strange foreigners. They quickly realized they had to start by building relationships and trust. After taking a step back to spend time playing soccer with the local kids, the locals became more comfortable and slowly warmed up to the students.[1]

When we are working with people and communities whose experiences are different from our own, *literally* getting proximate to the problem is an essential precursor to a good solution. If you're interested in exploring the topic further, a number of books on the topic of participatory research and ethnographic studies are available.

[1] Winnie Sun, "A Professor and His Students' Journey to Transform a Village," +Acumen blog, January 6, 2015, http://www.plusacumen.org/journal/professor-and-his-students-journey-transform-village.

CONSIDERING THE SYSTEM

Problems rarely exist in isolation. Most are influenced by a broad range of policies, market dynamics, and stakeholders. While the idea of addressing structural barriers to change has been around for some time, the importance of systems thinking – a holistic analysis of the complex interrelationships among elements of a problem – has become more widespread in recent years. Lasting change is not possible without considering all the layers of interactions that reinforce the existing state of affairs. One helpful tool is a system map – a visual representation of the interplay between the various actors, organizations, and policies, and how each connects, affects, and relates to the others. Figure 3.1 shows a simple example.

The journey of Little Kids Rock, a nonprofit based in suburban New Jersey, shows how engaging at a systems level can lead to massive impact. Founder David Wish has a sparkle in his eye and an infectious enthusiasm that makes you feel he's going to playfully push you out of your comfort zone at any moment. He calls himself an expert at first grade, as he took it twice himself, then taught it for 10 years. Growing up, he had a terrible experience in music classes, including being criticized for his rendition of "Hot Cross Buns" and having a violin thrust upon him when his preferred guitar wasn't available. It was only when a good friend taught him how to play cool tunes on a guitar in high school that he developed a passion for music.

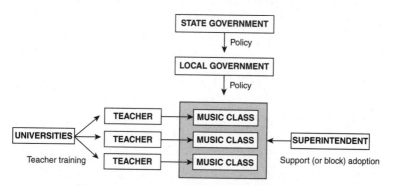

Figure 3.1   System map for Little Kids Rock (illustrative only).

The traditional way of teaching through music theory, scales, reading notation, and classical music leaves many kids bored and alienated. On a lark, as a first-grade teacher in Redwood City, David decided to give his class the opportunity to simply play songs they liked. It was a hit. Soon he had kids, parents, and teachers beating down his door to participate.

As an individual teacher, he realized he couldn't come close to meeting the interest his class had generated. So, he started teaching other teachers his technique. But demand continued to outstrip his ability to deliver. He soon recognized that he needed a different approach. As he considered the broader landscape, he recognized that university programs train massive numbers of teachers, state and local governments establish the curriculum through policy, and superintendents can support (or block) adoption of new teaching techniques. To leverage these existing systems, he created a new category of music education and called it modern band. Rather than focusing on individual educators, he worked with universities to train teachers and with government to include modern band in the curriculum. Today Little Kids Rock offers one of the largest music programs in US public schools, with over 2,400 schools in 45 states including modern band programs for their students.

A system map can reveal important insights into the stakeholders and their constraints, vested interests, and influences. From there, we can begin to identify potential points of intervention, who needs to be involved, what problems we could address, and what opportunities we could create.

WHO IS YOUR CUSTOMER?

Once you've collected insights through research, ethnographic studies, and system mapping, your target audience can be distilled into one or more customer segments. Each segment embodies the shared experiences, desires, and challenges that may be held by a set of beneficiaries or stakeholders. Avoid over-generalizing by selecting an entire organization or community, as individual reactions within a broad group may vary widely depending on their context. By evaluating a potential solution against the needs of people in similar roles or circumstances, we can gain an understanding of the potential value we could deliver.

Selecting a primary customer segment can bring focus to the early stages of design. Consider this the sweet spot – the people who stand to benefit most. If you can truly delight them, they will become your early adopters, share detailed feedback, and become evangelists. If you try to take too many diverse interests into account in the beginning, you may never fully satisfy anyone. It is far easier to expand your customer base from a dedicated following. Consider how Facebook built its audience by starting with an exclusive website for Harvard students and then expanding to Boston universities, to other Ivy League schools, to other universities, to US high schools, then to anyone with an email address. This allowed Facebook to focus on catering to the unique needs of each customer segment in turn. If Mark Zuckerberg had opened up his new social network to the general public from the start, Facebook might never have had the dedicated following to build momentum for its expansion.

One popular tool among Lean Startup practitioners is the Value Proposition Canvas introduced by Alexander Osterwalder in his book *Value Proposition Design* (see Figure 3.2).[2] The right half of the canvas represents a customer segment, and identifies jobs, responsibilities, and activities for that customer along with his or her existing pains (obstacles and challenges) and potential gains (desires and aspirations). These are then matched with a value proposition on the left side that describes how a proposed solution might relieve pains and create gains.

We used the Value Proposition Canvas in Hacking for Impact, a class I co-taught at the University of California at Berkeley in the fall of 2017. The class was modeled after Lean LaunchPad®, an

[2] Alexander Osterwalder, Yves Pigneur, Greg Bernarda, Alan Smith, and Patricia Papadakos, *Value Proposition Design* (Hoboken, NJ: Wiley, 2014).

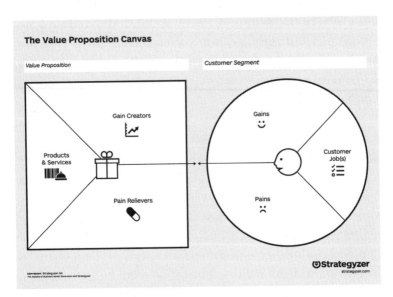

Figure 3.2   The Value Proposition Canvas. Source: Strategyzer AG.

experiential methodology for teaching entrepreneurship pioneered by entrepreneur-turned-educator Steve Blank. In his course student groups test the business proposition for a potential startup, validate their hypotheses by talking to at least ten customers a week, and present their findings back to the class for feedback and guidance. The more recent Hacking for Defense and Hacking for Diplomacy classes brought the same pedagogy to military and foreign policy challenges, respectively.

Our pilot class brought it to a fourth domain, social impact, working in partnership with nonprofit and government sponsors. Among the student groups was FirstGen, which aimed to increase the diversity of students studying STEM (science, technology, engineering, and math) subjects through an annual robot competition. The team started with a customer segment of disadvantaged students and discovered that they found existing STEM extracurricular activities boring and that after-school programs caused them to miss the only bus home. Next, the customer segment for teachers showed that they were overworked and didn't have the time or funding to serve as sponsors.

Given the transport issues and lack of teacher bandwidth, the FirstGen team struggled to identify a compelling value proposition. Although I was equally stumped as to the answer, I encouraged them to cast a broader net rather than stay wedded to their original approach. As the team explored further, they uncovered the potential of community centers, which were more conveniently located near the students' homes and always seeking new programs to offer. So, they pivoted. The customer segment of community center branch managers turned out to be far better positioned to serve as hosts.

In the world of human-centered design (HCD), interviews and observations may be synthesized into archetypes or common behavioral patterns that represent the range of customer segments. These insights can be used to inspire and crosscheck ideas throughout the design process.

IDEO.org took such an approach in its partnership with the Bezos Family Foundation to increase parental engagement and spur early childhood development. It started by conducting extensive interviews with low-income families, child development experts, and pediatricians around the country. These led to five insights that reflected the unique challenges the parents faced. Many had suffered abuse and neglect as children themselves and so had no positive role models for parenting and weren't aware of the type of stimulating interactions kids need. Others felt isolated from peer support networks, as they lived in dangerous neighborhoods. Teen parents faced particular challenges, such as finishing school and finding a job, without the maturity or resources to navigate them. All clearly cared deeply about their children's growth.

From these insights, the IDEO.org team found new opportunities to engage parents. For example, as some families were uncomfortable with the common prescription of reading aloud, they encouraged natural dialog between adults and children during routine, shared moments, such as sitting in the Laundromat or going shopping. Back-and-forth conversations promote brain development and strengthen the relationship between parent and child. The Bezos

Family Foundation incorporated these recommendations into the design and launch of Vroom, a nationwide initiative that takes early brain science out of the lab and puts it into the hands of parents.

There is no one right tool for gaining insight into the customers or beneficiaries you hope to reach. What's important is to recognize the limitations of our own instincts and to understand the motivations that will affect customer adoption of any intervention. This usually involves a mix of quantitative data to capture what is happening and qualitative techniques to explain why.

DON'T FORGET YOUR OTHER CUSTOMER

When Caitlin Baron was tapped to be the first CEO of the Luminos Fund, a social enterprise to help out-of-school children get back to school, she wanted to establish an innovative culture up front. She eagerly bought and read *The Lean Startup* from cover to cover. Then, she felt stuck. The principles made sense, but she found that most donors expected her to have the "entire path to impact mapped out before you even begin." Many were interested in bringing Luminos's program to new countries, but required "committing to proposals with very locked-down operating models" – even small refinements to adapt to local conditions, such as offering midday meals or textbooks, were painful to make. Finding support to experiment with new, related interventions was even more difficult. Luminos is fortunate to have received long-term, unrestricted funding from the Legatum Foundation, which is giving it the flexibility needed for its entrepreneurial journey.

Caitlin's story is all too common. One of the biggest factors that makes innovation harder in the social sector is the need to satisfy two completely different types of customers – your user (or beneficiary) and your funder. In business, the same customer usually both benefits from and pays for the product or service, so interests are naturally aligned. Investors and lenders place a bet on a company based on its business plan, team, and track record, and rarely get involved in the day-to-day details of how money is spent or how products and services are designed.

On the other hand, grants from foundations or governments, a common source of funding in the social sector, typically require meticulous plans for activities, deliverables, staffing, and budgets to be specified in a grant proposal. If selected, you are expected to execute on that plan. Due to this enforced waterfall model, any changes to the original design can require painful renegotiation. I've heard too many stories of organizations that determine that what they're doing is not working but find that the path of least resistance is to continue anyway. Of course, this also gets in the way of applying lean techniques to build the best solution.

Funders come with their own agendas, which can be in conflict with what's best for the customer or your enterprise. For example, they frequently restrict support to a particular geography, demographic, technology, or sector. The need to raise money to keep the doors open can lead nonprofits to swallow such compromises. But, to satisfy all the crisscrossing priorities of multiple donors, organizations can end up tying themselves into a pretzel.

Chapter Eleven will explore ways to navigate these and other funding challenges in depth, while Chapter Twelve will delve into recommendations for how funders can better support innovation and ultimately greater impact at scale. In the meantime, suffice it to say that the need to satisfy two different customers, the beneficiary and the funder, can pull you between conflicting priorities. Still, both must be considered.

PROBLEM DISCOVERY

Kinari Webb loved orangutans and became passionate about protecting the rain forests in Indonesian Borneo where they live. But rather than jumping into a typical conservation project, she decided to start by engaging in something she calls "radical listening" – trusting community members to identify their own challenges and needs, asking for their ideas, and implementing their solutions. She wondered, Why were people cutting down the rain forest? And, How could it be stopped?

She discovered that much of the deforestation was happening when a health crisis would force a family to raise large sums quickly to send their loved one to a far away, expensive hospital. By understanding the dynamics in the community, Kinari was able to home in on the underlying causes of habitat destruction as a basis to determine the best solution. The result? She started Health In Harmony to build a local health clinic and develop alternative livelihoods. Today, the number of households that participate in logging has dropped by over 89% through this nontraditional approach to conservation.

Too often, we leap to a solution before fully appreciating the multidimensional nature of the problem at hand. Without a deeper understanding, making positive impact is a crapshoot, and interventions may even lead to negative, unintended consequences.

One technique for understanding a problem is called the 5 Whys. Through an iterative inquiry that asks why repeatedly, we can move from symptoms to the root-cause problem. Originally conceived by Sakichi Toyoda as a critical element of the Toyota Production System, it takes a scientific approach to determine the underlying nature of a problem.

For Kinari, the path forward was revealed along these lines:

Why is the number of orangutans declining? Their habitat is being reduced.

Why is their habitat being reduced? People are cutting down the rain forest.

Why are people cutting down the forest? They have to raise money quickly to send a family member to the hospital.

Why do they have to go to an expensive hospital? There is no local health clinic.

Why is there no local health clinic? The area is poor, remote, and ignored by both government and the private sector.

Having a deep, immersive engagement with your target customers, as Kinari did, is ideal. Absent that, even a simple interview can add depth and nuance to your understanding of their pain points and desires. In our Berkeley class, we required each team to conduct at least ten interviews a week, to learn from real customers and stakeholders.

In interviews to validate a problem, the most important criteria is to not mention your solution – no matter how excited you may be. Once the discussion turns to a solution, the conversation will inevitably revolve around its plusses, minuses, and practicalities. The real problem may not surface. If Kinari had approached the community with a conservation project, she might never have heard about the connection to health crises. Instead, ask about customers' challenges, pains, and frustrations. How do they currently handle them? Have they tried other alternatives? Have they encountered anything that has helped?

Falling in love with your problem means getting to the root cause, wherever it may lead. When we don't stop to understand the underlying drivers, we can waste time perfecting a solution that merely addresses a symptom and doesn't lead to sustained impact. Problem validation should not be a one-time endeavor. Throughout the evolution of an intervention, it's important to stay curious and vigilant for indications that the original assessment was incomplete or that the nature of the problem has evolved.

Chapter Four
Finding the "Big Idea"

When most people think of innovation, they picture brainstorming sessions, cocreation workshops, and hackathons replete with colorful Post-its stuck on every bare surface. Once you have established your goal, identified your target customers, and understood their problems, it's time to turn to potential solutions. A good ideation process can elicit creative, out-of-the-box thinking that is firmly grounded in customer understanding, injects new perspectives, and goes beyond traditional approaches.

Brainstorming new ideas can be heady and fun. However, if your goal is to maximize impact, good solutions to your problem may already exist. Although they are among the most innovative companies on the planet, Google didn't invent Web search and Facebook didn't invent social networking. What they did was dramatically improve upon the algorithms, user experience, and features of their predecessors. Similarly, before we leap to the conclusion that what's missing is a dose of inspiration, we should be open to the possibility that what's actually missing may be the perspiration required to improve, adapt, expand, operationalize, or replicate an existing intervention.

Lean Impact: How to Innovate for Radically Greater Social Good, First Edition. Ann Mei Chang.
© 2019 Ann Mei Chang. Published 2019 by John Wiley & Sons, Inc.

The fallacy of the big idea is that it will change everything. A good idea is indeed important. But we are more likely to achieve our goals if we don't become too wed to any one solution, including our own. Instead of looking for *the* answer, think of each as an option to try, and allow data from performance in the real world serve as your guide. We'll take an in-depth look at how in Part II.

INSPIRING SOLUTIONS

Many of the modern techniques for ideation stem from design thinking (also known as human-centered design, or HCD), which was popularized for the business context by design firm IDEO. A good ideation process encourages divergent thinking and nurtures all ideas, even outlandish ones.

Think of ideation as a form of improv theater, where the stance is one of "Yes, and…" Defer judgment. Acknowledge each contribution, expand on it, and leave opinion, personal interests, and rank at the door. The CEO's perspective is no more valuable than that of the line staff who work directly with customers every day. A typical ideation session might start with individual or small-group brainstorming. Requiring a minimum number of ideas can push teams to move beyond the obvious solutions and encourage out-of-the-box thinking. In the beginning, the aim is quantity over quality.

Once new ideas are exhausted, the convergence process starts. Ideas can be synthesized, grouped together, and further developed. Here's where the Post-its help. Write each idea on a Post-it, stick it on a wall, and group related concepts together. These groups might spark new ideas in turn, combining and building on elements of different solutions. One technique for winnowing down options is to give each person a fixed number of stickers to vote on the ideas they find most promising. Figure 4.1 illustrates how a hypothetical ideation session for Health In Harmony (described in Chapter Three) may have looked.

Not every idea will be worth pursuing, but unexpected gems can emerge. Some may represent a radical departure with transformative

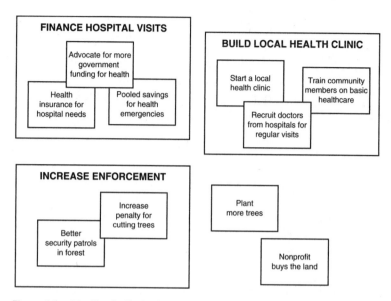

Figure 4.1   Ideation for Health In Harmony (illustrative only).

potential; others may simply add a fresh dimension to an established intervention. Avoid the temptation to either latch onto or dismiss any potential solution too quickly. For each, consider the value proposition to the target customer. What pain points does it address? Who will benefit and how? Also balance the risk relative to the potential impact. A highly speculative idea may be worth trying if it has the potential to be a game changer. Finally, consider the cost and potential for mass adoption. If a high-touch option would only reach a small number of people, would something more scalable be better? These questions will later map to the hypotheses you'll want to validate before a solution is taken forward.

The people who participate in an ideation session can be more important than the exact format. Great ideas often blend a direct need with a creative vision and technical expertise. Those closest to the problem may be unable to see beyond existing constraints, unaware of how related problems have been tackled elsewhere, or unfamiliar with the potential of a disruptive technology. On the other hand, experts from other fields may come with fancy gadgets but may not fully appreciate the realities and dynamics involved: a perfect recipe for collaboration.

Representatives from the communities you seek to serve can bring invaluable insights into how potential interventions fit into their lived realities. Stakeholders from partners and government can offer expertise on supply chains, existing structures, and potential barriers. Even competitors or experts from other geographies can introduce an important perspective. I imagine this to be a bit like the Indian parable of the blind men and an elephant – every person feels a different part of the elephant's body and can only describe the piece they touch. When we bring all these experiences together, we can form a fuller picture.

On the other hand, people from other domains of expertise can introduce new tools and techniques. You might consider including a behavioral scientist, technologist, educator, anthropologist, MBA, policy maker, or artist. Toss in a few wildcards. While they might not land on an appropriate solution directly, fresh perspectives can help the group think out of the box. What emerges may be surprising.

At USAID during the Ebola outbreak in West Africa we recognized that our current tools were insufficient and ran a Grand Challenge in conjunction with the White House and the Centers for Disease Control (CDC) to search for new innovations. One problem was that the standard-issue personal protective suits were designed for air-conditioned buildings. In the hot and humid climate of West Africa, healthcare workers could only wear the suits for 40 minutes at a time, suffering in heat of up to 115 degrees Fahrenheit. Safe donning or doffing required two people and 20–30 minutes. After sweating so profusely, workers could literally pour the sweat out of their boots. Miserable conditions for fighting a terrifying disease.

Among the Grand Challenge winners was a redesigned protective suit from Johns Hopkins University and health nonprofit Jhpiego. Their team convened a hackathon that included everyone from freshmen to robotics experts to a sportswear manufacturer and even a wedding-dress maker. These unconventional thinkers came up with a one-piece suit that could be taken off safely in five minutes with a single move akin to unfurling from a cocoon. It also included an integrated cooling system and a larger fog-resistant viewing area. A licensing agreement has since been signed with DuPont for commercialization.

Numerous resources are available to assist you in the ideation process, from books to paid facilitators to freely available online content. When you have one or more promising solutions in hand, don't forget to stay in love with your problem.

PROVEN SOLUTIONS

Funders and entrepreneurs alike are naturally drawn to creating something they can call their own. However, if your priority is impact, building on an existing, proven solution can entail lower risk and higher reward.

Academic and government institutions make enormous investments in research but often don't have the capacity, infrastructure, or incentives to take even highly successful interventions forward. For example, the US National Institutes of Health (NIH) and the CDC spent over $200 million to conduct an extensive study that demonstrated that the incidence of type 2 diabetes could be cut in half for high-risk individuals through a series of lifestyle changes, supported by individual counseling from a healthcare professional. Despite these compelling findings, which were published in the prestigious *New England Journal of Medicine*, there was no clear path to expand the program beyond the small pilots.

When one of the original researchers from the NIH study had a happenstance meeting with a senior staff member from the YMCA (now the Y) of Greater Indianapolis, a light bulb went off. The Y had local presence, knowledgeable staff, and a mission to promote health and wellness – a strong foundation for deploying a chronic-disease prevention program. Would it be possible to modify the NIH intervention to work in the context of the Y? Over two years, the Y and Indiana University collaborated to refine the best approach for the Diabetes Prevention program, finding that comparable outcomes could be achieved in a group-based format, led by trained staff, at a fraction of the cost. With this adapted protocol, the Y began to replicate the program across its national network. Today, more than 200 Ys across the United States are offering the YMCA's Diabetes Prevention Program. The Y's pioneering work led to a historic decision by Medicare to make the Diabetes Prevention Program a covered benefit beginning in 2018.

There is a natural tension between the goals of academia and the goals of a service-delivery organization. Even with an empirically validated solution, lean experimentation is still necessary to build out operations and adapt to different contexts. There is little incentive for academics to do this more practical work. On the other hand, nonprofits and social enterprises can fall victim to "not invented here" syndrome, preferring to invest in their own ideas.

One exception is Evidence Action, a nonprofit that has deployed a number of evidence-based solutions that originated in academia. It seeks to turn research studies that demonstrate successful results into institutionalized, cost-effective, scalable programs. In Bangladesh, Evidence Action tested an intervention based on Yale University economics professor Ahmed Mushfiq Mobarak's research on offering small transportation stipends to encourage farmers to migrate to towns or cities where they are more likely find work during the lean season – the months between planting and harvesting when they have little food or income. Its experiments have cut the costs for the program in half, streamlined operational systems and processes, and improved targeting based on the discovery that people were more likely to migrate if their neighbors do. With these enhancements, the program, No Lean Season, is rapidly expanding, with 40,000 disbursements in 2017 and concrete plans to reach over 200,000 by 2020.

To facilitate the use and dissemination of evidence-based solutions by both policy makers and practitioners, the UK government launched the What Works Network in 2013. The network consists of seven independent centers focused on areas such as health, education, crime, aging, and economic growth. Many other related initiatives also exist, such as the What Works Clearinghouse run by the

US Department of Education and the Abdul Latif Jameel Poverty Action Lab (J-PAL). Before investing in a new idea, take a look at what has been tried, and what has succeeded and failed, to best target your efforts.

MISSION FIRST

When we ask people to invest in a business venture, we have a responsibility to maximize financial returns. When we ask people to donate money, or beneficiaries to put their time and trust in us, shouldn't we have a similar obligation to maximize social benefit? In all cases, we are stewards. If we can't provide the best possible results, we should make room for better alternatives.

At times, personal or organizational priorities can lead to suboptimal social returns. Even when services could be delivered at less cost or greater scale, mergers of nonprofits are rare, as executive teams and boards are loath to relinquish identity, culture, and control. Too often, teams reinvent the wheel to make their own mark, when successful solutions exist that could be replicated. Fierce competition for grants can lead to hoarding insights as a competitive advantage, rather than collaborating towards a shared purpose. And, political or publicity priorities can trump impact, leading to flashy pilots that make a splash and not much else.

I've had a long-standing debate with a friend who started a boutique social enterprise that sources and sells handicrafts from her native state in India. She runs the business part-time, organizing local craftswomen when she is in country and seeking retail outlets to sell their goods in the United States. I asked her why she didn't connect those women to established distribution channels for local artisans or help expand the sales outlets for existing networks of craftswomen who could benefit from greater access to markets. Either would create greater economies of scale and thus more benefit for more women. Her response? "I enjoy running the business, and doing so my way."

Finding the best solution can mean keeping our egos and organizational priorities in check. This is yet another reason that it is crucial to establish a goal as a North Star that points to the impact we will relentlessly seek. If our goal is to provide better livelihoods for millions of women, what is the best way to do so?

AGAIN AND AGAIN

With a promising solution in hand, teams naturally become emotionally attached. After all, they've done the research, poured in their hearts and creative juices, gotten others excited, and found something that could make a big difference. Sadly, innovation often ends with the big idea. Ideation can be fun, but it is only one step on the long journey to radically greater social good.

As the experience of most social innovators tells us, it's rare for an idea to work perfectly on the first try. Even if a solid kernel exists, many rounds of refinement may be needed before arriving at a validated solution that fully addresses a complex and multidimensional problem. Customers may not embrace it, costs may be too high, or other forces in the ecosystem may prevent the expected social impact from being realized. The messy reality of the real world rarely matches the theory in the lab.

Expect to land back here, again and again. Remember the Lean Impact principle to relentlessly seek impact? Think like a scientist. A new drug may have all the hallmarks of success, but what matters is how it performs in clinical trials. If you become too attached, you may hang on too long and waste precious time and money while ignoring signs that it's time to pivot. Innovation is a continuous process of following the evidence while staying focused on the goal.

Chapter Five
Lessons from *The Lean Startup*

Now that you have a potential solution for your problem, remember that it is only the starting point, or the 1% inspiration. What comes next is the core of innovation – the 99% perspiration that turns a theoretical concept into cold, hard results through experimentation and learning. This book builds upon the process for continuous innovation introduced by Eric Ries in *The Lean Startup*,[1] which has helped companies "create long-term growth and results."

Lean Startup itself builds on the precepts of lean manufacturing pioneered by Taiichi Ohno and Shigeo Shingo at Toyota, which eliminates waste by empowering workers, accelerating cycle times, and delivering inventory just in time. Eric's work was also heavily influenced by his mentor Steve Blank, whose Customer Development methodology is described in *The Four Steps to the Epiphany*.[2]

---

[1] Eric Ries, *The Lean Startup* (New York: Crown Business, 2011). This chapter builds on many concepts from the book.

[2] Steve Blank, *The Four Steps to the Epiphany: Successful Strategies for Products that Win* (Pescadero, CA: K&S Ranch Press, 2005).

Lean Impact: How to Innovate for Radically Greater Social Good, First Edition. Ann Mei Chang.
© 2019 Ann Mei Chang. Published 2019 by John Wiley & Sons, Inc.

Before we dive into how we can employ these same techniques to deliver results in the form of social impact rather than profits in Part II of this book, let's review the five basic building blocks of Lean Startup. We'll explore each in a mission-driven context and refer to them throughout the rest of the book.

1. *Identify assumptions.* What must go right for your solution to work, and what could possibly go wrong?
2. Build a *minimum viable product*, or *MVP*. Run one or more experiments to test the riskiest assumptions as quickly and as cheaply as possible.
3. Use *validated learning.* Gather data from your MVP and compare it to expected success criteria to determine what works and what doesn't.
4. *Build, measure, and learn.* The strongest indicator for success is how quickly you can complete each iteration cycle.
5. *Pivot or persevere.* On a regular basis, step back to take a hard look at whether you are at the point of diminishing returns and need to consider a new tack or are gaining traction and can proceed with more elaborate experiments.

In essence, Lean Startup applies the rigor of the scientific method to systematically test the biggest risk factors that might cause a product or service to fail. By doing so efficiently, you can deploy precious resources to their greatest effect. Don't think of this as a linear process, but rather a set of techniques to employ, driven by the knowledge gained through experimentation. What's important is to stay focused on your goal, be honest about what you do and do not know at any stage, and constantly find ways to learn and improve.

I know several mission-driven organizations whose teams have read *The Lean Startup* and immediately embraced it. They have tended to be technology-centric enterprises, social startups, for-profit businesses, or a combination of all three. I've heard from far more who have been inspired by the concept, but who were unsure of how to proceed given the nature of their funding, culture, or area of focus.

They all have one thing in common: a desire to make a bigger difference by moving the needle on a social cause.

In fact, a grassroots community called Lean Impact sprang up several years ago as an offshoot of the Lean Startup movement, bringing together hundreds of practitioners. What has been missing is a framework that answers the common questions that arise when theory meets reality. How do I experiment when my funding is based on activities and deliverables that are predefined? How can I create a feedback loop when it takes years for true impact to become evident? Is it responsible for us to experiment on people who are already vulnerable? Where do I find the resources to test and iterate when I can barely make payroll?

Lean Impact begins where *The Lean Startup* ends, introducing new tools, reframing the methodology for this new context, and addressing barriers unique to the complexities of social innovation.

HARAMBEE'S STORY

To see Lean Startup in action, let's take a look at Harambee Youth Employment Accelerator, an impressive social enterprise in Johannesburg, South Africa that I visited for a couple of weeks last year. Youth unemployment has hit crisis proportions in South Africa, with almost 40% of young people (officially defined as ages 14–35) not in employment, education, or training.[3] This poses a dire threat to social cohesion, political stability, and an entire generation's ability to lead productive and meaningful lives. To bridge the gap, Harambee seeks to match disadvantaged youth who have never held a formal job with employers seeking qualified talent.

Its CEO, Maryana Iskander, is a small woman who packs a punch. She lifts the office with her peppy enthusiasm and huge

---

[3] Department of Higher Education and Training, Republic of South Africa, *Fact Sheet on "NEETs,"* February 2017, http://www.dhet.gov.za/Planning%20Monitoring%20 and%20Evaluation%20Coordination/Fact-sheet-on-NEETs-Final-Version-27-Jan-2017.pdf.

heart, yet can quickly zero in on the incisive question that needs to be asked. This rare combination makes her a compelling nonprofit leader, coming from prior stints as a consultant at McKinsey and COO at Planned Parenthood.

Maryana embraced a philosophy of experimentation from the start, with a requirement that every idea that is tested has a measurable target. Walking down the hallways, you can't help but notice the walls are plastered with names, scores, and rankings. Everything is measured here from the moment a young person steps through the door. The data helps Harambee constantly improve its algorithms to select the best candidates for the jobs on offer.

Harambee began by talking to both youth and employers to understand their pain points. It turned out that many youth had neither the social networks to connect with job opportunities nor the soft skills – such as punctuality, teamwork, and self-motivation – that were needed to succeed on the job. On the other hand, employers tended to hire the first person through the door, not the best person for the job, only to then suffer from high attrition. A clear opportunity. Harambee decided that its value proposition to employers could be to provide more work-ready candidates, with higher rates of retention. It started with the obvious and did what employers do – administer basic assessments for math and English – and found that very few of its candidates could meet these requirements. A sad legacy of poor schooling.

So, it pivoted. Rather than continuing to test for school-based knowledge, it instead focused on aptitude and sought providers who could assess learning potential. Armed with this new data, the team could select youth who had the personality traits and underlying ability to learn the necessary skills and then train them to fill any knowledge gaps. Employers were happy to receive more qualified candidates and hired many of them.

Harambee has continued to bring this rigorous focus on its goals, deep understanding of its customers, and appetite for constant experimentation and iteration to its work. To date, it has helped over 50,000 youth find their first jobs. We'll return to Harambee's story throughout this chapter to see how it has applied the Lean Startup to maximize its impact.

1. IDENTIFY ASSUMPTIONS

Most mission-driven organizations work under conditions of extreme uncertainty. The existence of gross suffering, injustice, or basic unmet needs in a community usually means that both markets and government have failed. This is where the social sector and philanthropy come in.

We may have lots of ideas about what *might* work, but how do we determine what *will* work? In the face of complex problems and untested solutions in dynamic contexts, we can maximize our chance of success by systematically addressing risks. This begins with an inquiry, adapted from the well-established scientific method, to tease out the key assumptions that are likely to make or break our solution. By testing these potential points of failure up front, we can increase our confidence before considering a greater investment.

For example, Harambee operates in a two-sided market that matches unemployed youth with potential employers. One of its ideas was to offer a training program, called a "bridge," to fill gaps in both soft skills and hard skills for job seekers. Among its key assumptions was that employers would be pleased with the resulting candidate pool and thus hire the candidates. Its first test included 43 job seekers, a single-job family (financial services), and three clients willing to be early adopters. To limit its risk and upfront investment, Harambee outsourced the entire process, identifying candidates through a labor recruitment agency and hiring contractors to perform the training. It worked! 39 of the youth were placed into jobs, and the companies were delighted. With this basic hypothesis validated, Harambee was then able to proceed to testing additional assumptions related to job retention, lowering the cost per candidate, and working with other types of employers.

What Could Go Wrong?

When we land on a promising solution, it's natural to become emotionally attached. After all, we could have a way to alleviate enormous suffering or open the door to tremendous opportunity. On the other hand, naysayers may shoot you down, seeing your nontraditional approach as impractical or even crazy. The trick is to find the balance between faith and dismissal. Let's call it cautious optimism.

One of the classic failures in global development was the PlayPump. The initial launch received big donations and numerous awards based on this creative idea to replace hand pumps in Africa by harnessing the energy of children playing on a merry-go-round to pump water into a storage tank. Too good to be true? It was. After installing 1000 PlayPumps, new deployments were stopped in the face of withering criticism. It turned out the extravagant claims of providing clean drinking water to 10 million people with 4000 PlayPumps by 2010 would have required a full 27 hours a day of "play." And, kids lost interest quickly, given the force required to turn the merry-go-round, leaving the humiliating task to women in the village. Tens of millions of dollars were spent on this scheme.[4]

Before making a big investment in even the most exciting idea, it's prudent to identify our underlying assumptions first. You might articulate these in the form of sentences that begin with "I believe." Or, answer tough questions, such as:

- What could possibly go wrong that could cause this to fail?
- What has to go right for this to work?
- Will people want to buy, use, or adopt it?
- Will they be enthusiastic enough to come back and bring their friends and family?
- Is it more cost effective than existing alternatives?
- Does it lead to lasting positive change?

[4] Andrew Chambers, "Africa's not-so-magic roundabout," The Guardian, November 24, 2009, https://www.theguardian.com/commentisfree/2009/nov/24/africa-charity-water-pumps-roundabouts.

This is the time to play devil's advocate. The same team members and stakeholders who helped to brainstorm new ideas can also help to identify key assumptions. Bring on the skeptics and break out the sticky notes! They will see important angles that you might miss. Don't see this as shooting down your idea, but rather making it stronger.

But don't go overboard. It's not necessary to delineate every last possibility that might cause a hitch. Most of those can be accommodated as they arise. What we are looking for are the *biggest* risk factors, or killer assumptions, that will determine success or failure. Start with the most obvious, continue to ask hard questions along the way, and allow others to emerge as you learn.

Three Hypotheses

The Lean Startup points to the *value* hypothesis and the *growth* hypothesis as the two most important assumptions entrepreneurs need to validate. When it comes to social innovation, we also need to consider a third: the *impact* hypothesis. In other words, does it work? For a solution to produce a substantial social benefit, we have to deliver on all three. This means explicitly identifying the key assumptions for each, validating whether they are true or false, and continuously improving on our results.

Value, growth, and impact are the three essential pillars for a successful social innovation. A mission-oriented solution must deliver *value* to its customers or beneficiaries so they will try it, embrace it, and recommend it to friends and family. Otherwise, trying to convince people to use a product or service they fundamentally don't want will leave you swimming upstream. Additionally, without an engine that will accelerate *growth* over time, an intervention will likely fall far short of the need and remain expensive in the absence of economies of scale. Finally, our ultimate responsibility is to deliver social *impact*. Are we not only improving lives, but doing so to the maximum degree possible?

For example, Harambee started out by testing its dual value hypotheses of helping youth find job opportunities and employers identify work-ready candidates. Its growth hypotheses might include one about the willingness of employers to pay for job placements. And, a first step for its impact hypothesis might involve its ability to place and retain youth in jobs, as a step towards reducing youth unemployment. Part II includes a full chapter on each of these three hypotheses and explores them in detail, along with a wide range of examples.

Once you have articulated your core assumptions around value, growth, and impact, it's time to validate and learn. Of course, there are probably dozens of assumptions you could test, so start with the riskiest. This will help you to identify potential points of failure and improve your approach before you make a bigger investment to build infrastructure, hire a team, or manufacture a product.

So, how do we go about validating assumptions? That's where an *MVP* comes in.

2. MINIMUM VIABLE PRODUCT (MVP)

With a set of prioritized assumptions in hand, the next step is to formulate one or more hypotheses that will validate or invalidate them. While an assumption represents a general belief about what will happen, such as "I believe people will buy my product," a testable hypothesis precisely articulates a provisional theory that can be proven or disproven, such as "If 20 people are offered my product for $10, then 60% will agree to buy it." This if–then structure is one way to make your test (the "if" piece) and the expected result (the "then" piece) explicit. A hypothesis should be objectively measurable so that success or failure is not a matter of debate.

Each hypothesis can be tested through controlled experiments using one or more MVPs. Think of an MVP as the cheapest and quickest prototype or proxy that can enable learning. The faster we can learn, the less time and money we are likely to waste pursuing a fruitless path. An MVP consists of running a test and comparing the results to the original hypothesis to prove it right or wrong. If the test fails, the experiment can be tweaked using different messaging or targeting based on what was learned, then rerun; in some cases, the solution may require a more significant redesign or need to be scrapped altogether.

Alas, in the social sector, many powerful forces are aligned against starting small. What happens instead? Sadly, it means millions of laptops, food packages, cookstoves, or other goods are distributed to people who don't like, know how to use, or maintain them. It means training people on skills that are irrelevant or quickly forgotten. It means running costly and time-consuming evaluations only to discover a fundamental flaw. It means deploying a solution that may work, but which is so expensive that it never reaches more than a few. Or, it means designing and deploying an expensive, multidimensional intervention that results in little impact, or even negative unintended consequences.

The goal of deploying an MVP is to reduce risk. If we can uncover a big or small issue with 10 people before we rolling out to thousands, we'll save money, make faster progress, and avoid alienating potential customers. With a small audience, we can also build a bespoke MVP that is handcrafted to elicit the learning we need, before investing in costly design, production, and infrastructure.

Hypotheticals Versus Behavior

When testing a hypothesis, observing actual behavior is far more accurate and revealing than asking hypothetical questions. This is where the MVP comes in. The aim is to create a simple prototype, mockup, or simulated experience to see how people react. Are they confused? Uninterested? Or do they beg you for the product itself?

In fact, Nexleaf Analytics, a nonprofit that builds and deploys wireless sensors, has found significant differences between actual and self-reported behavior. Early on in its work, it sought to encourage the usage of biomass cookstoves in order to reduce the harmful emissions that contribute to the deaths of over four million people a year. To do so, Nexleaf installed rugged sensors to measure the duration and frequency of cookstove use in poor areas of India. They discovered that when women were asked to report on their own usage, their answers did not match the sensor data. In fact, women both underreported and overestimated their usage.

Ultimately, Nexleaf found the most accurate responses were elicited by combining actual usage data with interviews. In one rural Indian village in which some households were not using cleaner cookstoves, this technique uncovered problems that made the stove design unappealing. Women complained that wood had to be chopped into small pieces and that the batches of fuel sometimes didn't last long enough to complete their cooking.

Obtaining fully honest feedback can be particularly difficult for mission-driven organizations, as we often work with disadvantaged populations in which a cultural barrier or power differential may exist. Thus, people may be too polite or afraid to offend you, and instead say what they believe you want to hear. The social enterprise d.light found that showing potential customers a single solar lamp model would rarely elicit any negative feedback. But when it offered three different versions to compare, people were more comfortable sharing what they preferred about each.

We don't need to go so far as to install sensors for every MVP, but by finding ways to observe people's behavior we can gain a far more accurate picture.

Types of MVPs

There's no hard-and-fast rule for what makes a good MVP, other than that it enables you to learn as quickly as possible. So, how do you design an MVP? Ask yourself, What could you do to learn more about your biggest risk if you *had* to do something tomorrow? How about next week or next month? If you're spending more than a few hours, you're probably overanalyzing. MVPs are intended to be imperfect. If you're not sure, try it. Getting out of the building and seeing how customers behave will open your eyes, even with an imperfect experiment.

What is most important is to shift your mindset from one of building to one of learning. This is not as easy as it sounds, as we've been trained our whole lives to build things. I've often watched teams begin with a simple prototype that quickly grows in complexity based on customer excitement. Soon they're focused more on running the product or service than validating the remaining high-risk assumptions.

The most common approach to building an MVP of a product is to create a rough prototype with minimal functionality. In the case of software, a paper mockup or interactive storyboard can be used to see how users respond to the features, interface, and flow. In the case of hardware, a prototype might consist of cardboard, string, duct tape, or whatever is on hand that can convey the experience of the product.

At the other extreme, an MVP could take a more expensive existing product to test questions around feature set, willingness to pay, or acceptance for a different use or demographic. While testing with a pricey proxy may seem counter to lean, remember that the aim is to avoid wasting time and money. Once we learn how users respond, we can invest more heavily to reduce costs for a design that will be more likely to work.

For an MVP of a service, you might create a flyer or Web page to describe the service, make a special offer for early signups, and see who bites. To test the service itself, you could invite a small cohort to participate in a bespoke experience. Or you might outsource provision, as Harambee did, and avoid building up costly staff and infrastructure. In the case of distribution, you could showcase a catalog and fulfill orders manually to learn about product mix before investing in a streamlined supply chain.

You can also design an MVP to test paths to scale. For example, if you hope to grow your organization quickly, you might put out a job ad and confirm the availability of the talent you need at the price you can pay. If you hope to scale through replication, you might recruit a typical organization and see how well they are able to preserve the fidelity of your offering with minimal training. Or, if you hope to scale through government, you might engage with a current or past official to understand timeframes and criteria for changing policies and winning procurements, then test those.

These are only a few examples of the vast possibilities. A single MVP can often shed light on multiple hypotheses. Have fun, and be creative. Just remember to start small. You'll find many more detailed examples of MVPs in Part II, "Validate."

3. VALIDATED LEARNING

The process of *validated learning* looks at hard data on what works to confirm a hypothesis. It cuts through the emotion and politics that can often drive decision-making and instead focuses on empirically demonstrated evidence.

Harambee knew that placing youth into jobs was not enough. To provide real value to employers, it had to address the pain point of poor retention. If it could do so, companies would be willing to pay Harambee a placement fee and would keep coming back. This required it to beat the typical retention rates for each sector. So, it tracked candidates after being hired to determine if they stayed in their jobs and followed up to understand the reasons behind any departures.

One sector in which it saw high attrition was retail and hospitality. After interviewing the youth, Harambee discovered that they simply weren't physically prepared to stand all day as part of their jobs. As a result, Harambee modified its bridge program so that candidates would regularly stand during their five days of training. This gave youth a chance to get comfortable with that job requirement before showing up to work. Those who couldn't adjust self-selected out, so employers only received candidates who were truly prepared.

Before deploying an MVP, document the key hypotheses you are testing, what data you will collect, and – most crucially – the measurable success metrics. In Harambee's case, improving retention was key. Establishing your criteria in advance will keep you honest and prevent confirmation bias, in which attachment to an idea can lead teams to find some evidence that it's working. These same criteria can also form the basis of an agreement with executives or funders on the results needed to unlock further investment.

Vanity Metrics

There's a crucial distinction between what *The Lean Startup* calls *vanity metrics* versus *actionable* or *innovation metrics* (see Table 5.1 for an example). Vanity metrics tend to reference cumulative or gross numbers as a measure of reach. In the absence of any data on the costs entailed and ensuing impact achieved, they give no indication of whether an intervention is working or better than another alternative. With enough time or money, reach can be increased through brute force. Big numbers may simply mean someone is good at telling a story and raising money.

On the other hand, innovation metrics measure the value, growth, or impact being delivered at the unit level. In the business world, this is analogous to the unit economics – the profit made on each sale – as opposed to the aggregate users or revenues. During the dot-com bubble, startups fueled by plentiful venture capital built up big audiences at a financial loss. Of course, they soon came crashing down, as the fundamentals weren't there. For a mission-driven organization, the equivalent metrics are the unit costs along with the unit yields – such as the rate of adoption, engagement, and success that will bring about the intended social impact. These data points drive

Table 5.1 Examples of vanity versus innovation metrics.

Vanity metrics	Innovation metrics
• Raise $5 million from donors. • Train 10,000 youth in job skills. • 100 employers agree to participate.	• Value: 90% of participants refer a friend. • Growth: Employers are willing to pay a placement fee that covers the cost of training. • Impact: Over 80% of trainees are hired and stay employed for at least six months.

feedback loops, can be tested and improved through experiments, and indicate whether a solution is on track. When the targets are achieved, scaling becomes far easier and more cost effective.

Vanity metrics have spread throughout the social sector like a communicable disease. If you go to the website of your favorite mission-driven organization, I bet what you'll see highlighted is the number of people it has served or reached. While at USAID, I constantly railed against the continual pressure to share the number of people we'd "touched." It's meaningless.

Most workforce development organizations will tell you how many people they've trained. Some may even share how many job placements they've made. But, with enough outreach you can find people in need, with enough funding you can run large numbers of trainings, and with enough participants a certain number will find jobs. What matters is how much you spend to train each person, what percentage of them get jobs, and whether they stay and grow in those jobs. If you can make the biggest difference in long-term employment with the fewest dollars spent, you will have a meaningful competitive advantage and a way to magnify impact.

How metrics are used can also make them more or less meaningful. Many mission-driven organizations collect reams of data – primarily for the purpose of accountability and reporting, as required by their funders. Don't mistake such compliance data with the innovation metrics that you need to learn and drive improvement. There's a difference between doing things right and doing the right things.

Innovation Dashboard

Beyond tracking learning for each MVP, consider replacing your traditional project dashboard that highlights vanity metrics with one that tracks progress against innovation metrics. This can rally stakeholders, ensure transparency, and build engagement.

To do so, it's important to determine how you aspire to be better than the alternatives. If people are burning kerosene today, is your value proposition to offer a less polluting option at the same price? If another nonprofit has a program for reducing gang violence, do you propose to expand reach with a lighter-weight model that can make a similar impact at a dramatically lower cost? If you aim to create a movement, do you have a message that engages more people to take more effective action than other groups? If you can't clearly articulate how you are better than what's out there, think hard about whether you should be competing for scarce funding and attention.

Innovation metrics can be used to track the success criteria that must be met for your unique model to work. These in turn can be broken down into testable hypotheses and MVPs that will move you closer and closer to your goal.

In Harambee's case, an innovation metric dashboard might include the cost of training per job seeker, percentage of candidates hired into jobs, and average retention rate, each with an associated target. Experiments can then be run to test a hypothesis: for instance, whether modifying the training so that students stand all day does in fact lead to higher retention. Based on results, the success criteria may need to be adjusted but should always show a plausible path to the overall goal in aggregate. For example, if Harambee learns that its price point is too high, it might simultaneously reduce the fee it charges employers, its training expenses, and the expected success rate. The strategy remains the same: to demonstrate that it can deliver more value for money than the alternatives.

4. BUILD, MEASURE, AND LEARN

Now that we've identified our hypotheses, built a minimally viable product, measured the results, and started to learn, it's time to do it all over again. After all, the build–measure–learn feedback loop (see Figure 5.1) is at the core of the Lean Startup model.

Engineers such as myself can get stuck building ever-more-elegant solutions, scientists can get stuck gathering and analyzing data, and academics can get stuck delving deeper and deeper into

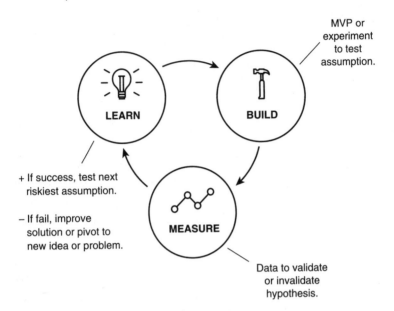

MVP or
experiment
to test
assumption.

+ If success, test next
riskiest assumption.

– If fail, improve
solution or pivot to
new idea or problem.

Data to validate
or invalidate
hypothesis.

Figure 5.1   The build–measure–learn feedback loop.

research. But it's time to put aside the perfectionist in all of us, as the most critical indicator of successful innovation is the *speed* of iteration. The faster we run through the entire cycle, the faster we learn, and the faster we improve.

Alas, traditional grants are not designed to support this model. Many global development programs run for three or five years, with midline and endline evaluations. This means that a five-year program only starts to seriously validate the intervention after two and a half years. And, this is no MVP – the evaluation can take a whole year itself. The upshot is that it can be three and a half years before any meaningful insights emerge on what is working. By then, it's a bit late to change much. In reality, such evaluations are more about ensuring compliance and preventing fraud than learning and improving.

When we think fast feedback loops, we tend to focus on the early startup stage in which we are running rapid experiments to home in on product–market fit for a new solution. This usually involves lots of lightweight MVPs and little scaffolding. But establishing the culture and infrastructure for ongoing build–measure–learn cycles can also help drive continuous innovation and improve performance for more mature products and services.

Iterating for Good

Accelerate Change, an incubator for social enterprises, ran through numerous iterations of the build–measure–learn cycle to develop a service for its client, the Fair Immigration Reform Movement. As lead entrepreneur, Veronika Geronimo set out to learn what low-income immigrants to the United States wanted and needed. She discovered that the greatest demand was simply to learn English.

It turned out that existing classes were slow, expensive, and not always effective at improving language skills. Free or low-cost options often had long waiting lists, and apps were hard to download and easily forgotten. Veronika and her team looked for a better way, quickly testing and failing many times with multiple ideas. They discovered class space was too expensive and that many students found it difficult to access online content and make digital payments.

Veronika's team believed that the best way to learn a language wasn't attending a few isolated classes each week, but rather using English in real-world settings for multiple hours a day, every day. They realized that free content was widely available – on TV, radio, and the Web – and immigrants only needed encouragement and guidance to turn practicing English into a consistent habit. In order to test their hypotheses while limiting bureaucracy and brand risk, they launched the service under a new name, Revolution English.

Through text messages, Facebook Messenger, and email, students receive tips, reminders, and resources for do-it-yourself immersion strategies that can be used throughout their daily lives – while watching TV, listening to the radio, or talking with friends and family. The experience is constantly optimized and improved using experiments that are carefully tracked and analyzed. Although it is free for users, the service has become profitable, primarily through ad revenue, and thus scalable.

By listening to users, constantly experimenting, rigorously measuring results, and developing a business model, Revolution English created a solution that both works and scales. One study found that students who supplemented their ESL classes with Revolution English increased their practice time by over eight hours per week, and that greater engagement correlated with higher final-exam scores. Revolution English now serves over 400,000 people with its free service and expects to reach a million by the end of 2018.

5. PIVOT OR PERSEVERE

After taking a few spins through the build–measure–learn cycle, how will you know when to claim success, keep going, or acknowledge failure? On a regular basis we need to step back, consider what we've learned, and draw conclusions from our experiments. Knowing when we have hit the limits of our current path and need to pivot is essential to innovation.

Identifying success is easy. After running tests and making improvements, have you met your success criteria – the targets for conversion rate, referrals, changed behavior, cost structure, etc. – that indicate your model will work? If so, it's time to take the next step. By starting small, you will have learned important lessons that make a bigger investment appropriate, though of course risks will remain. But don't think for a minute you are done experimenting. Rather, you're simply ready to move to the next stage of learning that incorporates a more realistic scenario, higher-fidelity solution, or expanded audience.

On the other hand, if you haven't reached your targets but are making substantial headway, productively learning through experiments, and have additional ideas to test, buckle down and persevere. However, don't fall victim to wishful thinking. Think of how microwave popcorn is made – the pops start slowing down. If there is a gap of more than two seconds, you better hit stop or your popcorn will burn. Deciding whether to pivot or persevere is similar.

When the pace of learning and progress towards your success criteria has stalled for a while, it's a good time to reevaluate. Is your learning resulting in new improvements that are just as or more promising than your previous ones?

If a key assumption has been invalidated or your model continues to fall far short of your success criteria, it's time to pivot. In *The Lean Startup*, Eric defines a pivot as "a change in strategy without a change in vision." Remember loving the problem rather than the solution? Here's a good opportunity to practice. Stay focused on the goal you defined in Chapter Two, but it may be time to consider a new path. Is there another promising solution that may use an alternative business model, positioning, technology, or delivery mechanism? If not, as another strategy to reach your goal you may need to pivot and tackle an altogether different underlying problem.

As Harambee continued its experiments to improve retention, it found that some young people would stop showing up for work during their first month, even after completing the training. It turned out that many youth were simply running out of savings before receiving their first paychecks and couldn't pay for transport to and from work. To address this, Harambee educated employers and encouraged them to structure a payroll advance that could tide their new employees over.

With its recognition of the importance of transportation costs, Harambee looked further and discovered a strong correlation between poor retention and workers who had to take two or more mini-buses to commute to work. These youth were spending too much time and money to make a low-paying job worthwhile. As a result, Harambee tuned its matching algorithm to make transport and geography deciding factors for lower-paying jobs.

But, even this wasn't enough for those living in the isolated and desperately poor township of Orange Farm from the apartheid era, who were simply too far from any meaningful economic activity. For these youth, Harambee had hit a dead end. It was time to pivot and think out of the box. Then the idea hit the team – cruise ships. Where you live doesn't matter if you will be posted at sea for months at a time. International cruise liners turned out to be a great option for a first job as well as an opportunity for adventure.

A Pivot to Greater Impact

TOMS Shoes is an early pioneer among the growing number of modern companies seeking a double bottom line – to do well while doing good. An essential element of its brand is the One for One model it popularized. For every pair of shoes purchased, another pair is donated to a woman or child in need. Customers can purchase stylish footwear and feel good about fighting poverty at the same time.

Despite giving away more than 60 million pairs of shoes to date, TOMS came under criticism that its charitable model wasn't necessarily making a meaningful difference. To TOMS's credit, it responded by investing in a rigorous study to evaluate its impact. The research showed that donated shoes were not reducing poverty, or even the number of shoeless children. Instead, it had created a mindset of dependency and risked displacing local manufacturers as local shoe purchases declined.[5]

With this stark realization, it pivoted. While TOMS continued to give away shoes, it sought to have them manufactured locally to build local industry and create local jobs. It also diversified its giving to provide more of what communities wanted – eyeglasses, clean water, and training and supplies for birth attendants.

Reaching a lot of people or making a profit does not equate to social impact. The evolution of the One for One model is a valuable lesson in the importance of validating our assumptions, and being willing to pivot based on what we learn. By taking its impact seriously, TOMS is doing more good today as a result.

---

[5] Bruce Wydick, Elizabeth Katz, Flor Calvo, Felipe Gutierrez, and Brendan Janet, "Shoeing the Children: The Impact of the TOMS Shoe Donation Program in Rural El Salvador," World Bank, September 2016, https://openknowledge.worldbank. org/handle/10986/25133.

Evaluating Progress

Deciding whether to pivot or persevere often entails a tough discussion that can affect people very personally. It's difficult not to have an emotional attachment to a solution you've been pouring your heart and soul into for weeks or months. Understandably, the tendency is to kick the can down the road, hoping for an ever-diminishing likelihood of better news. This is particularly true in the social sector, where almost anything we try is helping someone at least somewhat, making it even harder to discontinue a solution that is showing a benefit.

Scheduling regular meetings in advance about whether to pivot or persevere can ensure this important reflection happens, while relieving the day-to-day pressure of continuous scrutiny. A couple of failed experiments in a row may just be a natural part of the cycle. Instilling the discipline to step back regularly, perhaps once every month or quarter, will yield valuable perspective. Ask the question, What evidence do we have to indicate our presumed solution will solve the problem and achieve our goal?

One approach Reprieve, the London-based human rights advocacy organization, has taken is to empower small teams to experiment with multiple approaches as they tackle big problems. As a counterbalance to this autonomy, the teams come together quarterly for a pivot-or-persevere session to review data and evaluate how well each effort is working. Having a regular mechanism to step back and assess helped prevent people from becoming too attached to their own programs. We'll learn more about Reprieve's groundbreaking work in Chapter Nine.

LEAN STARTUP FOR SOCIAL GOOD

The experimental, learning-oriented approach described in this chapter has become pervasive in Silicon Valley at both startups and more established companies. Beyond tech, businesses of all stripes are embracing lean methodologies. Eric Ries' second book, *The Startup Way*, highlights stories from one of the biggest, GE, and shows how larger organizations can integrate a "system of entrepreneurial management."[6] There is a growing recognition of the need for new tools in the face of the accelerating change and uncertainty in our world today.

Through my interviews and direct experiences with over 200 organizations, I have seen this movement begin to take root among those working to achieve social good as well. Make no mistake, this still largely consists of early adopters, whether smaller social enterprises and philanthropists or innovation teams at larger organizations. Yet, they are starting to deliver better solutions and tangible results. People are taking notice.

The rest of this book delves into the unique challenges, contexts, and constraints that have, to date, limited the adoption of lean approaches to social good. My hope is that by learning from the paths these pioneers have blazed, we will unlock the latent potential to deliver dramatically greater social impact at scale.

---

[6] Eric Ries, *The Startup Way: How Modern Companies Use Entrepreneurial Management to Transform Culture & Drive Long-Term Growth* (New York: Currency, 2017).

Part II
Validate

Setting an audacious goal, understanding the problem, and identifying a solution are the necessary first steps towards social impact at scale. Consider your goal, as defined in Chapter Two, as the North Star that captures your aspirational vision for a better world. In Chapter Three, we saw the importance of getting close to your customers and working with them to validate their underlying problems. Chapter Four followed with techniques to identify promising solutions. Then, Chapter Five explored the Lean Startup methodology for validating a solution: identifying the riskiest assumptions, forming measurable hypotheses, then testing these through one or more MVPs. As you may recall, Figure 1.2 illustrated the relationship between these elements in the Lean Impact workflow.

Now Part II dives deeper into validation – the iterative process of testing, learning, and improving that lies at the heart of Lean Impact. For this phase of the innovation journey, curiosity and humility will be essential. After all, we are working in complex ecosystems on long-standing, intractable problems that involve a high

Lean Impact: How to Innovate for Radically Greater Social Good, First Edition. Ann Mei Chang.
© 2019 Ann Mei Chang. Published 2019 by John Wiley & Sons, Inc.

degree of risk. Thus, the likelihood that any idea will be perfectly crafted from the start and optimally deliver the desired impact is infinitesimally low.

That doesn't mean we should throw in the towel and go home. What it does mean is that we must proceed with a healthy dose of skepticism, adopt a learning mindset, and find ways to reduce risk each step of the way. In essence, we must walk before we run. The good news is that there is a time-proven process to do so – the scientific method. Just as for a scientific inquiry, we'll identify implicit assumptions, formulate a hypothesis, predict the anticipated outcome, run experiments, and analyze the results. Chapter Six tackles the nuts and bolts of validation, with an eye towards starting small and speeding up our feedback cycle.

In the three chapters following Chapter Six, we'll explore in depth all the critical dimensions of validating interventions for social good, along with a wide array of practical, real-world examples. What types of assumptions do we need to test? How do we collect data? And, what do MVPs look like in a mission-driven context? A full chapter is dedicated to each of the three key pillars of social innovation: value, growth, and impact. Chapter Seven focuses on the value we deliver to our customers and beneficiaries. Chapter Eight explores the diverse range of potential paths to accelerate growth and scale. And, Chapter Nine tackles the challenges associated with assessing social impact. Throughout Part II, we will examine the common barriers to innovation in the social sector and the successful strategies organizations have discovered to overcome them.

Whenever we run an experiment, we risk embarrassment or disappointment. We put ourselves on the line by introducing a visible measure for success or failure. It can be tempting instead to plow ahead blindly, and hope for the best. Yet, the only way to learn is to be willing to fail. And, learning as fast as possible is what drives innovation.

Chapter Six
Start Small, Iterate Fast

Validation works best when you start small. The faster you can iterate, the faster your pace of improvement and innovation. By learning important lessons early, you can save time and money by avoiding investments in unnecessary infrastructure, manufacturing, and deployment. You can also minimize any potential risk from unintended consequences, particularly if you are working with vulnerable populations.

Programs in the social sector are often planned in painstaking detail, then deployed through large rollouts. This places a big bet on getting everything right off the bat. Inevitably, we don't. Lean Impact replaces this linear process with an iterative one based on the scientific method. Design and implementation are melded into staged tests, each one building on the lessons of the last. Your solution should evolve, not from debates in a conference room, but from the data collected from the reactions and behaviors of real customers and stakeholders. Failure is a natural and essential part of the process.

This chapter will make the case for the Lean Impact principle of starting small, walk through the process of validation, and explore ways

Lean Impact: How to Innovate for Radically Greater Social Good, First Edition. Ann Mei Chang. © 2019 Ann Mei Chang. Published 2019 by John Wiley & Sons, Inc.

to accelerate learning. Once you confirm that you can deliver on all three pillars of social innovation – tangible customer *value*, an engine to accelerate *growth*, and meaningful social *impact* – you have a solid foundation to do more. As the saying goes, "Nail it before you scale it."

LEARNING FROM FAILURE

Over the past 30 years the world has made dramatic progress, reducing the number of people living in poverty by more than half. Most of those gains were made in Asia, leaving extreme poverty increasingly concentrated in Africa, which is now home to half of the world's poor.[1] The majority live in rural areas and depend on agriculture for their livelihoods.

Smallholder farmers, who grow subsistence crops on small plots of land using family labor, are among the poorest and most neglected people on the planet. Despite numerous well-meaning aid programs, the majority still live on less than two dollars a day and do not have access to the modern farming tools and techniques that have the potential to dramatically increase their crop yields and incomes. In 2006, after completing their MBAs at Northwestern University's Kellogg School of Management, Andrew Youn and Matt Forti started the One Acre Fund with an aim to bridge this gap.

The One Acre Fund offers smallholder farmers in Africa a complete bundle of agricultural services, including delivery of improved seeds and fertilizer, training on good farming practices, and access to markets and crop storage facilities to boost their profits. By taking advantage of financing, farmers pay small amounts over time, covering most of the costs. As of 2017, One Acre's core program was serving over 600,000 farmers, increasing their incomes on supported activities by an average of over 50%. It aims to bring these benefits to over a million farmers by 2020.

---

[1] World Bank, "No Poverty," *Atlas of Sustainable Development Goals 2018*, accessed July 23, 2018, http://datatopics.worldbank.org/sdgatlas/SDG-01-no-poverty.html.

But it's not resting on its laurels. The One Acre Fund has constantly sought ways to improve its offerings, and thereby farmers' lives. Early on, in 2008, the team learned of an international buyer for passion fruit as an ingredient for drinks. Research and financial modeling indicated strong economics and potential profits. So they offered passion fruit as a new crop option to their farmer network.

Alas, the realities in the field didn't match the idealized conditions of the researchers' theoretical assumptions. Farmers were wary of this unfamiliar crop and needed extensive training to cultivate it properly. The result was poor quality fruit that fetched far lower prices than anticipated. Transport to ports from inland farms was also more expensive than projected. All in all, it was a failure.

The failure not only impacted the One Acre Fund as an organization, but also a large number of farmers who were already quite vulnerable. Andrew vowed to not let this happen again. He had learned that desk research wasn't reliable and placing such a big bet on an unproven intervention was too risky. By staging risk more gradually, starting with small experiments, he could identify issues earlier and adapt as needed. This led him to create a new innovation framework.

Today, the One Acre Fund sources innovations from across its organization and network. Each idea is evaluated based on potential impact, the percentage of farmers likely to adopt it, the simplicity of the model, and operational feasibility. The best ideas are prototyped with a small number of farmers to learn from their real world experiences. This allows One Acre to iterate at a small scale and apply any necessary changes quickly, cheaply, and with less disruption. What fails, fails small. After prototyping, One Acre validates each of its four criteria through gradually larger trials and more realistic conditions – first a nursery setting, then a few dozen farmers' fields, and finally at the scale of a district with thousands of farmers. Many innovations that initially appear promising are discontinued based on the results. By the time a new product is rolled out to the full farmer network, most of the potential risks are understood.

This process for research and development (R&D) has paid off. Based on the impacts achieved to date, the One Acre Fund estimates that it has generated a four- to six-fold return on investment. One Acre is highly unusual in the nonprofit sector for its commitment to innovation, dedicating 7% of its annual budget to R&D. In the private sector, investors typically consider a company's R&D spending to be a sign of health and a leading indicator of potential future growth. We should value R&D investments in social innovation and their potential to unlock far greater future impact similarly.

PRESSURE TO GROW

Common sense tells us that it's better to fail small than to fail big. When we start by testing a solution with just a few customers, we can reduce risk, refine our idea, and abandon it if necessary without putting a lot of time, money, or reputation on the line. Then we can deliver a much better, validated solution to more and more people over time. So why do so many social interventions start to scale before they're fully tested?

While all of us can get caught up in the thrill of a new innovation and be tempted to get ahead of ourselves, mission-driven organizations face some unique pressures. For one, they're typically either working with people who are suffering today or trying to avert a potential calamity tomorrow. Thus, the need to do something, anything, feels quite urgent. We get into this line of work because we want to make a difference, not stand on the sidelines. Our hearts and our spirits call us to action.

So when there is an opportunity to improve a situation, even just a bit, it is a natural human inclination to want to do as much as possible for as many as possible. Never mind that the consequences are unclear, the work is unsustainable, or a more cost-effective alternative may exist. As a result, organizations tend to land on a solution that is "good enough" to help with the most immediate needs, then stick with it. Yet, by slowing down, starting small, and validating first, we could create far more benefit for far more people over time.

During my time as chief innovation officer at Mercy Corps, a global humanitarian aid nonprofit, I experienced this phenomenon firsthand. Our Social Ventures team raised an innovation fund in 2014 to invest in building our own social enterprises. Think of these as startups for social good. The goal was to create financially sustainable, mission-aligned businesses that would continue to grow and thrive long after the initial funding was spent. Among the first was KibaruaNow, an online marketplace similar to TaskRabbit, that connected disadvantaged youth to short-term work in Nairobi, Kenya. The youth-population bulge and resulting high levels of unemployment is one of the biggest social challenges in Africa, so this business was well aligned with our mission.

It started out well. We found an amazing Kenyan leader with a passion for the business, experience tackling youth unemployment, and a postgraduate degree from a top African university to boot. She quickly recruited a local team of youth who were eagerly seeking work and clients who were willing to pay. The team created a simple vetting process to screen so-called taskers and was off to the races. After testing a range of possible tasks, they learned that without a trusted relationship, customers were uncomfortable fronting the necessary cash for errands or entrusting a stranger with their children. So, KibaruaNow decided to focus on housecleaning.

Each day new taskers were sent to clean homes, and many youth earned two or three times more than they could before. The business started to grow. There was one problem. KibaruaNow was losing money on every transaction and headed towards a financial cliff. Although the team had agreed on metrics for success and was given clear direction to stay small until the unit economics were validated, no one on the team could bring themselves to turn away the youth who arrived in desperate need of work. More and more effort became focused on running the business rather than experimenting with ways to bring costs down and improve revenues. We never landed on a viable business model and ultimately had to shut down the enterprise.

Oftentimes the pressure to grow is not internal, but external. Most funders want to see tangible results for the money they provide, and that means numbers – the bigger the better. The websites of nonprofits, social enterprises, foundations, government agencies, and impact investors are littered with vanity metrics on the number of people, communities, schools, or small businesses that have been reached. Yet such raw numbers only indicate activity, not whether the intervention was effective.

Some organizations may go further to include aggregate measures of benefit, such as lives saved, kids educated, or incomes increased. This is a significant improvement as we can attribute a positive effect. But, does it merely reflect prolific fundraising? Could another entity have made a far greater impact with those same funds? I once came across a program that claimed to have raised the aggregate incomes of smallholder farmers in a community by 1 million dollars, which sounded fantastic until I discovered that 10 million dollars had been spent to do so.

Harsh financial realities can also cause a premature shift from validation to delivery. Nonprofits and social enterprises operate on a shoestring. Sometimes accepting a strategically misaligned grant can mean the difference between making payroll or layoffs. There is no shame in this. But don't let yourself be perpetually caught up in funding cycles and donor priorities, and lose sight of your ultimate goal. If you can explicitly acknowledge when you decide to make a temporary compromise and keep it within tight constraints, you can map a path back to your vision and the validation required to get there.

VALUE, GROWTH, AND IMPACT

In the business world, recognizing the signs of success is simple. If users love a product or service, they will buy it, tell their friends, and come back for more. Because the user of a product or service is typically also the purchaser, assumptions regarding value and growth tend to be well aligned. As a result, most commercial design practices focus on validating customer value.

The job of a mission-oriented organization is far more complex. Not only do value and growth frequently involve different customers with divergent priorities, but social impact, rather than profits, is the true goal. Thus, a successful solution must fulfill all three of the

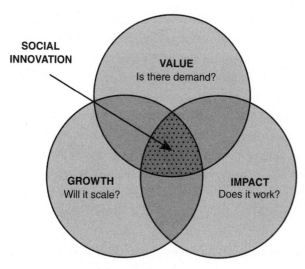

Figure 6.1   The three pillars of social innovation.

sometimes conflicting pillars of social innovation: value, growth, and impact (see Figure 6.1).

We typically start with value. After all, if we don't deliver value to our beneficiaries, our solution may not be used, bought, or recommended to others. When evaluating value, what people do is far more revealing than what they say. If someone is asked a hypothetical question about whether they like a product or service, a positive response may merely indicate a reluctance to offend. But if users are beating a path to your door and bringing their friends, you're likely onto something. The more your users find value in what you are offering, the easier it will be to drive growth and ultimately impact.

In concert with value, we also need to consider the engine that can accelerate growth over time. Too often, interventions are scaled through brute force with grant money, and sustainable models for scale are only evaluated after the limits of charitable funding are exhausted. The problem is that injecting a new growth strategy can have significant implications that may force you to completely redesign your solution. For a market-driven business model, you may need to target a lower price point based on ability to pay. Replication or franchising will only work with a simple, well-defined intervention that can be delivered equally well by a third party with far less training and expertise. Or if deploying through government, your costs and processes must conform to existing budgets, policies, and politics. By testing the engine for growth early, your solution can evolve in ways that will enable it to scale over time.

Of course, our ultimate goal is to deliver social impact. People may demand potato chips and you might have a compelling business plan to sell them, but what social benefit does it offer? The impact hypothesis can often be the most challenging to validate, as conclusive impact may take years to prove – think of challenges such as increasing high school graduation rates, reducing recidivism, combating climate change, or ending the cycle of violence or poverty. Yet, lighter-weight proxies can often give an indication of whether you are on track sooner and help you to refine your approach so that success is more likely down the line. Compelling impact will also increase perceived value, further fueling adoption.

What does it look like when one of these three pillars is missing? If users don't perceive sufficient value and thus don't want or demand a solution, you might find yourself in the same situation as those trying to provide polio vaccinations in Nigeria and Pakistan. Though the vaccine has proven effective and is funded for worldwide administration, some families refuse treatment due to religious beliefs, false rumors of health risks, or distrust of workers. A similar lack of perceived value has at times hampered clean cookstoves, toilets, mosquito nets, and numerous other interventions from being used as intended.

If no viable path exists to accelerate growth, the result might resemble the first incarnation of EARN, a nonprofit helping low-income Americans save money that we learned about in Chapter Two, when a highly effective and desirable solution was only reaching a tiny fraction of those in need. This is all too common in the social sector, where the scale of most solutions begins to plateau far short of the need. Not only does this leave out many who suffer, but the overall value for money is significantly lower without economies of scale.

And if the intended social impact does not materialize, an intervention might become widespread without delivering the promised benefit. As we'll learn about more in Chapter Nine, in the case of microfinance decades passed and hundreds of millions of customers were reached before rigorous evaluations contradicted the original claims of increased incomes and women's empowerment. The fascinating book *Poor Economics*, by Abhijit Banerjee and Esther Duflo, chronicles numerous such failures in the global development arena.[2]

Few mission-driven organizations embrace and validate all three pillars of social innovation from the start. As a consequence, precious time, money, and even lives are being wasted. This is one reason the sector as a whole vastly underperforms relative to its potential. By investing in more diligence upfront to ensure solutions meet real user needs, have a sustainable engine for growth, and achieve the desired social impact, far more social benefit can be created over time.

Some trailblazing entities have stepped in with tools and techniques to deliver on value, growth, or impact. Each has their aficionados and advocates, along with associated funding, luminaries, and consultants. Yet, this expertise largely remains siloed and rarely are all three considered in concert. At the forefront is value, or desirability, which is moving into the mainstream, driven by HCD and behavioral science. The importance of evaluating impact continues to gain traction, bolstered by development economists, the effective altruism movement, and a collection of evidence-first nonprofits and funders, although it is not often integrated into an iterative learning process. Perhaps least prevalent are growth models that enable solutions to reach true scale, with leadership coming from social entrepreneurs exploring innovative business models, some larger nonprofits engaging with governments, and others (such as the Skoll Foundation) who promote systems change.

[2] Abhijit J. Banerjee and Esther Duflo, *Poor Economics: A Radical Rethinking of the Way to Fight Global Poverty* (New York: Perseus Books Group, 2011).

As the next frontier, Lean Impact proposes a holistic approach that incorporates value, growth, *and* impact from the start. There are no shortcuts. To realize social impact at scale, we need to deliver on all three.

STAGING RISK

How do you determine which assumptions to test first? There's no simple formula, but it is important to consider risk, time, and cost. The goal is to eliminate the greatest degree of risk with the least investment of time and money (see Figure 6.2). A good place to start is by identifying the killer assumptions – the biggest risks with the potential to make or break your solution. Both internal and external skeptics may have something to say on this topic. Give them a chance to voice their concerns.

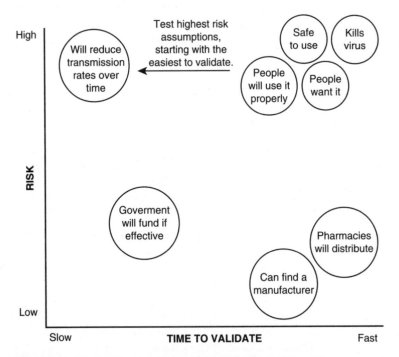

Figure 6.2   Prioritizing assumptions for Tenofovir (illustrative only).

Your killer assumptions can each be broken down into one or more hypotheses, which are in turn tested using one or more MVPs. With a dose of creativity, an MVP can be quite simple. Consider the roughest prototype, fewest people, and fastest experiment that could help you learn. While an individual test might only shed light on one dimension of an assumption, it may provide sufficient insight to immediately invalidate a particular path or give you the confidence to proceed with more expensive tests.

Of course, some assumptions realistically take more time to test than others. Long-term impacts, such as educational attainment, breaking the cycle of poverty, or improved health may take years to fully manifest. And, obtaining rigorous evidence of such impact through randomized control trials (RCTs) or similar tools can be slow and costly. But that doesn't let you off the hook to learn as much as possible first. If you find that your killer assumptions are landing in the upper-left corner of Figure 6.2, look for ways to break them down into early indicators that are predictive of those eventual outcomes and can be tested more cheaply and quickly. We'll explore this more when we delve into the impact hypothesis in Chapter Nine.

In certain situations – such as for medical drugs, devices, and procedures – regulations may even require that an RCT be completed before a solution can be deployed. But that doesn't mean we should plow forward blindly. Consider the case of Tenofovir, a vaginal gel intended to prevent the transmission of HIV. Through early clinical trials in a highly-controlled environment, it was found to be safe to use and effective in killing the virus. Given these promising results, large aid donors paid millions of dollars for a three-year phase-3 clinical trial called FACTS 001 that was undertaken in South Africa as the final step for regulatory approval. The result? No statistically significant difference between the placebo group and the treatment group.[3] How could that be?

It turned out that the women in the trial didn't use the gel consistently both before and after every sexual encounter as required.

[3] Helen Rees, "Results of the FACTS 001 Tenofovir Gel Study," AVAC Webinar, March 9, 2015, https://www.avac.org/sites/default/files/u3/after_facts.pdf.

While Tenofovir worked in a controlled clinical setting, the messy reality of life made it undesirable and impractical. Given cultural dynamics, stopping to apply the gel in the heat of the moment often wasn't possible. Of course, skipping the phase-3 trial was not an option. But a much shorter and cheaper test could have been conducted first to understand the women's preferences and realities – verifying value before impact. If that had been done, the researchers might have redesigned or abandoned the drug before investing in such a big trial.

The order of testing can be just as important as which assumptions are tested. Start as small as possible with the biggest risks. Then add more complex, expensive experiments after eliminating the more obvious ones.

FASTER ITERATION

Once you have identified the first assumption to test, your validation cycle begins. For each iteration, start with an assumption, formulate a hypothesis to validate or invalidate the assumption, build an MVP to test that hypothesis, run experiments to measure the response, and learn whether your hypothesis is in fact true. Even if the initial results are positive, you may want to consider additional dimensions, different conditions, or a larger sample size. Or, if you have gained sufficient confidence, it may be time to move onto the next riskiest assumption. On the other hand, if the results are negative, take a step back and consider whether to refine your test, improve your solution, or make a more significant pivot.

The most crucial factor for success is not designing the perfect experiment, but rather the speed at which you can execute each turn of your feedback loop. A cycle is the basic unit of learning. When we don't consolidate learning until months or years into a program, we miss opportunities to course correct along the way. Imagine sailing a boat without checking the direction, speed, location, and wind regularly. You'd be unlikely to take an efficient route. By reducing the time for each iteration, we can learn and improve more quickly.

Prototypes and feedback loops are easy if you're running an online service. It's no coincidence that the accelerated pace of progress in Silicon Valley corresponds to the transition from boxed software for personal computers to online services in the cloud. Companies such as Google and Facebook are able to deploy hundreds of A/B tests every day as controlled experiments to compare the performance of their current service (the control, or A) with a new version of their user interface or algorithm (the variation, or B). Some of these may be minor tweaks in layout, language, or color. Others may include new features, modified algorithms, or more dramatic redesigns of the product or service. Today, almost all online sites stage their rollouts by first running A/B tests with a smaller cohort to ensure that any change works well and represents a real improvement.

Of course, many, if not most, social innovations don't involve an online service. Realistically, this means tests will require more manual effort and not be quite so instantaneous. But the same principles apply. Iteration time can be reduced by starting with a small cohort and designing the simplest MVP that will shed light on a hypothesis. Summit Public Schools reconfigured a classroom for a week, Nexleaf Analytics tried different cookstove designs with a small number of women, and the One Acre Fund now tests new crops with a few farmers first.

When Kudoz first prototyped its service, it asked 20 adults with a cognitive disability to select from options in a mocked-up catalog. Within a week, it delivered the first experiences by having existing team members serve as hosts. As most of its clients were nonverbal, it created a range of visual and tactile materials that could be used to self-identify emotions before and after an experience and took photos to look at body language. This allowed Kudoz to measure changes in motivation, capabilities, and engagement to determine how its offerings were being received and whether it was having a positive effect.

In the following three chapters, I'll share numerous other examples of how organizations tested their value, growth, and impact hypotheses.

COLLECTING DATA

Through their extensive work with early-stage social entrepreneurs, the venture philanthropists at the Draper Richards Kaplan Foundation have found that a culture of rigorous data collection is one of the primary drivers for greater impact. Good, timely data gives us an unbiased view into experiments so that decisions can be made scientifically rather than be based on potentially biased opinions. It can also be used to monitor ongoing performance, drive continuous improvements, and quickly surface any issues.

Although my own background has been in the tech sector, I've tended to shy away from leaping to technology-based solutions for global development challenges. In low-income countries, too often basic access or literacy doesn't exist. And a cool gadget can divert you from first understanding the underlying need. I have generally found it more fruitful to start with an analog solution, iterating on it to convincingly understand a problem, and only then consider digital automation as a means to lower distribution costs and increase scale.

Where I *have* found technology to be a consistent game changer, however, is for data collection. There simply is no substitute for the speed, accuracy, and flexibility of capturing, sharing, and analyzing data digitally. During the Ebola outbreak in Liberia, one of the biggest challenges was obtaining accurate information on transmission rates, geographic spread, and health service availability. A member of my team at USAID who was deployed to the country found that data was often collected on scraps of paper, transmitted by motorbike, and entered multiple times into incompatible health information systems. A slow and error-prone process.

Timely, accurate data is the fuel that drives your feedback loop. The purpose of experiments and MVPs is not the prototype itself, but rather the resulting data that tells you what works and what doesn't work so you can learn, adapt, and improve.

> The *Lean Data*^{SM} initiative at Acumen, a nonprofit global venture fund, uses low-cost technologies to collect data for social enterprises on customer feedback and social indicators. Its aim is to drive feedback loops that deepen impact with more timely and relevant insights than traditional measurement tools can offer.
>
> More resources, including a field guide, online class, and newsletter, are available at http://www.acumen.org/lean-data.

In Chapter One, we learned how Summit Public Schools uses a technology platform to manage curriculum, assessments, and student information. By analyzing this data, Summit gains rapid insight into what is working or not, so they can quickly adapt. While most attention focuses on the transformative potential of user-facing technologies, such enterprise data systems can make a huge difference in accelerating innovation and improving results.

Given the proliferation of mobile phones and the increasing sophistication of big data tools, collecting and analyzing data digitally has become feasible almost everywhere. When Living Goods was founded in 2007 to improve rural healthcare through a network of Avon-like health entrepreneurs, only 30% of the Ugandan population had mobile phones. Five years later, with mobile penetration at 70%, the organization reinvented itself to be digital first. Founder Chuck Slaughter found the shift transformative, moving "data at light speed versus bicycle speed." Using digital tools, Living Goods has been able to reduce costs, improve accuracy, and decrease the turnaround time of getting data back from the field, thus dramatically increasing its pace of learning.

One experiment with 30 community health promoters tested a prototype Android app built by two Kenyan programmers for under $2000 to register pregnant mothers. Using the streamlined user interface of this new smartphone app, health workers dramatically increased the number of pregnancies they accurately identified and captured from 35% to 85%. This early identification enables Living Goods to reduce complications by providing health and nutrition tips, flagging risk factors, monitoring danger signs, and making referrals to a health facility if necessary.

The decreasing cost and increasing sophistication of sensor technologies and the Internet of Things opens up new possibilities for low-cost data gathering. Nexleaf Analytics is building cloud-based sensors to remotely monitor cold-chain storage of vaccines and usage of clean cookstoves. Smaller steps can also be taken with technology-enabled solutions that are not fully automated. In refugee camps in across Africa, the American Refugee Committee (ARC) has deployed a real-time feedback system called Kuja Kuja to track customer satisfaction with water distribution, healthcare, and other services. Refugees employed by ARC stand at service locations with mobile-enabled tablets and ask two simple questions: Are you satisfied with the service, and do you have an idea to make us better? The results are shared transparently on a public dashboard.

A common complaint for many programs is the lack of data on outcomes beyond the end of an engagement. By following up via text messages every four months for two years, Harambee Youth Employment Accelerator has been able to keep its fingers on the pulse of the trajectory for its job seekers in South Africa. Youth report whether they secured employment, were promoted, lost their job, or found Harambee helpful in finding a job. With a 30% (and growing) response rate, it's been able to glean significant insights it can use to tune its products and services.

As organizations collect, collate, and analyze more and more data, new possibilities will open for analytical tools to better predict trends, understand correlations, and identify opportunities. Perhaps one day, the same algorithms that Amazon uses to predict the next product you will want to purchase will be used to predict what intervention is most likely to transform someone's life for the better.

SUCCESS CRITERIA

Objective success criteria, established before experiments are launched, are important to counterbalance the groupthink that can arise from enthusiasm or exhaustion. Determine these targets based on what will be necessary to reach your goal rather than what seems possible for you to achieve. This will typically reflect a combination of appreciable improvement relative to the status quo, a cost structure that can be scaled, and a realistic assessment of how the pieces come together to deliver the intended outcome. How many doors do you have to knock on to get a positive response? What percentage of recipients need to correctly use the goods or training to improve health, reduce crime, or protect the environment? How often do people come back for more or bring their friends?

It is important to note that each of these *innovation metrics* is based on unit measures. That is, for each 100 attempts, how frequently does the desired result occur? In contrast, *vanity metrics* typically report on absolute numbers and are easy to game simply by pouring in more dollars, time, or people. Table 6.1 illustrates a simplified set of success

Table 6.1   Success criteria example.

Success criteria	Hypotheses (to test)	Target
Value: 50% of all farmers in the region will participate	Percentage of farmers approached by sales staff who will sign up	30%
	Average number of referrals after first growing season	2
Growth: Net contribution margin of $10 per farmer	Amount farmers are willing to pay for seeds, fertilizer, and training	$200
	Percentage loan repayment rate	95%
	Cost of raw materials and staff	-$180
Impact: Average income increases by 70% for participating farmers	Average percentage increase in crop yields	90%
	Percentage of crops spoiled or unsold	20%

criteria for a hypothetical intervention to improve smallholder farmer incomes. One way to reach 50% of all farmers in a region could be to hire sales staff to do outreach. Perhaps the pitch will be compelling enough for 30% of the farmers to sign up right away, and the remaining 20% might come later through referrals. To be financially sustainable and allow for growth, we might seek a small net profit from each farmer who participates. They'll need to be willing to pay more than our marginal costs, and if we offer loans we should also factor in default rates. Finally, if the overall goal is for average income to increase by 70%, perhaps crop yields will need to increase by 90%, to allow for some spoilage or dysfunctional markets.

Notice that each of these discretely measurable hypotheses can be validated through experiments. If they all prove to be true, then the associated success criteria will likely be met. If not, the strategy may need to be adjusted. For example, if only 20% of farmers respond to recruiters initially, the success criteria of 50% participation could still be achieved if each then refers a larger number of friends. Similarly, higher costs or default rates could work if greater revenues can be generated. And if markets or transport options prove to be highly unreliable, even higher yield increases may be required. Throughout the validation process, keep an eye on your success criteria, make adjustments based on your results, and recognize if all likely paths become blocked and it's time to pivot.

DIMINISHING RETURNS

For validation, starting small is essential. But you also don't want to only run experiments forever. Certainly, if you aren't making good headway towards your success criteria for value, growth, and impact, it may be time to consider a pivot. However, if you have successfully validated your killer assumptions, continuing to test every last hypothesis will soon run into the law of diminishing returns.

Don't let yourself get too comfortable. Remember, the reason we want to start small is to spend the least amount of time and money learning the lessons we need to learn. It's a waste to fail with 1000 when we can fail with 10. It is also true that as our remaining assumptions become less and less risky, running lots of small experiments, even cheaply, can be a different waste of precious time and money. We want to always sit on the edge of comfort, so that we continue to learn as fast as possible. That means that once we have gained reasonable confidence, we should aggressively take on more risk in the form of greater scale, a more realistic deployment, or new contexts.

The goal is not to validate a solution to 100% confidence. That will never happen. The goal is to answer the make-or-break questions and to do so with the smallest investment possible.

Chapter Seven
Value

Over the years I have heard far too many stories of well-meaning investments being made in goods or services that people simply don't like or want. Homeless people may choose not to stay in available shelters or visit free clinics, villagers may use a mosquito net for fishing rather than protection from malaria, and unemployed youth may forgo training and ignore resource guides. Earlier I shared the examples of clean cookstoves, a water-pumping contraption, and an HIV-prevention gel that all went unused. What we want to offer may not be desired or needed. Or it may simply be too inconvenient, poorly designed, distasteful, or embarrassing.

This shouldn't come as a surprise. After all, how many of us do everything that we're told is good for us? I know I should eat more vegetables, meditate, and do yoga, but I don't. For a social innovation to provide real value it must tap into users' real wants and needs, not only what we believe is good for them. People don't always choose what is in their theoretical best interest.

One reason undesired interventions persist for longer in the social sector is because frequently it is *funders* rather than consumers

Lean Impact: How to Innovate for Radically Greater Social Good, First Edition. Ann Mei Chang. © 2019 Ann Mei Chang. Published 2019 by John Wiley & Sons, Inc.

who are paying for them. Without the important signal that a purchase decision sends to confirm perceived value we can be lulled into believing something is wanted when it is not. A company knows immediately it has a problem if no one buys its product or service. But if we are giving something out for free, how do we know what people really think? Some organizations have even imposed a nominal charge as a way of affirming interest in their offerings.

Our aim shouldn't be merely to provide *some* value, but rather to offer something beneficiaries demand, use, and encourage their family and friends to adopt. If users see compelling value, it will be far easier to achieve impact at scale.

In the business world, validation of value is typically a two-dimensional problem, sometimes referred to as customer discovery or product–market fit: that is, finding the sweet spot to delight a customer by matching the design of the product on one hand and the target market segment on the other hand. In the social sector, the target customer is frequently fixed due to the organizational mission, funding source, or most pressing needs. Thus, identifying the value proposition primarily involves modifying only one dimension – the proposed intervention. As Josh Harvey, director of research and design at CARE, puts it, "Your customer already exists. You can't choose your own customer by moving to a more attractive market."

This chapter focuses on the value hypothesis, the first pillar of social innovation. Are we providing something our beneficiaries merely accept, or do they want it, choose it, and prefer it? Validating your solution typically starts with the value hypothesis, as we won't get far if no one wants what we're offering.

THE ACCIDENTAL MVP

When you put yourself out there and deliver compelling value, customers will find you, even if what you're offering is imperfect. In 2016, Ezra Levin and Leah Greenberg were 30 years old, married to each other, and former congressional staffers. After the US presidential election, they saw a wave of grief and frustration across the country. Many people who had never been involved in politics before became energized to resist the new Trump administration, but had no idea how to get started. While working on the Hill, Ezra and Leah had seen firsthand the emergence of the Tea Party in the 2000s, the tactics it employed, and the outsized effect it had on Congress and President Obama's agenda. Over Thanksgiving, as part of their own therapeutic process, they pulled together some friends to create a simple online advocacy guide with hopes of sparking progressive action.

Half an hour after Erza tweeted a link to their 23-page Google Doc, it went viral. The document kept crashing, and a flood of emotional emails expressed gratitude for a path forward and a way to connect with others. Press and celebrities fueled further attention. The guide served as a rallying cry for people across the country seeking a sign of hope. Indivisible was born. To date, the Indivisible guide has been viewed or downloaded over two million times, over five thousand local affinity groups have been registered, and chapters have rallied activists across the country at marches and town halls. Indivisible was credited as a major force in preventing the repeal of Obamacare.

Ezra and Leah's Google Doc was an MVP, assembled over three weeks and still containing embarrassing typos. Although they had not intended to create an organization, the overwhelming reaction to their unintentional experiment demonstrated a real need. If you *are* considering starting a movement, get out early to learn if anyone is interested before hiring people, investing in infrastructure, and raising funds.

There is a place for planning and research, but it's easy to get stuck in analysis paralysis. As Lean Startup guru Steve Blank recommends, "Get out of the building." Research lives in the realm of theory and can inform context, understanding, and ideas. But there is no replacement for seeing how actual users respond to a product or service. Real-world data can cut through long debates and get a project on track fast.

Remember, asking is not the same as doing. If a bunch of American aid workers show up to ask some Indian villagers what Internet service is of most interest, they'd probably be embarrassed to answer if it's pornography. And if Ezra and Leah had asked activists what they wanted in a guide, they might have gotten bogged down for months debating the design and content. For an MVP, the goal is to approximate one or more elements of the anticipated experience to see how people respond in real life. With any luck, they'll be clamoring for more, as with the Google Doc that led to Indivisible.

DESIGNING WITH USERS

When we not only consider but also collaborate with users to design solutions, the process of ideation, feedback, and validation can become seamless. In Chapter Three, we saw how Proximity Designs in Myanmar engaged farmers from the start to design an affordable treadle pump that would be lighter weight and more portable. Proximity practices HCD, perhaps the most widespread framework for designing with and for users. As one of its early pioneers, IDEO describes HCD as sitting at the intersection of empathy and creativity. I see HCD as a close cousin to Lean Impact – both are customer centric, utilize rapid prototyping, and seek fast feedback loops. The main differences are in terminology and emphasis, with HCD particularly well suited for understanding and delivering customer value in the earlier stages of design.

Human-centered design (HCD), also known as design thinking, is a creative approach to design that aims to incorporate the human perspective in every step of the problem-solving process. It puts the customer or beneficiary front and center to ensure solutions fully consider their wants, needs, and perspectives.

IDEO.org, a nonprofit spun out from famed design firm IDEO, offers free online tools and case studies tailored for the social sector at www.designkit.org.

For the same reasons we saw in Chapter Three that proximity is crucial to understanding problems, integrating customers throughout the validation process can yield solutions that are more usable, appropriate, and broadly adopted. New Story, a nonprofit that builds homes for poor families, has adopted such a participatory design approach. Cofounder Alexandria Lafci was shocked to discover ghost towns around the world, where millions of dollars have been wasted on homes that lie empty, as they don't meet the critical needs of families, such as proximity to their income sources and social networks. When she interviewed these families to ask where they would like to have their homes built and how buildings should be arranged, she was met with surprise – they were not used to being asked for their opinions and had become accustomed to simply receiving whatever was given, whether useful or not.

New Story has embraced Y Combinator's simple but essential motto, "Make something people want." In the gang-infested neighborhoods of El Salvador, its team learned that mothers were deeply concerned that their children would be recruited into lives of violence. Using moveable paper cutouts of buildings, New Story and families worked together to explore different community layouts. They landed on one in which houses are clustered around a common space, with doors facing towards the center. This created a neighborhood feel and a sense of safety and security.

For the San Diego Food Bank, keeping up with the work of serving 370,000 people a month left staff with so little bandwidth that they found it difficult to do more than react to issues as they arose. Then a longtime donor, the San Diego Foundation, sponsored the team to attend a multiday innovation bootcamp led by Moves the Needle. As they took a step back to consider the problem of low retention among volunteers, they wondered what would encourage more to come back. Food bank managers assumed that their noble mission was the main hook and giving out schwag might be a good incentive. But when they started interviewing volunteers, they discovered that it was the interaction with people – both staff and other volunteers – that mattered. They realized that a better reward would be lunch with the CEO or a social event with food bank staff and other volunteers.

Sadly, while not necessarily expensive, raising money for participatory design can be difficult. Most donors prefer well-defined solutions, to minimize risk and uncertainty. Fortunately, forward-leaning funders have started to experiment with more flexible mechanisms. Among them is the Federal Transit Administration (FTA), which has started awarding small planning grants to develop new ideas using a design-thinking process through its cooperative agreement with the National Center for Mobility Management, an FTA-funded technical assistance center.

The United Way of Buffalo and Erie County in New York State received one such $25,000 grant in 2015. In a focus group with expectant mothers, transportation surprisingly emerged as the most significant pain point. As its team learned more from the women, they discovered that many did not have sufficient savings to purchase monthly bus passes and as a result were paying up to 50% more than necessary for transport. This led them to propose a matching savings account to help pregnant mothers manage their money and take advantage of more economical transit payment options.

By involving customers, stakeholders, and beneficiaries as much as possible and as early as possible, we are far more likely to arrive at designs that serve their needs well.

DESIGN IN CONTEXT

Even better than designing with users is users designing for themselves and their communities. They understand the problems and context intimately and are personally motivated to make positive change. This is relatively rare in the social sector, particularly when working with disadvantaged communities who frequently lack the resources, education, and confidence to promote solutions and access funding. There is vast untapped potential.

At the USAID Lab, we continually sought to engage more local innovators through capacity building, accelerators and incubators, and more accessible funding streams. Among these is the Securing Water for Food Grand Challenge, which seeks to help farmers around the world grow more food using less water. In the fourth Global Call for Innovations, which closed in the fall of 2016, we were delighted that 74% of applicants came from developing countries.

One awardee from the first round of awards was Claire Reid, founder of Reel Gardening in South Africa. As a 16-year-old girl in Pretoria, Claire struggled to plant a vegetable garden on a small patch of land. Each type of seed had to be planted at a certain depth, spaced a particular distance apart, and supplemented with the right amount of fertilizer. It was a tedious process in which so much could go wrong. She was also frustrated by wasting precious water, as well as having to buy seeds and fertilizer in far larger quantities than she needed. She knew that many low-income families couldn't afford the expense and risk of failure to invest in growing their own fresh vegetables.

Claire came up with an ingenious solution. She took seeds along with the necessary fertilizer and encased them in strips of paper, spaced an appropriate distance apart, with markings indicating the depth for planting. Through tests with the University of Pretoria, she determined that her method could save up to 80% of the water required for germination by only watering judiciously at the marks where the seeds were buried. As the concept began to gain traction, Reel Gardening received a grant from Securing Water for Food, which was willing to take the risk to invest in her growing business. Today, Claire's Garden in a Box is available through a variety of distribution channels, including the Girl Scouts of America catalog, stores in South Africa and the United Kingdom, as well as through direct donations to schools and low-income communities.

Through the Lab's Development Innovation Ventures (DIV) program, we supported another inspiring innovator, Sanga Moses. Sanga did not even have shoes when he was growing up in a village in Western Uganda. But he worked hard, was the first from his family to graduate from college, and landed a coveted bank job in the capital city, Kampala. One day when he went home to visit his family, he found his 12-year-old sister walking by the side of the road carrying a huge bundle of firewood. When she saw him, she started to cry. She had walked six miles, and was tired of missing school.

Sanga was so upset that he quit his job to find an alternative source of fuel that wouldn't require girls to spend hours each day collecting firewood for cooking. After a year of research, he invented a machine to turn abundantly available agricultural waste into fuel briquettes that burn longer, are cleaner, and cost 50% less than wood. In 2010, he launched Eco-Fuel Africa to train farmers to start their own microbusinesses using the Eco-Fuel press machine to supply villages with less polluting, cheaper energy. Sanga's deep knowledge of his community and the challenges they face enabled him to create a symbiotic ecosystem that takes advantage of an underutilized fuel source, gives women a new product to sell at their kiosks, and offers communities a better option for sustainable fuel.

NUDGE

Another way to maximize customer value is to build on existing research into motivations and behavior. This is the domain of behavioral science, thrust into broader consciousness in 2008 with the publication of *Nudge* by Richard Thaler and Cass Sunstein.[1] At the core of the book is a recognition that people are quirky and don't always behave rationally or in their own self-interest. One common example is encouraging desired behavior, such as enrollment in a retirement plan or consenting to organ donation, by changing the default choice to require users to opt out rather than ask them to opt in. This seemingly trivial adjustment can significantly increase the number participants by reducing friction.

[1] Richard H. Thaler and Cass R. Sunstein, *Nudge: Improving Decisions about Health, Wealth, and Happiness* (New Haven, CT: Yale University Press, 2008).

Piyush Tantia, co-executive director at the nonprofit behavioral science firm ideas42, sees behavioral design as a way to "turn art into science." Starting ideation with a blank sheet of paper can be daunting, needlessly disconnected from existing knowledge, and overly reliant on the creativity and intuition of the participants to generate good ideas. Behavioral research can give us a head start on likely hypotheses for interventions based on what has worked in other related circumstances.

> *Behavioral science* is an interdisciplinary approach to human behavior that incorporates elements of economics, psychology, sociology, anthropology, and neuroscience. Rigorous experiments to understand how people behave, and why, have been captured in extensive literature. By building off these insights, interventions can be designed to encourage people to make decisions that will benefit themselves and others.
>
> A beta of the Behavioral Evidence Hub at www.bhub.org seeks to make research, previously buried in academic journals, more accessible to all.

Insights from behavioral science can shape social policies, programs, and products to work with, rather than against, people's natural proclivities, thereby increasing engagement and follow through. Perhaps the most prominent early adoption of these techniques for social purposes was the establishment of the Behavioural Insights Team (BIT) by the UK government in 2010 to improve policy and services. This so-called Nudge Unit was spun out in 2014 as a social purpose company. It encourages desirable behaviors by making them easy, attractive, social, and timely and validates impact with rigorous evaluation methods.

For example, BIT Australia partnered with the Victorian Health Promotion Foundation to discourage the consumption of unhealthy sugary drinks (labeled "red") at the Alfred Hospital. It brought together established behavioral research and lean approaches to run two experiments. In the cafeteria, red drinks were moved to a less prominent location so that a greater effort was required to choose one. And in vending machines, the price of red drinks was increased by

20% to discourage purchases, corresponding to a sugar tax proposed by public-health bodies. Both changes resulted in approximately 10% fewer purchases of unhealthy drinks, offset by a corresponding increase in those of a healthier variety. As their overall net proceeds were not impacted, vendors were happy to accept the change.

BIT has also used behavioral interventions to reduce patient referrals at overbooked hospitals, decrease household energy consumption, and increase the number of eligible, disadvantaged students who apply to selective universities. As with HCD, behavioral science is another valuable and complementary tool for incorporating user understanding into the design of programs.

MVPs FOR VALUE

There is no better way to validate customer value than to put a potential solution in the hands of users. Real responses by real people will give you far more accurate data on whether you've hit the mark than research, surveys, or even experts. The social sector seems particularly prone to overanalysis, with organizations spending months or years on research and design. Resist the temptation. In most cases, the fastest way to learn is by doing. Concrete data points from your intended customers can introduce an important perspective and shortcut a long debate. This is where an MVP is helpful.

Cecilia Corral, VP of product development at CareMessage, set out to design a health management system for underserved populations suffering from diabetes. Patients at free health clinics tend to have poor health outcomes, in part due to a lack of regular visits, poor disease self-management skills, and inconsistent adherence to drug regimens. As studies had shown that use of text messaging was inversely proportional to income, she believed an SMS-based solution might serve CareMessage's low-income target customers well.

For the first few iterations to refine content, Cecilia would send messages to her own family to see how they reacted. Would they listen to nutrition advice from a text message? What seemed to matter most was feeling that someone cared, as with messages worded as if from a trusted friend. As she scaled up her tests, she started recruiting patients from the nearby St. Anthony's free medical clinic in San Francisco's Tenderloin district. At one point, this involved cutting and pasting text messages for 100 people. She learned that new patients were often in a state of shock for the first few weeks after receiving a diagnosis. If she bombarded them with too much information at once, they couldn't absorb it all. Instead, she structured simple messages in a logical series of steps to be delivered over time.

CareMessage has now reached over two million patients through more than 175 partner healthcare organizations. Partners consistently report a reduction of 5–12% in missed appointments, and pilot studies have found improved adoption of nutrition and exercise recommendations that results in significantly greater weight loss.

Given the origins of Lean Startup in Silicon Valley, it is not surprising that most MVPs (as with CareMessage's) have centered on validating demand, feature set, and user experience as a precursor to making the investment to build expensive software. Yet MVPs can be equally valuable to accelerate learning for virtually any type of intervention. In all cases, the key is to start with the fewest people, shortest time, and cheapest prototype or proxy that can unlock the next stage of learning. Beginning with early adopters who feel the need most acutely and may thus be more forgiving of imperfections can make this easier. If even they are not excited, others are less likely to be.

In the following pages we will explore the creative approaches organizations have taken to validate their value hypotheses through a wide range of MVPs. These include some of the most common archetypes to get you started, but there are no set rules or limitations. Feel free to mix and match among the techniques or make up your own. Be scrappy, and find new ways to learn faster.

The Marketing MVP

The simplest and cheapest way to validate customer demand is to promote a theoretical product or service and gauge the response. Do people clamor to be first in line? Will they sign up to be part of a beta trial? Would they even put money down to place a preorder? For a marketing MVP, nothing at all may exist beyond a compelling description. If no one bites, far better to know before investing the much larger sums required to build the real thing.

The rollout of Tesla's mass-market electric car, the Model 3, is a classic example. Based on nothing more than a marketing brochure, photos, and specs, over half a million people were willing to put down $1000 to reserve a car. Tesla could invest the huge sums required for design and manufacturing, confident that customers would buy its car. Kickstarter takes a similar model to the masses, allowing anyone to launch a crowdfunding campaign for his or her new product. Such promotion can both validate interest and simultaneously raise the funding needed to bring a project to fruition.

Though it is less likely to raise large sums of money, a marketing MVP can quickly validate the perceived value of interventions intended for social benefit as well. Think crowd validation versus crowd funding. A flyer, poster, or video can be used to depict the value proposition on offer and garner data on the number of inquiries or purchases, level of enthusiasm, or degree of word-of-mouth buzz. These indications of genuine interest, or lack thereof, can then guide improvements to the design and features before larger investments are made in production, infrastructure, and rollout.

Off Grid Electric, a social enterprise in Tanzania, took this approach to determine the best pricing and appliance bundles for the pay-as-you-go home solar systems it sells to poor families who don't have access to electricity. Cofounder and CEO Xavier Helgesen created posters describing the value proposition for each option, set up shop, and tracked inquiries and orders. Would customers prefer the cheapest option with just a few lights? A radio? Would they pay more for a TV? (Hint: people like to be entertained.)

In the enterprise domain, TaroWorks offers a mobile customer relationship management system to manage field operations in low-connectivity settings. While developing the initial concept at the Grameen Foundation, Emily Tucker was told by an advisor that the best way to test your hypotheses is to sell your product. To start, she mapped out six customer segments, corresponding to a matrix of small, medium, and large nonprofits and social enterprises, with a proposed value proposition for each. Then she started to sell. After presenting the product to a prospect, Emily would ask them to sign a beta agreement to determine whether they felt a sufficiently compelling need for the product. She quickly learned that while large nonprofits had the most money, most of it was tied up in inflexible, project-based grants. In contrast, fast-growing social enterprises were highly motivated to reduce their distribution costs as they scaled in order to reach financial sustainability. TaroWorks was perfect for them.

Of course, selling a mockup has its limits. If customers are interested in the idea, will they like the actual product or service? Other types of MVPs can serve to mimic the experience in part or in whole, with varying degrees of fidelity.

The Concierge MVP

When you're scaling a finished product, minimizing the costs of production and distribution is essential. But if you're testing an early concept, sometimes it can be more efficient to start with an expensive, completely manual mode of delivery. How can something be both efficient and expensive at the same time? The cost of such an experiment may be high per instance, but with only a limited number of users that's okay. The cost of extensive human intervention will still be far less than the investment required to build, automate, and roll out a product or service that may not work. And, you can get something running far more quickly. Certainly, this is not a model that can make sense at scale, but in the early stages of development it can accelerate learning. Being in direct touch with customers and the mundane details of each interaction can also allow teams to gain intimate insights into user responses, introduce new variations, identify and fix issues, and know when to abandon failed experiments.

Mercy Corps offers MicroMentor as a free online mentoring service with the aim to create jobs by supporting small-scale entrepreneurs in starting new businesses. One of its key performance metrics is the percentage of newly signed up users who start engaging with potential mentors. If too few become active, the costs of recruitment for each successful match are too high. Despite its low-cost, low-touch business model, the team wondered how important some personal connection might be. So a few team members scheduled 10-minute introductory calls with randomly selected new users. It worked. The conversion rate shot up by 178%. Talking to a real person clearly made a difference, though it was far too expensive to do at scale. Based on this knowledge, the team started to explore a semiautomated way to add a personal touch for the highest potential entrepreneurs who register but do not take action.

In the early days of Off Grid Electric, the concept of a lease-to-own payment model was still quite novel in Tanzania. Would people be willing to buy a home solar system this way? Would they continue to pay? These were important questions to answer before making the big investment required to build the hardware and software necessary to process payments using the mobile money network. So, Off Grid Electric's first pay-as-you-go system consisted of a Maasai tribesman walking from village to village in his traditional bright red shuka to collect money. Having a large network of Maasai warriors process payments would be unaffordable and was never intended to be part of the design. Yet, it was a great way to learn. After proving that people would continue to pay for the service over time, Off Grid Electric could more confidently invest in scalable technology.

The visible human intervention involved in a concierge MVP can affect people's responses, and thus may skew how they might react to the final solution. For that, using a Wizard of Oz or hardware proto-type MVP can move a step closer to the anticipated user experience.

The Wizard of Oz MVP

In California, only about two-thirds of eligible families have enrolled in the state food stamp program, CalFresh, leaving two million people struggling unnecessarily to afford healthy food. One major barrier is the online registration form, which includes 200 questions, takes an average of 45 minutes to complete, and is abandoned by half of those who start the process.

Code for America, a nonprofit that helps governments harness technology to solve community problems, believed it could dramatically simplify the signup process if only the most essential information contained in the form had to be filled in, as a subsequent interview process would cover the rest. But would counties accept submissions with missing fields? Rather than building a Web application and backend integration that might have to be abandoned, it used a classic Wizard of Oz MVP to configure an off-the-shelf Web form with only 18 critical fields. Upon receipt, staff manually reentered the data on the relevant government website and submitted it. Code for America used online ads to recruit applicants to try the system. All this happened in a matter of days, at minimal cost.

It worked. The application approval rate was comparable to existing applications and far simpler for applicants. With this validation, Code For America built its GetCalFresh site, cutting the application time down to eight minutes and improving completion rates to more than 70%.

The user experience with a Wizard of Oz MVP may resemble a full-fledged solution, but the processes and intelligence are manually handled behind the scenes. Of course, this is expensive and isn't scalable, but it can be up and running in a matter of hours or days. Once demand is validated and the requirements are better understood, a larger investment can be confidently made to streamline and automate the backend systems. This style of MVP is commonly used for software, using a simple user interface and doing all the real work behind the scenes by hand. It can also work for services that are not technology based.

Take Copia Global, which tested a service to offer low-income villagers access to a far wider variety of affordable consumer goods. When former CEO Crispin Murira moved back to Kenya to start building the company, he had limited funds and a short runway. He also had the humility to recognize that he had no idea what would work. The first version of the service consisted of a paper catalog with pictures of products from a supermarket in Nairobi along with prices. A small number of shopkeepers were recruited to display the catalog and place orders with him via SMS. Upon receiving the text, Crispin would run to the supermarket, purchase the product, and bring it to the shopkeeper in the village. From a customer perspective, the experience was almost like using Amazon – they could select from a wide array of products and have their purchase arrive days later.

As for Crispin, he was able to validate whether people would order from a catalog and which products were in highest demand. In addition to understanding the preferences of end users, he also learned how to identify the best selling agents. It turned out that while existing shopkeepers talked a good game, they were more focused on selling the inventory already sitting on their shelves. On the other hand, entrepreneurs who ran complementary businesses, such as hair salons, made far better agents.

The Hardware Prototype MVP

To test the value proposition for a physical product, placing an elf inside to pull the strings is unlikely to be a viable option. Instead, a series of prototypes with increasingly high fidelity can be used to test individual features or the product as a whole. As with other forms of MVPs, the aim is to answer the simple questions as cheaply as possible, then progress to more complex questions that require greater investment.

This might start with the shape and appearance. Is it too heavy or too light? Do users find it appealing? How does it integrate into the context where it will be used? Simprints, a nonprofit biometric identification tech company, has a goal of helping the over one billion people without access to essential services due to a lack of formal identification. When it started working in Bangladesh, it quickly became clear that off-the-shelf fingerprint scanners from the West were untenable, as farmers who did backbreaking physical labor had distorted hands that prevented them from placing their fingers flat on a sensor screen.

So Simprints went back to the drawing board and started testing foam models through its partners. By watching videos of how people used them in different countries, they learned how to make the reader more ergonomic and intuitive. After multiple iterations to refine its foam model, Simprints progressed to a 3D printed model, then a prototype with a wired sensor, and a final version with a wireless sensor. Simprints has optimized its hardware and software to be over 228% more accurate for these rugged environments than five industry-leading systems.

To design its first solar lantern, d.light didn't even need to build a custom prototype for many of its experiments, as existing lanterns that would otherwise be too expensive or were not solar powered could be used as proxies to understand the market. For example, to determine the preferred color and brightness, families were shown different types of lanterns in their homes at night. Unexpectedly, people strongly preferred those with a bluer color temperature. While in Western markets people find yellow lighting to be warmer and less harsh, for these families a light in the home was highly aspirational. Yellower lights reminded them of their old kerosene lamps, whereas they associated bluer, brighter light with the fluorescent bulbs they knew from the town.

This theme of aspiration is one I have heard over and over again. We often make the mistake of assuming that because people are poor, they will choose the least expensive option. Yet, dignity and pride are strong human drivers, regardless of condition. When PATH gave low-income families in Cambodia a choice between the cheapest water filter and a nicer design that was double the cost, three times as many people bought the premium design in shops. It turned out that people were embarrassed to have something that resembled a garbage pail in the middle of their homes. This is yet another reminder to not impose our own values in assuming what customers will want.

Whether it is a lantern, water filter, or other type of product, offering potential customers three or four options will elicit far more honest and meaningful feedback. With only one product, people can be hesitant to voice criticisms that might offend, particularly when power dynamics and cultural differences are involved. A wider range of variations allows them to express what they like best about each, as well as display contrasting levels of enthusiasm.

Even commonly used products can sometimes be improved through experimentation. Jibu took a different approach to expanding access to clean water in East Africa – building a network of locally owned franchises that sells safe, filtered water in sealed, reusable containers. While water jugs have existed for ages, Jibu watched women struggle as they carried home two 10-liter bottles. On the other hand, two 5-liter bottles were quite easy to handle. By experimenting with filling the larger containers with varying amounts of water and observing different women, they landed on an optimal size of a nonstandard 7 liters, approximately the weight of two gallons of milk.

Social innovation often doesn't require a new breakthrough invention or technology. In many cases, what is game changing is simply adapting an existing, proven product by dramatically reducing costs and making it more culturally and contextually appropriate.

The Improv MVP

The best experimentation is scrappy and doesn't always fit in a tidy box. The prior sections covered some common techniques for MVPs but are far from exhaustive. Sometimes the best approach to test your hypothesis is to fly by the seat of your pants. What matters is getting out of the building, learning in the real world, and scientifically measuring your success.

When Katy Ashe arrived in Bangalore in 2012 to do research for her Design for Extreme Affordability class at Stanford University, her erstwhile hosts had altogether forgotten a group of students would be arriving. So Katy and her three classmates took it upon themselves to wander the halls of the low-cost hospital and interview staff, patients, and their families. Given her background in fluid dynamics, Katy had assumed she would work on queuing and flow-management issues. Instead, she found two nurses struggling to cover an entire ward filled with hundreds of patients, while crowds of confused, anxious, and helpless relatives camped in waiting rooms for weeks. Families were afraid to go home, and medical staff were afraid to discharge patients to families. Everyone suffered.

Katy and her team wondered, What if we could repurpose this massive waste of human resources to provide better care to patients both in the ward and at home? They began to experiment with ways to teach family members about and engage them in patient care, starting with physical therapy, where the stakes were lower. Would people come to a class? Some did, but many, particularly women who play a primary role in caregiving, found the classroom setting intimidating. What kind of pedagogy would work best? When presented with a variety of existing health-education videos, people liked and remembered those that included a relatable narrative. Through these and other lessons, the team evolved their strategy. Trainings were moved from classrooms into the wards and used simple videos that the team recorded on a cell phone in a parking lot.

As families took their new skills home, a small independent study found readmissions were reduced by 24% and complication rates by 36%. Based on these positive results, the team went on to found the nonprofit Noora Health, which was selected as one of the top 50 most innovative companies by *Fast Company* in 2016. Its mission is to train patients and their families in caregiving skills to improve outcomes and save lives.

On the other end of the spectrum is Roca, a nonprofit in Massachusetts founded more than 30 years ago with a mission to disrupt the cycle of incarceration and poverty by helping young people transform their lives. Despite having a well-defined, rigorously evaluated four-year intervention model, it has had to stay nimble to adapt to the fluid contexts in which it operates.

For example, when Roca started its program in Boston, its ongoing monitoring discovered that a full third of high-risk youth weren't able to safely come into the offices and participate in sessions due to their strong ties to street gangs. Thus, this long-established program went back to prototyping. Starting with a handful of clients, it experimented with sending staff for home visits, meeting in small trusted groups, and shutting down the building to serve only one youth at a time. The result has been a new model: so-called portable programming, which takes place in homes or other safe locations, tailored to the participant's situation.

Whether an organization is large or small, early or late stage, or in rich or poor countries, an MVP can accelerate learning and reduce waste when delving into a new, uncertain intervention. Be creative, start small, and learn from the data.

ENGAGING STAKEHOLDERS

In the social sector, delivering value requires not only meeting the needs of the end user but of all the stakeholders in the broader ecosystem who can make or break an intervention, whether they be governments, existing nonprofit or business actors, or respected community leadership. Of course, funders play a particularly crucial role, and will be discussed in detail in Part III.

After over 30 years of working at United Way, Michael Brennan left his job as CEO of the Southeastern Michigan office with an aspiration to explore new paths for impact outside the constraints of an established, historic organization. Civilla, his nonprofit based in Detroit, is on a mission to transform the work of social change using HCD. As he got started, the power of small teams hit him between the eyes, and he noted, "So much of change work in the caring profession is done with a backhoe rather than a garden shovel."

One of the biggest barriers to accessing public benefits in Michigan is a daunting 42-page application process, the longest of its kind in the United States. The form includes over 1000 questions, including one that asks for the date of conception of each child. Five thousand caseworkers at the Michigan Department of Health and Human Services (MDHHS) organize their work lives around this form.

Through extensive field research, observations, and interviews with both residents and caseworkers, Civilla gained a deep understanding of their experiences and the bottlenecks. These lessons led to the creation of an immersive experience that chronicled the arduous process. When the state's leadership team came to visit, they entered a converted hallway simulation of the MDHHS office and were handed the 64-page form to complete. Three-quarters of its members had never done so. Afterwards, a 100-foot-long journey map led them through the experiences of and activities for both applicants and staff. It was crystal clear that the current state of affairs wasn't working for anybody. People on all sides saw the role of MDHHS as one of preventing fraud rather than providing a helpful service.

Giving the stakeholders at MDHHS a visceral experience of the real challenges helped Civilla develop a collaborative partnership and unlock funding to dramatically improve the process. At the beginning of 2018, after a prototype and pilot, a new application that met all regulations with 80% fewer words and questions rolled out to over 100 offices throughout Michigan.

As with Civilla, identifying your key stakeholders early and engaging them to speak with users, participate in design sessions, or deploy prototypes can build invaluable buy in. Having committed partners in your ecosystem with a shared sense of purpose will pay dividends as you scale.

NET PROMOTER SCORE

One widely used instrument that has been found to be a strong indicator of customer loyalty and satisfaction in the corporate sphere is the net promoter score (NPS). It is based on answers to the question "How likely is it that you would recommend our [company, product, or service] to a friend or colleague?" Users are typically asked to respond on a 0–10 scale, with those who record a 9 or 10 considered promoters who are likely to come back, engage more deeply, and recruit others.

Asking this simple question and calculating the NPS can be a helpful tool to evaluate your value MVP. As a complement to observed behavior, it will give you an indication of the degree of enthusiasm you have generated. Beyond assessing MVPs, mission-driven organizations are increasingly incorporating the NPS on an ongoing basis to understand how beneficiaries perceive the value of their offerings. For example, solar company d.light performs a randomized weekly NPS poll and reports the results on the company dashboard.

The Fund for Shared Insight is a donor collaborative consisting of 78 funders that grew out of conversations initiated by the Hewlett Foundation. It seeks to systematize high-quality feedback loops between nonprofits and their clients as a way to increase social impact. The collaborative's Listen for Good initiative provides small grants and technical assistance to client-facing nonprofits to implement a five-question survey based on the net promoter system. To date, over a hundred organizations have participated in the beta program, and there are plans to eventually make the survey tool publicly available. Over time, these consistent data sets will make it possible for nonprofits to benchmark their performance relative to others in their sector.

GAUGING TRACTION

One day, Jesse Moore, CEO and cofounder of M-Kopa Solar, was eating at a dusty restaurant miles away from the community where he was testing his new pay-as-you-go solar systems. When a group of Maasai, having heard about his product, approached him to ask when M-Kopa would be available in their village, he knew he was onto something.

At the end of the day, how do we know if we are delivering sufficient value to our customers? The answer will inevitably entail a mix of the subjective and the objective. Ultimately, the perceived value should be substantially greater than the status quo or existing alternative to justify the cost and potential disruption of building and distributing something new. Don't let pride of ownership get in the way of making a levelheaded assessment about a fairly marginal gain.

On the subjective side, users will demand, come back, and tell others about a truly compelling product or service. If there isn't a constant stream of people asking for more, they're probably not all that interested. Additionally, objectively measurable data helps us to avoid bias. For the value hypothesis, common success criteria include adoption rate, purchase rate, retention rate, and the NPS.

Building awareness and acceptance of any new solution is a heavy lift. If you deliver compelling value that results in high engagement and positive buzz, achieving your audacious goals for scale and impact will be far easier.

Chapter Eight
Growth

O ver the past 20 years the world has made slow but steady progress in expanding access to crucial services, such as clean water, electricity, and sanitation. Yet despite hundreds of nonprofits, social enterprises, companies, and governments each doing their bit, on average access to these vital services has grown by less than 1% of the global population each year (see Figure 8.1). As of 2015, this has left over 700 million people without clean water, one billion without reliable power, and two billion without proper sanitation.

In contrast, adoption of mobile phones has skyrocketed around the globe (Figure 8.1). Despite the challenges of reaching poor communities, growth has resembled that of the classic hockey stick graph. In my travels, I've seen a Maasai warrior herding cattle in a remote village in East Africa with a mobile phone strapped to his belt and a smallholder farmer in rural Indonesia fish a phone out of her pocket. Today, far more households have access to a mobile phone than a toilet.

The story of mobile phone adoption shows that massive scale is possible, even in the most challenging contexts. How could we achieve this kind of growth trajectory for matters of social good?

Lean Impact: How to Innovate for Radically Greater Social Good, First Edition. Ann Mei Chang.
© 2019 Ann Mei Chang. Published 2019 by John Wiley & Sons, Inc.

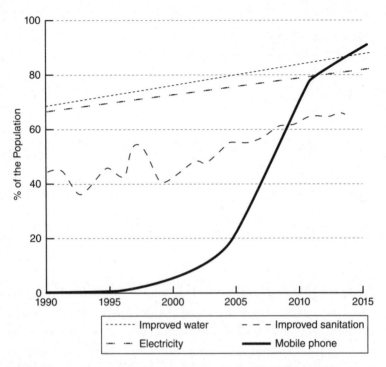

Figure 8.1   Accelerating the pace of progress. Source: World Bank, World Development Report 2016: Digital Dividends (Washington, DC: World Bank, 2016), http://www.worldbank.org/en/publication/wdr2016.

What's the difference? To start with, people clearly see the value of a mobile phone, whether to stay in touch with loved ones, find job opportunities, or access markets. So much so that many will choose to spend their meager earnings topping up their phone credit before buying food. In addition, there is a market-driven business model for both the hardware and cellular services that continues to drive growth. The resulting profits provide the means to finance big investments in infrastructure, distribution, and product development. Yet it was only when prepaid service plans rolled out – allowing small purchases of minutes as needed – that usage in developing countries took off. Traditional monthly contracts were too expensive and required credit verification that often was not possible.

In contrast, growth that depends on grants and donations will rapidly hit natural limits. Even if, as the nonprofit charity: water estimates, only $20 can provide clean water for each of the 10% of people who don't yet have it, that adds up to approximately $15 billion. With its online fundraising prowess, charity: water raised an impressive $243 million in its first 11 years, improving the lives of over seven million people.[1] Yet this still represents merely 1% of those in need.

Factoring in electricity, sanitation, and other basic needs will require an even greater investment. Aside from a few notable exceptions, charity and aid can only put a small dent in most big problems. The result is a growth curve that looks more like an inverted hockey stick, or logarithmic graph, with rapid initial growth as donors flock to a fresh idea. Growth then flattens out as available philanthropic sources are exhausted, which usually occurs long before reaching anywhere close to the size of the need (see Figure 8.2).

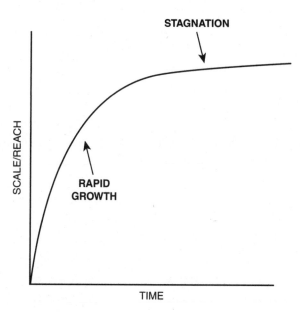

Figure 8.2   Inverse hockey stick.

[1] charity: water, *2016 Annual Report*, charity: water (2016), 38.

Growth is the second pillar of social innovation, as our aggregate impact arises from a combination of the *breadth* of how many we reach and the *depth* of change we deliver. A powerful solution that only benefits a few will fall far short of its potential. However, that does *not* necessarily equate to scaling your organization or program. What matters is scaling the social benefit, which might come from growing an entity, but equally if not more likely from replication, government adoption, or policy change.

As we saw in Chapters Two and Six, mission-oriented organizations face many pressures that run counter to thinking big and starting small. After all, there's no potential initial public offering on the horizon, but rather a constant need to bring in the next grant or donor to keep the doors open. The result? Over and over, nonprofit leaders are forced to make the understandable tradeoff to prioritize short-term deliverables over the potential for long-term growth.

Staying small while you are validating your growth hypotheses can reduce the likelihood that you'll hit a wall down the road. Otherwise, it's easy to waste time perfecting a solution that may deliver value and impact but does not have the means to reach a substantial portion of the need. For a market-based business model, at what price point will customers find enough value to buy? For publicly funded services, does the design fit within the government budget, process, and policy constraints? For replication or franchising, is the model simple enough for others to successfully copy? For ongoing aid or charity funding, are there sufficient pools of money available? The answers to any of these questions could have significant implications for the design of a solution.

In this chapter we will explore a wide range of potential paths for growth and how to test their viability, along with examples of each model in action. Of course, scale takes time. And typically, it takes far more time than in the private sector, given the perverse incentives, more limited funding, and need to navigate market and policy failures. Just as with value, validating your growth hypothesis isn't a one-time event. Lessons will continue to emerge with new audiences, new partners, and increased reach.

A WAKE-UP CALL

Solutions to social challenges are often designed to address a narrow, immediate problem without sufficient consideration of the broader ecosystem or how growth will be achieved over time. But the Lean Impact principle of starting small must be paired with thinking big, such that experiments test for the potential to scale over time. The history of mobile phone health application (mHealth) pilots in Uganda is an example of what can go wrong when growth is an afterthought.

As mobile phones began to proliferate across developing countries, interest in the potential of harnessing this new device to improve healthcare in underresourced environments also grew. Across sub-Saharan Africa and Asia, mHealth pilots were deployed by a plethora of organizations tackling different diseases and using different technologies. Applications included diagnosis tools for community healthcare workers, SMS reminders for appointments and drug regimens, SMS health tips of various kinds, tracking systems for drug stockouts, electronic patient records, and many, many more. Yet a 2013 article in *PLoS Medicine* found that despite hundreds of pilots, few mHealth services ever reached any degree of scale.[2]

The trouble was, organizations ran their own pilots in isolation. The duplication of effort meant that very similar experiments took place in different contexts and that the same lessons were learned over and over again. Worse yet, the systems didn't communicate or integrate with either each other or with local government systems. Thus, a pregnant woman with HIV might have to register with one SMS service to receive maternal health tips and a completely different one for reminders on her HIV medication. Health providers would have no idea this was the same person.

[2] Mark Tomlinson, Mary Jane Rotheram-Borus, Leslie Swartz, and Alexander C. Tsai, "Scaling Up mHealth: Where Is the Evidence?" *PLoS Medicine* 10, no. 2 (2013): e1001382, https://doi.org/10.1371/journal.pmed.1001382.

In a shocking wake-up call in 2012, the government of Uganda issued a stop work order, effectively declaring a moratorium on any further mHealth projects. This relatively small country had become inundated with dozens upon dozens of organizations implementing programs that were overlapping and duplicative, addressed narrow niche problems, lacked a viable path to scale, and did not work together. Supporting these scattershot efforts simply took too many scarce resources. Instead, the health ministry required new programs to integrate with government health systems and to coordinate their efforts to build evidence of what worked.

The situation of mHealth is an extreme case, but it highlights a tendency to focus on niche problems without a clear path to scale. If each pilot had considered what would be required to succeed across the entire country, let alone across the entire continent, they would have recognized any number of growth hypotheses that needed validation. Doing so early might have led to a pivot to build on the existing government systems, take a more holistic approach to healthcare needs, or partner with other players.

As you begin to test your solution, you can avoid falling into trap of being a subscale, niche intervention by identifying and validating your assumptions for growth up front. Who will pay for the ongoing costs of your products or services? Who will carry out the work? Will you need to integrate with existing systems in your domain? What is your unique and significant differentiator relative to other options?

THE LIMITS OF CHARITY

Most mission-driven programs get their start through some form of charitable funding. This early seed money is essential to develop, validate, and pilot programs. But it's rare that grants alone can provide sufficient dollars to meet the full scope of needs. Thus, the path to scale typically requires a shift from depending on donors to tapping into other larger and more sustainable financing streams.

This is the essence of the growth hypothesis – testing whether you have an engine that can accelerate growth over time.

For developing countries, the funding landscape has shifted dramatically over the past 30 years, with donors becoming a fast-diminishing piece of the pie. As of 2014, foreign aid and philanthropy amounted to $147 billion and $64 billion per year, respectively, while remittances and foreign investment have grown to approximately $224 billion and $513 billion, respectively.[3] What dwarfs all of these are the increased private and public resources being brought to bear locally: over $3 trillion in government spending in developing countries[4] (excluding China) and an estimated $3.7 trillion in investment by domestic companies.[5] When you add these up, at less than 3% of the aggregate financing in developing countries, foreign aid and philanthropy are clearly insufficient in themselves to solve problems at scale.

Of course, there are a few exceptions. Among the largest is the global collaboration to improve childhood immunization coverage being coordinated through the Global Alliance for Vaccines and Immunisation (Gavi). With leadership from the Bill and Melinda Gates Foundation, this unique public–private partnership was created to bring together UN agencies, governments, and the vaccine industry. As of 2017, Gavi has received over $20 billion in commitments and estimates nine million deaths have been averted since its

[3] Carol Adelman, Brian Schwartz, and Elias Riskin, *Index of Global Philanthropy and Remittances 2016*, Hudson Institute (February 15, 2017): 5–6, https://www.hudson.org/research/13314-index-of-global-philanthropy-and-remittances-2016.

[4] Daniel F. Runde and Conor M. Savoy, *Domestic Resource Mobilization: Tax System Reform*, Center for Strategic & International Studies, August 16, 2016, https://www.csis.org/analysis/domestic-resource-mobilization-tax-system-reform.

[5] *Public-Private Partnerships in Foreign Aid: Leveraging Taxpayer Dollars for Greater Impact and Sustainability, Before the Senate Subcommittee on State Department and USAID Management, International Operations and Bilateral International Development* (July 12, 2016) (testimony of Eric G. Postel, Associate Administrator of USAID), https://www.usaid.gov/news-information/congressional-testimony/jul-12-2016-eric-g-postel-aa-public-private-partnerships-foreign-aid.

inception in 2000. Other similar partnerships include the Global Fund's effort to end AIDS, tuberculosis, and malaria and the Global Partnership for Education. But not much else comes close to the impressive global scale these funds have achieved.

In the United States, the Edna McConnell Clark Foundation (EMCF) brought together 12 funders to form Blue Meridian Partners, one of the largest domestic donor collaboratives. Blue Meridian plans to invest at least a billion dollars in large, multiyear grants to scale programs with the strongest empirical evidence for serving children and youth who live in poverty. But even such a relatively large fund doesn't come close to what is required to pay for all the necessary services. Instead, Blue Meridian provides growth capital to build the institutional capacity of organizations and test financially sustainable paths to scale that can dramatically increase their impact nationwide. This typically involves finding ways to tap into regular and ongoing local, state, and federal government funding, as well as influencing policies of the welfare, educational, and judicial systems that affect children's lives. For perspective, federal, state, and local government spending on social benefit programs in the United States adds up to almost a trillion dollars a year.[6]

Of the more than 200,000 nonprofits founded in the United States since 1975 (excluding hospitals and universities), only 201 had grown to at least $50 million in annual revenues by 2008. Of these, only a handful was primarily supported by foundations. The vast majority drew most of their funding from government or by charging ongoing service fees.[7] Compare this to the tens of thousands of for-profit companies with revenues over $50 million.

If you truly believe that donor funding will be sufficient to address the long-term size and scale of your problem, then your

---

[6] Michael Tanner, *The American Welfare State: How We Spend Nearly $1 Trillion a Year Fighting Poverty—and Fail*, Cato Institute Policy Analysis No. 694 (2012), https://ssrn.com/abstract=2226525.

[7] Peter Kim and Jeffrey Bradach, "Why More Nonprofits Are Getting Bigger," *Stanford Social Innovation Review*, Spring 2012, https://ssir.org/articles/entry/why_more_nonprofits_are_getting_bigger.

growth hypotheses should confirm your expected unit costs, size of need, source and availability of donor funds, and the realistic share your organization can expect to attract over time. Receiving a large grant may be sufficient to carry out work for a few years, but without a long-term plan for growth, it may only be staving off the day of reckoning. In most cases, another engine besides grants will be needed to reach true scale.

ENGINES FOR GROWTH

While most private sector companies are based on a business model where customers pay directly or indirectly for a product or service, in the social sector, the potential engines for growth are far more diverse. In some cases, a market-driven business model may in fact be possible. However, when aiming to serve disadvantaged populations or deliver broader public goods, this is often not realistic.

The good news is that a wide range of creative paths to scale exists. The key is to move from a linear, brute-force mode – in which each unit of expansion requires additional dollars to be raised – to one in which an engine for growth can accelerate adoption over time. Otherwise, our total impact will remain plodding, marginal, and expensive.

One of the people I most admire in global development is Kevin Starr, managing director at the Mulago Foundation, a private foundation focused on scalable solutions to the basic needs of the poor. He's identified two simple questions that tidily capture the options: Who is the doer at scale, and who is the payer at scale? For each, he posits that only four realistic answers exist. The doer could be you, lots of nonprofits, lots of businesses, or government. The payer could be customers, government taxation, private philanthropy, or foreign aid. Based on the limits of charity I covered in the prior section, I'm skeptical of these last two sources in most cases.

Using Kevin's framework, the growth hypotheses boil down to: Can and will the doer do, and can and will the payer pay? For example, if your assumption is that other nonprofits and businesses will replicate or franchise your solution, it would be important to validate both their motivation and capability to do so at high fidelity. Or, if you assume that the local government will fund your solution through its budget, it would be important to validate that the intervention fits within its cost parameters, policies, processes, and politics. If not, it's better to find out early, and pivot.

There are innumerable variations on these basics, as well as hybrids between them. I expect new models will continue to emerge. Regardless of which you choose, there will be implications for your design, structure, and positioning. Thus, you will save time and money in the long run if you identify and validate your growth hypotheses early, and adapt your solution accordingly. This will likely require slower expansion at first in order to realize the potential for dramatically greater scale down the road.

Let's look at some of the most common engines for growth that have been successful in scaling social innovations: market driven, voluntary contributions, cross-subsidy, replication, commoditization, government funding, government adoption, and big donors.

Market Driven

Home solar company Off Grid Electric was the first organization to receive all three tiers of grant funding through the USAID Lab's DIV program – first $100,000, then $1 million, then $5 million. The earlier-stage grants helped it to test and prove its innovative business model, in which families pay a small amount each month via the local mobile money system to keep the lights on. Later, to offset the perceived risk of repayment for these small consumer loans as Off Grid Electric began to scale, the final $5 million grant was "coinvested" in a pool of working capital, catalyzing $40 million in private debt. Based on its proven track record, Off Grid Electric has raised a total of over $150 million in private debt and equity and is now primarily financed through commercial sources, with over a hundred thousand systems sold, and counting.

Of course, the most simple and straightforward engine for growth is a traditional market-driven business model. There are big benefits when the customer and funder are one and the same. Interests are naturally aligned and purchase decisions provide clear feedback as to the perceived value of the product or service.

In many ways, is looks not at all unlike the private sector, where at the core, the unit economics of the business must work – the associated revenue exceeds the direct costs of delivering each good or service by a sufficient margin. Although nonprofits may seek income streams to improve their sustainability, they tend to adopt a cost-recovery mindset and construct financial statements with expenses on top and revenues and grants below, which net out to zero. Instead, a growth mindset starts with revenues, deducts expenses, and aims for sufficient profits to invest in the leadership, marketing, infrastructure, research, and expansion into new markets needed for scale.

Beyond the basics, running a business with a social purpose involves several challenges. Assuming goods or services are being sold into poor or otherwise disadvantaged markets, the ability of customers to pay will likely be far more constrained. This can limit the potential financial upside and thus decrease the degree of risk a private investor is willing to take. To offset this risk, many social enterprises, such as Off Grid Electric, receive some degree of donor funding in the beginning to build a track record before seeking private financing.

The limited ability to pay may also require companies to make deeper investments in financing options for customers than is typical for a for-profit business. For Off Grid Electric and similar household solar companies in developing countries, this has meant developing the hardware and infrastructure to amortize costs through mobile money payments. Other situations might call for investment in lending or savings programs that enable customers to afford a product or service.

The mechanism for customer acquisition is another important dimension to validate, whether through paid marketing or distribution, viral growth via referrals, or repeat usage. The higher the cost is to reach each new beneficiary, the lower the profits and potential for growth. When customers enthusiastically demand your offering, growth becomes far easier.

Sometimes, the best path to market may involve leveraging the infrastructure, networks, and expertise of an existing company, rather than building a new one. If mission comes first, the loss of some control can be a worthwhile tradeoff in order to deliver more benefit sooner. For example, Jorge Odon, an Argentinian car mechanic, was the unlikely inventor of a low-cost obstetrical instrument to assist in obstructed birth. Through research funding from USAID and other donors, early testing showed that it could become a safer alternative to the long-standing use of forceps, particularly in low-resource settings with minimally trained midwives. But running clinical trials, manufacturing, and distribution was not Jorge's expertise. Instead of taking the slow and risky path of building a new medical device business, he licensed the design to Becton Dickinson, a large American medical technology company, to bring it to market.

For all the hype about triple bottom line businesses that seek financial, social, and environmental returns, real tradeoffs do exist. On one hand, selling into slightly more affluent markets will likely yield higher profits. On the other hand, reaching those who are most disadvantaged and remote will likely be more expensive. While impact investors may have a higher degree of patience, when returns come under threat, pressure can build to focus on more lucrative opportunities to the detriment of social benefit. To formalize these noneconomic commitments, in 2007 nonprofit B Lab began to certify B Corps – for-profit companies that meet rigorous standards for social and environmental performance, accountability, and transparency. Soon thereafter, in 2010, the first legislation was passed in the United States to establish a formal corporate structure for benefit corporations.

One certified B Corp is Inflection, a Silicon Valley company that performs identity and background checks. Its GoodHire platform sells employment-screening services to companies. At the same time, its social mission is to contribute to a more diverse and inclusive society by promoting fair hiring practices. Many individuals with criminal records struggle to find jobs, are perpetually shut out of the system, and then end up back in jail. GoodHire's True Me feature allows people to view what employers will see about them in a background check and to add their own commentary to paint a fuller picture. This personal touch creates an opportunity to build the trust that is essential in any hiring decision. As a result, Inflection can provide companies with high-quality background screening while helping people get a second chance.

Voluntary Contributions

A nonprofit variation on a pure market-based business model is to solicit contributions on a voluntary basis. Voluntary contributions can range anywhere from large university alumni donations to small "tips" to a nonprofit in lieu of a set fee-for-service. While few for-profit businesses can run on the uncertainty of discretionary payments, the goodwill created by nonprofits can inspire generosity. And, by breaking the direct correlation between payment and benefit, the most needy will not be turned away. It can also alleviate the temptation to move upmarket.

The donation, or tipping, model is common among nonprofit crowdfunding sites. For example, DonorsChoose helps teachers raise money for the supplies needed to run classroom projects that can enhance children's education. From the start, it encouraged, but did not require, donors to allocate 15% of their donation to fund DonorsChoose itself. Most do. After 10 years, it was able to fully cover its own expenses, and it has started to generate profits that are channeled into its own classroom projects. A remarkable 77% of public schools have at least one teacher who has posted a project on its site.

As with a market-driven engine for growth, a contributions model also requires sufficient profit margins and drivers for customer acquisition in order to reach significant scale.

Cross-subsidy

Yet another variation on a pure market-driven business model is cross-subsidization, in which profits from one product or customer offset part or all of the costs of another, typically for lower-income populations. One impressive example is the Aravind Eye Hospitals in India, the largest provider of eye care services in the world. Early on, after a disappointing experience raising funds from donors, Aravind committed to sustainably financing services for those who can't pay with earned income from those who can. This self-imposed constraint gave it control over its own destiny.

Rather than means testing, patients self-select from a range of payment options for surgical procedures, with the primary differentiation based on their choice of accommodation – from a free, shared ward to a full-priced private air-conditioned room. All patients receive the same high-quality care from the same doctors. By dramatically reducing its costs and improving efficiency, Aravind is able to generate sufficient margins from each patient who can afford to pay full price to cover the costs of three or four others who cannot. With its relentless focus on purpose, it has continually expanded outreach to underserved populations. In 2017, it performed approximately 300,000 cataract eye surgeries, two-thirds of which were either free or highly subsidized.

The cross-subsidy model is appealing, as it can be easier to derive and redirect profits from sales to higher-income customers than to garner sufficient earnings purely from selling to low-income customers. In Aravind's case, it has led to a degree of scale that would not have been possible had the hospital chain been reliant on external donors.

With the millennial generation increasingly willing to pay a premium for brands aligned with their social and environmental values, offering social benefit can also become a strong marketing asset. Despite some issues with the initial distribution of free shoes by TOMS, its One for One model propelled significant consumer interest. Warby Parker, a socially responsible eyewear brand, took a somewhat different approach. Rather than attempting to run both a profitable business and a charitable endeavor simultaneously, its Buy a Pair, Give a Pair program works with independent nonprofits that specialize in underserved markets. For every pair of glasses purchased, it makes a donation to an organization such as VisionSpring. VisionSpring in turn uses the funds to subsidize a pair of affordable glasses for someone in need. In this way, Warby Parker and VisionSpring each stay focused on their core missions, while profits are plowed into scaling a promising social enterprise.

BioLite puts its own twist on this approach with its model for parallel innovation. The company leverages a common pool of world-class talent and capital to build products for both relatively wealthy outdoor enthusiasts and families living in energy poverty. For example, the BioLite CampStove is a portable biomass stove sold to campers, while the BioLite HomeStove is a biomass cookstove that offers a cleaner alternative to open fires in developing countries. While the two markets BioLite serves are in some ways on extreme ends of the spectrum, there are many similarities in the technologies and skills required to build the products. The opportunity to work on something meaningful is a bonus for top engineers and designers who are normally difficult to recruit and retain.

Although the developing-country business intends to become profitable, finding investors who are tolerant of the greater risk and longer timescale of such a venture on its own would be extremely challenging. And relying on erratic grant funding cycles wouldn't provide the predictability needed to keep permanent staff onboard through the long R&D process. With parallel innovation, BioLite is able to leverage its consistent cash flow in the United States to offset both the risk and longer time horizon of its mission-oriented offerings.

Replication

Alcoholics Anonymous (AA) boasts over two million members who participate in over a hundred thousand groups worldwide who support each other to recover from alcoholism. Despite this impressive scale, there is no formal organization aside from two small operating bodies that handle literature and basic administration.

Each AA group is independent and self-supported through voluntary donations of time and money from members. Massive impact doesn't necessarily require a massive entity or massive funding.

If this were a problem tackled by the private sector, companies would likely compete by designing proprietary systems, marketing to the most desirable audiences, and creating incentives to refer more customers. One advantage of the social sector is that we can share our assets freely while working towards a common goal. Yet too often, organizations feel compelled to go it alone due to pride of ownership, a desire to maintain control, or the need for a competitive advantage when applying for grants. To maximize social good, replication should be encouraged, not discouraged.

For replication to work, as in the case of AA, an intervention has to be easy enough and cheap enough. If the design is too complicated, others might find it difficult to deliver with high enough fidelity to preserve the original value and impact. And if the intervention is too expensive, others may struggle to raise the necessary funds. AA published a guide to its 12-step program, enabling people to start a group in their own communities with a few volunteers, modest donations to cover the costs of a meeting space, and a pot of coffee.

Another approach to replication is franchising, in which one organization maintains the brand, intellectual property, and design of a product or service and agrees to license the bundled enterprise to others. Think McDonald's for social good. Unfortunately, without a profit motive, few people are willing to give up control to operate under another's brand. So, more often a company or nonprofit will adopt and replicate existing best practices under its own name. For example, after microfinance was successfully pioneered by Grameen Bank and BRAC in Bangladesh, numerous nonprofits and for-profit companies proliferated the model around the world.

What is more common than traditional franchising is a narrower version called "microfranchising," particularly in developing countries. Here, a company or social enterprise offers a small, prepackaged business opportunity to drive sales and distribution of its product. A kiosk selling scratch-off cards to top up mobile phone minutes might be the simplest and most common microfranchise. Others include the farmers making and selling fuel briquettes for Eco-Fuel Africa, the "vision entrepreneurs" who perform exams and sell glasses for VisionSpring, and the shopkeepers selling products from Copia Global's catalog. In each of these cases, the franchisees are typically low-income individuals who benefit from an additional source of income.

Commoditization

A strategy that is also not usually seen among for-profit companies is deliberately commoditizing a market to drive down costs. When PATH sought to permanently reduce the price of water filters to make them more accessible to low-income households around the world, it designed and open-sourced a standard universal interface rather than selling its own product. This meant that any standard-compliant replaceable cartridge would be compatible with any compliant filter, eliminating the premium vendors were charging for proprietary parts. An analog in the United States might be standardizing printer ink cartridges to drive down the overall costs of printing.

With a no-cost license, PATH was able to recruit smaller businesses interested in breaking into the market. Eventually larger companies, including Kohler, also came on board. While PATH didn't produce products itself, the benefit was significant – broader availability, lower prices, and a sustainable market.

Government Funding

A fascinating experiment has been taking place in Liberia, one of the poorest countries in the world. Besieged by 14 years of civil war followed by the Ebola crisis, Liberia's schools have been failing. Estimates are that less than 40% of school-age children attend primary school, and that half of the country's youth are illiterate. In a shock to the nation, zero students were able to pass the entrance exam to the University of Liberia in 2013.

Faced with this crisis, Liberia's forward-thinking education minister at the time, George Werner, recognized it was time to consider radical new ideas and launched the Partnership Schools for Liberia (PSL) in 2016. PSL awarded contracts to eight nonprofit and for-profit organizations to operate 93 public schools. The schools are free to students, with the government paying teachers' salaries plus an additional $50 per student per year to the operator. After the first year, a rigorous third-party evaluation found that students in the partnership schools learned 60% more than in government schools. While open questions remain about whether results will endure over time, costs will be sufficiently reduced with scale, and the political winds can be navigated, the hope is that the program will be expanded nationally over time to dramatically improve the education system.

For basic public services, such as education and healthcare, government tends to be the largest provider, and purely market-driven business models may not be viable. Thus, tapping into existing government funding streams can often be the most promising path to reach massive scale. To do so, a provider must fit into the government's budget, policies, and processes, or work to change them.

Among the PSL schools is Bridge International Academies, a social enterprise company that runs over 500 low-cost schools in Africa. It seeks to provide better education than is available in many public schools through innovation and technology. While Bridge operates private schools in most countries, it ultimately hopes to demonstrate that high-quality education is possible within limited public-education budgets even for disadvantaged communities. In essence, its schools serve as pilots to demonstrate the benefits of a new model to governments, with the hope that it will eventually lead to public schools that are free, effective, and available to all children.

In Chapter Seven, we learned how Code For America created GetCalFresh to vastly simplify applications for food stamps in California. This improved experience landed it a Food and Nutrition Service outreach contract, allowing for the use of government funds to pay for its ongoing recruitment, operations, and service. Rather than seeking donations to meet the nutritional needs of low-income

Californians, GetCalFresh taps into unclaimed government budget already set aside for food stamps. Code For America estimates that for every $10 invested, $180 in food benefits has been unlocked for a client.

You might not think that the first drone delivery service operating at national scale would be in Africa, but that's exactly what Zipline has done in Rwanda. And as a venture capital–backed company with high expectations for returns, this is no charitable project. Given Rwanda's poor infrastructure and mountainous terrain, supplying crucial blood products for emergency transfusions often required driving for hours to a regional center, reaching many patients too late. Attempts to strategically pre-position blood supplies led to frequent stockouts in underprovisioned areas and expiring products being wasted in overprovisioned areas. Through a contract with Zipline, the Rwandan government was able to centralize supplies and deliver them by drone, on demand, within 30 minutes. Though it may sound expensive, this innovation is actually helping the government save money – factoring in prior transport, wastage, and inventory costs – while providing improved healthcare.

In each of these examples, demonstrating greater bang for buck served as an entry point for accessing government funding. When applied successfully, impact can be massive. Philanthropic dollars can play a crucial role in funding early pilots, but governments have far bigger wallets to scale and sustain successful solutions.

Government Adoption

Sometimes scale can be achieved through government adoption rather than government funding. In the United States, there are over 22 million federal, state, and local government workers, amounting to 16.7% of the national workforce.[8] Improving how and what they deliver can make a big difference.

---

[8] G. Scott Thomas, "Governments Employ 20 Percent or More of Workers in Nine States," Business Journals, May 14, 2012, https://www.bizjournals.com/bizjournals/on-numbers/scott-thomas/2012/05/governments-employ-20-percent-of.html.

Over years of running a small number of charter schools in California, Summit Public Schools questioned every traditional assumption about education and eventually completely redesigned its schools to focus on the skills, knowledge, and habits that students need to live a fulfilled life. With its strong results in hand, in 2015 Summit began to work on influencing the public education system across the United States. As of the 2017–2018 school year, more than 300 predominantly public schools from 40 states are participating in the Summit Learning Program. By integrating its techniques into these existing schools, Summit has crossed an inflection point to scale and is on the way to dramatically magnifying its impact.

The infrastructure and reach of existing government programs can serve as a platform for delivering additional benefits to society too. Over 800 million children worldwide are at risk for parasitic worm infections that can pose a serious threat to their health, ability to learn, and future productivity. Yet scientific studies have shown that school-based deworming programs can protect a child for less than 50 cents. The Copenhagen Consensus Center, a think tank, believes "the benefits of deworming can be up to 60 times higher than the costs."

It would be difficult for any nonprofit to build the distribution network needed to tackle this problem economically or at a global scale. Instead, the Deworm the World Initiative at Evidence Action advocates for deworming to policy makers and offers technical assistance to design and implement effective programs at a state and national level. Through its support of India's National Deworming Day alone, the program treated an astounding 260 million children in 2017. By taking advantage of the existing government schools and staff, the program can reach more children at far lower cost than would have been otherwise possible.

Big Donors

As I indicated at the start of this chapter, although I am skeptical about the potential to achieve significant scale purely through donor funding in most circumstances, there are a few exceptions. These generally fall into one of two categories: either when vast donor funds have been mobilized that are sufficient for the scale of the need or when interventions are so highly leveraged that costs don't expand significantly with scale.

Earlier in the chapter I shared some examples from the first category. There are a small number of global challenges where big donors have coordinated and committed massive funding. Most often, these efforts are anchored by governmental agencies, which have far greater resources and reach than even the largest private foundations. The potential for donor-funded growth can be easily validated by comparing the size of need and anticipated cost per intervention to the dollars available.

In some cases, the most cost-effective solution may be to prevent a problem from occurring in the first place. For example, significant sums are spent on food aid to alleviate the seasonal hunger that affects 600 million farmers around the world. As mentioned in Chapter Four, researchers at Yale University have found that providing a transportation stipend can lead to a significant increase in seasonal jobs, and thereby higher incomes and the equivalent of an extra meal per person per day. It turns out that buying a $20 bus ticket is 5–10 times more cost effective than supplying food after the fact for those who would otherwise go hungry. Thus, over time Evidence Action hopes to convince donors to invest in this program, No Lean Season, as an important complement to food aid.

Interventions that are relatively inexpensive and whose costs don't scale in proportion to reach may also be good candidates for ongoing donor funding. These are most often advocacy groups or technology platforms that do not directly distribute products or provide services. When their overall budgets are modest, even operating at national scale, donor funds may be sufficient.

Advocacy groups seek to influence policy or public opinion on an issue of interest. They can achieve outsized impact by directly or indirectly affecting norms, laws, regulations, and government spending. For example, the First Five Years Fund advocates for federal investments in early childhood education for an annual budget of approximately five million dollars, funded by a number of prominent US foundations. On the public-opinion front, GLAAD has sought to build acceptance of lesbian and gay people through fair, accurate, and inclusive portrayals in media for over 30 years, operating on an annual budget of approximately $12 million. Such organizations can punch well above their weight through individual or foundation support alone.

Technology-based solutions can also be highly leveraged, particularly when the value provided is in digital form. As with any number of for-profit online services, once a platform is built the incremental cost for adding more users is minimal. This attribute has driven massive growth in the tech industry and can do the same for social impact. For example, on a budget of just over $37 million a year Khan Academy provides free world-class education to nearly 12 million learners each month through its catalog of online courses.[9] By harnessing the power of technology, a class can be created once, then taken over and over again for only the pennies needed to run the website.

Despite these exceptions, think twice before relying exclusively on donor funding as your engine for growth. Are sufficient philanthropic dollars available to fully scale to the size of the need? If not, it is important to test the feasibility of other revenue streams early, so you can factor them into the design of your solution from the start.

PARTNERSHIP

During my travels across dozens of developing countries, I've had the opportunity to make field visits to large foreign-aid programs, tiny social enterprises, and everything in between. One challenge almost all have in common is last-mile distribution. Unlike the United States where we have so many options (from UPS to smartphone

[9] Khan Academy, *2017 Annual Report*, Khan Academy, accessed July 15, 2018, http://khanacademyannualreport.org.

apps) to reach almost any customer anywhere, in poorer countries reliable distribution can be a huge hurdle, particularly in remote rural areas. The problem is compounded by poor roads, low literacy, and scattered populations.

To cope with poor infrastructure and the lack of shared distribution services, organizations tend to create their own. In the same location, I've come across separate agents selling mobile airtime, solar systems, clean cookstoves, healthcare products, agricultural inputs, consumer goods, and much more. Every product line has to hire its own local reps, navigate transport options, and build trust with customers. On top of that, additional networks provide services such as microfinance, agricultural training, community healthcare, and women's empowerment. This tendency towards fragmentation is so strong that large donors have found themselves inadvertently funding independent supply chains and frontline delivery teams to treat separate diseases such as malaria, tuberculosis, and HIV.

Certainly it is not realistic for all these diverse activities to be handled by a single person or network. But funders, nonprofits, and social enterprises can achieve their goals faster by investing in shared infrastructure and collaborating across initiatives. Such a recognition led the Bill and Melinda Gates Foundation to establish its integrated delivery team in 2012 to supplement its vast investments in disease-specific interventions by building integrated delivery channels and strengthening health systems.

No doubt partnerships and coordination can slow progress in the short term. But just as taking the time to validate the engine for growth can lead to acceleration down the road, leveraging systems and infrastructure that are already at scale can do the same. For example, the Coca-Cola Company's Project Last Mile works with African governments to leverage its extensive refrigerated supply chain to deliver life-saving medication and vaccines to remote communities. In another powerful case, described in Chapter Ten, VisionSpring decided to leverage BRAC's extensive network of community health workers in Bangladesh to distribute eyeglasses, rather than painstakingly building out its own network. Yet another is the use of the Y's network of community centers to roll out diabetes prevention programs in the United States, described in Chapter Four.

Distribution is only one of many challenges to scaling solutions for disadvantaged populations, particularly in low-income countries. Michael Lwin, the managing director of Myanmar-based health and IT social enterprise Koe Koe Tech, puts it this way: "Being an entrepreneur is much easier if you're a smart, talented person in a rich country where you can sell to people with money to spend, build on established infrastructure, and depend on rule of law." Without these conditions, many endeavors become vertically integrated and are forced to master a wide range of expertise, increasing risk and slowing growth.

Admittedly, organizations can also get in their own way. Large funders and nonprofits tend to be structured around geographic or sector priorities, while smaller nonprofits and social enterprises tend to have narrowly targeted missions. Finding a meaningful intersection as a basis for partnership can prove challenging. Focus is essential to gauge progress and ensure accountability, but it can also lead to myopic thinking.

When faced with the need for systems or infrastructure that extend beyond your core value proposition, look for other players with similar needs who can share investment and operational costs. This could be a distribution network, backend IT system, supply chain, outreach, training, or any other elements that would benefit from greater economies of scale. Sometimes, an existing system can be dual purposed for both the original and new requirements, such as with Coca-Cola, the Y, and BRAC as described above. In cases where a system doesn't yet exist, bringing together nonprofits, entrepreneurs, and funders with related objectives to coinvest in a shared asset can reduce costs and gain leverage for all.

Remember, we share a common mission for social good. Innovation flourishes when we each focus on our unique value add. Rather than seeking control, seek scale.

ACCELERATE

If we agree a social startup should start small and think big, the growth hypothesis tests our assumptions for how that transition from small to big will occur. In the early days, grants can be sufficient for design, experimentation, and pilots. But, the pool is finite. At some point, we need to find sustainable and recurring funding sources that will accelerate growth if we hope to meet the scale of the need.

Newton's second law of motion states that the greater the weight of an object, the more force is required for acceleration. So to make your job easier, lighten the load by constantly driving down both cost and complexity. An intricately crafted intervention might make a big difference for a few. But would you make a greater impact by getting something slightly less comprehensive to a hundred or a thousand times more people? Don't let the perfect be the enemy of the good.

All too often, the social sector touts success with a vanity metric of an absolute number that represents reach. Remember, scale is not a static data point. Rather, it is the formula that can break out of the grant cycle, rev the engine, and start to accelerate, whether through a business model, government adoption, replication, or other means. Scale is making the shift from linear to exponential growth.

Chapter Nine
Impact

Microcredit, the extension of small loans to low-income borrowers, was a darling of the aid industry for decades following the birth of the modern movement in 1983, when Muhammad Yunus established Grameen Bank in Bangladesh. The promise was enticing: a relatively simple, financially sustainable intervention able to lift millions out of poverty. It earned Yunus and Grameen Bank a Nobel Peace Prize in 2006 "for their efforts to create economic and social development from below." By 2007, microcredit had blossomed into a global industry, with up to 25,000 microfinance institutions around the world serving perhaps over a hundred million borrowers.[1]

On one hand, the story of microcredit is one of the most impressive examples of achieving massive scale for social good, in this case through replication. On the other hand, some of the claims that fueled the hype have been disproven. Almost three decades after Grameen Bank was established, a number of rigorous evaluations were performed in different countries to measure the impact of

---

[1] Ina Kota, "Microfinance: Banking for the Poor," *Finance and Development* 44, no. 2 (June 2007), http://www.imf.org/external/pubs/ft/fandd/2007/06/basics.htm.

Lean Impact: How to Innovate for Radically Greater Social Good, First Edition. Ann Mei Chang. © 2019 Ann Mei Chang. Published 2019 by John Wiley & Sons, Inc.

microcredit on poverty. An analysis of six randomized control trials (RCTs) in the January 2015 edition of the *American Economic Journal: Applied Economics* found a "lack of evidence of transformative effects on the average borrower." While microfinance made some positive contributions, such as smoothing incomes, expanding access to credit, and increasing business activity, there was no evidence it increased income or reduced poverty overall.[2] Some poor households even became mired in debt, as they were unable to keep up with payments given the high interest rates typically charged by microfinance institutions.

The moral of the story is not that microcredit is all good or all bad. After all, it gives families more financial options and thus can empower them with more choices and improve their resilience to shocks. However, would the same billions of aid and investment dollars have been channeled here had we known it didn't reduce poverty?

One of the core principles of Lean Impact is to start small and validate before going big. For a purely for-profit business, testing the value and growth hypotheses is sufficient. But if we have a social or environmental mission, then there is an even higher bar. We must also test our impact hypothesis – the third pillar of social innovation.

DOES IT WORK?

Despite the billions upon billions that have been spent on foreign aid over the past 70 years, a heated controversy remains over whether in fact it works. An academic analysis of 97 econometric studies in 2009 concluded, "the preponderance of the evidence indicates that aid has

[2] Abhijit Banerjee, Dean Karlan, and Jonathan Zinman, "Six Randomized Evaluations of Microcredit: Introduction and Further Steps," *American Economic Journal: Applied Economics* 7, no. 1 (January 2015): 1–21, http://dx.doi.org/10.1257/app.20140287.

not been effective."[3] The reality is that across the incredibly diverse range of interventions, there have been stunning successes that we are quick to celebrate, dismal failures that tend to be hidden, and a majority of cases whose results are unclear. We should know the difference.

Impact is the ultimate aim of the social sector, so should be front and center when testing your solution. At the same time, in many cases it is reasonable and practical to test the riskiest value and growth hypotheses first, as they can lend themselves to cheaper and quicker experiments. After all, if no one wants to use or pay for something, whether it has social impact may not be relevant. But before expanding the size and scope of an intervention, it's important to answer the basic question – Does it work?

For most efforts at social change, the honest answer seems to be, We're not sure. The hungry may be getting fed, but are they becoming healthier? Kids may be going to school, but are they learning and growing up to lead more productive lives? We think we're helping, but how do we know?

Nonprofit GiveDirectly has received considerable attention for its promotion of unconditional cash transfers as a tool for reducing poverty. It gives cash grants directly to poor households and allows them the flexibility to spend the money on the needs they consider most pressing. Yet cofounder and president Michael Faye describes its true measure of success as "establishing a benchmark for impact in the social sector, as Vanguard did with the index fund for the investment industry." That is, GiveDirectly would like to challenge other interventions to prove that they work better for long-term poverty alleviation than simply giving out cash. For the same amount spent, if a complex program can't deliver more benefit than cash, is it worth doing? Michael doesn't expect cash to always come out ahead. But he hopes to inject more rigor and greater effectiveness in the industry over time.

[3] Hristos Doucouliagos and Martin Paldam, "The Aid Effectiveness Literature: The Sad Results of 40 Years of Research," *Journal of Economic Surveys* 23, no. 3 (July 2009): 433–461, https://doi.org/10.1111/j.1467-6419.2008.00568.x.

Even organizations that can clearly articulate their impact are often less certain when it comes to cost-effectiveness. Quantifying impact is an important first step. But to be meaningful we also need to ask, At what cost? While managing costs is an imperative for businesses, many nonprofits surprisingly don't have systems that can accurately track financial performance on a unit basis – how much is being spent per capita for an intervention. GiveDirectly's benchmark serves as a useful reference point. The pertinent question is not whether we are making *any* difference, but whether are we making the greatest difference possible for our investment.

Measuring social impact is a lot more complicated than tracking e-commerce transactions. Most software startups have a small number of straightforward indicators that determine their success: revenue, 30-day active users, conversion rate, etc. In contrast, social impact can take years or even decades to be fully realized. As a result, the prospect of evaluating impact can seem too expensive, too time consuming, and too daunting. More tangible and immediate priorities, including the pressure for measurable results from funders, can take precedence. Over time, organizations can fall into doing more and more without stopping to confirm or improve upon their actual impact.

On the other hand, those who take a rigorous approach to impact can sometimes make significant sacrifices in agility to do so. Gathering evidence through a comprehensive RCT can take years, during which time changes to a program are often discouraged or even prohibited. And once an evaluation confirms positive outcomes, both funders and providers can be hesitant to make changes that may invalidate the evidence base. Thus, some of the most impressive and impactful interventions stagnate over time.

How can we avoid the false dilemma between shooting blind and becoming slow and rigid? The better option is to break down the process of validation, just as with value and growth, by identifying the riskiest assumptions behind the desired impact. Validating impact isn't an all-or-nothing choice. Instead, we can take smaller steps to tier experiments, reducing risk each step of the way.

THEORY OF CHANGE

A theory of change is the most commonly used tool among non-profits, foundations, and governments to model, design, and evaluate social impact. In short, it maps the causal linkages between activities and their anticipated effects that lead step by step to the desired result.

Consider a goal of having your middle-school daughter admitted to a good university. Your theory might be: if I offer Emma a cash incentive, she'll be more likely to attend after-school tutoring sessions, the extra help will improve her grades, and better grades will make it more likely she'll get into Harvard. Now, your daughter may or may not cooperate. In fact, a 2015 study by Vanderbilt University studied just this and found that a cash reward made no difference. However, a certificate of recognition from the school superintendent for consistent attendance increased participation in tutoring sessions by 42.5%.[4] A theory of change articulates your assumptions, identifies what is expected to happen as a consequence of an intervention, and highlights what should be tested.

In its simplest form, a theory of change describes five major stages: inputs, activities, outputs, outcomes, and impact (see Figure 9.1). A list of *inputs* describes the resources required, such as money,

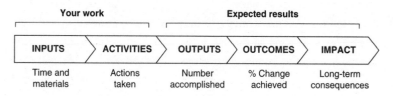

Figure 9.1 Theory of change.

---

[4] Matthew G Springer, Brooks A. Rosenquist, and Walker A. Swain, "Monetary and Nonmonetary Student Incentives for Tutoring Services: A Randomized Controlled Trial," *Journal of Research on Educational Effectiveness* 8, no. 4 (2015): 453–474, https://doi.org/10.1080/19345747.2015.1017679.

goods, and labor. The *activities* stage then deploys those inputs through an intervention. In combination, inputs and activities represent the work that is under your direct control. The *outputs* step then captures the most immediate result of those actions, typically an absolute number of people or entities receiving the goods or services. Based on those benefits, anticipated *outcomes* describe the change in well-being, behavior, or capacity of the recipients that results. Finally, the long-term (hopefully positive) consequences comprise the ultimately desired *impact*.

In the tutoring scenario, the inputs include the money for the reward and the tutor. The activity is the offer to pay students cash to attend tutoring sessions. As a result, the output is the number of students who participate in the program. The outcome would be the percentage increase in attendance at tutoring sessions. And the impact is hopefully manifested by an improvement in test scores or grades over time, with admission into a desirable university as the ultimate goal.

In clinical research terminology, the overall theory of change captures the *effectiveness* of an intervention – the beneficial effect under real-world conditions. The individual linkages should reflect all of the factors necessary to lead to the long-term desired impact. This includes *efficacy*, or whether the desired results occur under idealized conditions, along with other external variables, such as adherence, quality of implementation, and availability of resources.

A good theory of change should be rooted as much as possible in existing evidence. At most one or two new variables might be introduced at one time and tested to determine whether the intervention as a whole is likely to work. If virtually every linkage in the chain is speculative, you may be gambling more than innovating.

While articulating a theory of change has become commonplace in the design process and is required by many grant proposals, too often that theory is never fully validated. Instead, it can become reduced to a planning tool that is used to explain the rationale for a program. Once execution gets underway, ongoing reporting tends to focus on outputs as evidence of work being performed because they are relatively quick and easy to measure. Whether the intended outcomes or impacts are being achieved may not be known. In the case of microcredit, the rapid growth in the number of borrowers attracted global attention. Yet the notion that it would increase incomes and lead to a reduction in poverty went unquestioned for years. If you care about impact, you should test your theory of change early and often.

BREAKING IT DOWN

In line with Lean Impact principles, your aim should be to stay as small as possible while reducing risk each step of the way. Articulating a theory of change is the first step in moving away from an all-or-nothing approach to impact. We can further break down each stage by detailing the chain of events within it. In the tutoring example, we might have a string of assumptions for attendance to lead to better grades, such as "students pay attention," "tutors are competent," and "test scores increase." Each connection thus represents an assumption that can be tested that will lead to the intended impact. As some of these linkages may already be well established, such as good grades improving the likelihood of university admission, it is prudent to focus on the areas with the greatest unknowns.

For example, if you are distributing bed nets with the hope of reducing deaths from malaria, you might have a string of assumptions, including that people receiving nets will hang them properly, sleep under them, and thereby lower their exposure to malaria. As efficacy research has already established a causal relationship between sleeping under mosquito nets and a reduction in malaria transmission, the riskier assumptions are whether people will correctly hang and sleep under the mosquito nets.[5]

---

[5] Neil Buddy Shah, Paul Wang, Andrew Fraker, and Daniel Gastfriend, "Evaluations with Impact: Decision-focused Impact Evaluation as a Practical Policymaking Tool," 3ie Working Paper 25 (September 2015): 22, http://www.3ieimpact.org/media/filer_public/2015/10/01/wp25-evaluations_with_impact.pdf.

Fortunately, checking whether nets are being used is an experiment that can be run in a relatively short time, versus perhaps years to detect a perceptible reduction in disease burden. We can also quickly test variations that might increase the rates of adoption, such as pricing schemes, trainings, or messaging on health implications. The more people who sleep under mosquito nets, the fewer people are likely to contract malaria. In the fullness of time, we will still want to validate that malaria rates have in fact declined to confirm our impact, and make sure we haven't overlooked an unexpected factor. But by optimizing usage first, we will have reduced the risk of failure and increased the likely degree of improvement.

IDinsight, a groundbreaking leader in rapid-cycle evaluations, used this approach to help the Zambian Ministry of Health study ways to reduce distribution costs for insecticide-treated bed nets. Its research found that nearly all households were willing to travel to pick up nets at community distribution points, a far more cost effective practice than going door-to-door. In addition, it found that follow-up home visits by community health workers to hang any uninstalled nets resulted in no difference in usage after six months. Based on these findings, Zambia updated its national guidelines to use distribution points and eliminate home visits, saving an estimated 59% in staff costs with minimal impact on coverage.[6]

TIERED VALIDATION

To design an MVP for impact, start by articulating the steps in your theory of change, identifing the riskiest link, and then designing an experiment that can directly test that causal relationship. If a linkage will innately take a long time to manifest, look for ways to break it

---

[6] IDinsight, *Measuring Community-level Point ITN Distribution Dynamics and the Impact of CHW Hang-up in Rural Rufunsa District*, IDinsight, July 15, 2014, http://idinsight.org/wp-content/uploads/2015/02/ITN-distribution-and-hang-up-dynamics-3DE-Technical-Report.pdf.

down further into the substeps that will lead to the full effect. By validating and optimizing those precursors first, you can gain confidence that there will be a higher likelihood the desired impact will ultimately be realized. Your aim should be to reduce the greatest degree of risk relative to the cost of validation.

In *The Startup Way*, Eric Ries shares the story of building an MVP diesel engine at GE. Unlike prototyping an app, one-day iterations are simply not feasible when designing an engine. Yet by reducing the number of new features and leveraging an existing product, the GE team found a way to create a first test for the five-year project in less than six months, thus dramatically reducing complexity and risk.[7] Smaller experiments can confirm customer demand and identify design issues prior to making a bigger investment. Rather than spending five years only to potentially have the product flop, producing an MVP allowed GE to test and improve a simpler engine, then incorporate those lessons into the final design.

The complexity of social interventions can sometimes rival that of a jet engine. Similarly, even when a one-day MVP is not realistic, narrowing the scope of an experiment to the degree possible allows us to learn more quickly. Remember Tenofovir, the vaginal gel for preventing HIV transmission? Even though a phase-3 trial was required for regulatory approval, running shorter experiments on the major risk factors first could have identified and addressed flaws before the longer and more expensive evaluation.

While MVPs for value test the degree to which beneficiaries and stakeholders will participate and engage, MVPs for impact test for the likelihood of the desired benefit when they do. Achieving such impact typically takes longer, but experiments should still be the smallest, cheapest, and shortest necessary to learn. In the following sections, I'll cover strategies for handling some of the unique challenges that can arise when validating impact.

---

[7] Eric Ries, *The Startup Way: How Modern Companies Use Entrepreneurial Management to Transform Culture & Drive Long-Term Growth* (New York: Currency, 2017), 147–155.

Using Early Indicators

Some types of social impact may take years or even a generation to realize. Are we creating a more democratic society? Is the generational cycle of poverty being broken? Will environmental degradation be sufficiently contained? While it is impossible to accurately predict the answers to these questions, improving on early indicators of impact can decrease risk and increase the likelihood of a good outcome over time. Although the correlation with ultimate outcomes won't be 100%, it's a far better option than just crossing our fingers and toes.

Improving educational attainment falls into this category. Summit Public Schools' goal of having 100% of its students successfully graduate from college is a result that can't be fully confirmed for a decade. Yet it recognized the need for a faster feedback cycle: waiting to see the results for each cohort would be too slow.

Working with a small team of independent engineers at Facebook, Summit improved its technology platform to capture data on each student's journey on an ongoing basis. Did students choose to take a test? How did they perform? What did they do afterwards? The data, combined with regular mentor meetings and teacher feedback, gives schools an individual level view of student progress. Today Summit uses this information to continuously evaluate and improve every aspect of the educational experience while garnering immediate insight into the impact on learning.

One series of variations tested CEO Diane Tavenner's intuition that kids don't learn well from traditional stand-and-deliver lectures with a teacher planted at the front of the room. In the first week lectures became optional. Participation dropped somewhat, but assessments showed no difference in learning. However, some kids reported through surveys that they had some questions that weren't answered. The next week, the teachers added office hours and attendance at lectures declined even further. After seven weeks, only two kids were still going to lectures (and were now enjoying the benefits of personalized attention). At the same time, the tutoring bar proved immensely popular. Across the class as a whole, performance and satisfaction was higher. The model was a success.

By identifying and measuring the precursors to educational achievement, Summit was able to dramatically speed up its feedback cycle, test a range of approaches, learn what works best, and improve its model. While such early indicators can never guarantee the desired impact will eventually manifest, they can go a long way in reducing risk and increasing the likelihood of success.

Working with Constraints

Certain interventions by nature operate under constraints that must be accommodated when validating impact. Some activities can only take place at certain times of the year, while others may innately take a certain period of time. Both of these characteristics are true of agriculture: planting takes place only at the start of the growing season and vegetables simply need time to grow. Despite these challenges, the One Acre Fund has built innovation into its DNA to drive both incremental and transformative innovations on an ongoing basis.

In Chapter Six, I shared its journey to recognizing the importance of early testing and validation in its work with smallholder farmers in Africa. It has since developed a five-phase process for rolling out new products, starting with research and culminating with program-wide adoption for successful innovations. One such series of trials tested the potential of planting trees as an additional income stream for farmers.

Trees are a source of firewood, timber for construction, and livestock fodder. They can be planted on the borders of a farm plot, providing shade and protecting against soil erosion. In early research, the One Acre Fund estimated that if farmers waited for a full six years to harvest trees, a year's worth of planted seedlings could potentially net $390 in profit – a 1450% margin – an extremely high number relative to its goal of increasing farmer incomes. It was an idea worthy of further exploration.

Among the key factors for success is the germination rate. The more trees that survive, the greater the income generated. Thus, One Acre started by testing different planting methods in its nursery, seeking the ideal balance between maximizing yield and minimizing complexity for farmers. This included experimenting with seed sourcing, seed storage protocols, composition of the potting mixture, and timing for transplantation.

With success in the nursery, small farmer trials started the following year. Unfortunately, performance under real-world conditions didn't match that of the nursery and a far lower number of trees survived. Though still highly profitable, the results fell far short of what could be possible if more trees made it to maturity. This led to further experiments to improve seed storage, the mix of soil and fertilizer, and trainings for farmers. In addition, they introduced sockets to separate seedlings and decrease competition for nutrients, with the potential to double survivability.

The protracted growing cycle hasn't deterred One Acre from continuous experimentation. Beyond improving tree survival rates, it has tested behavioral interventions to encourage farmers to defer sales of their trees for six years, until they reach full maturity and maximum profitability. A fully grown tree is worth approximately eighteen times more than a seedling, making it a great long-term savings plan for farmers.

The One Acre Fund isn't satisfied with good impact. It is finding ways to deliver as much impact as possible.

Measuring Intangibles

Sometimes the challenge in measuring impact is not timeframe but discerning effects that are not so discretely measurable. This can be the case when seeking to influence policy or bolster intangible qualities such as resilience, empowerment, or a sense of well-being. Such complex effects don't lend themselves to an easy yes or no metric. But early indicators can still provide a meaningful signal as to whether you're on the right track.

Reprieve is a London-based organization that advocates for human rights and justice. It offers a different kind of product: creating a new narrative in order to shift public opinion. With only 41 staff and often fighting enormous opponents, it punches far above its weight by making the most of its agility. Former executive director Clare Algar has seen "a tendency in the sector to believe everything needs to be done perfectly to achieve credibility, which gets in the way of trying lots of different things to find the campaign that works."

Whether a campaign will work is difficult to anticipate, but Reprieve has found that the level of press interest is a good early indicator as well as a big factor in driving public engagement. Thus, an MVP can simply consist of running a new idea by a trusted press contact. If the reporter is hooked and wants to do a story, that's a good sign. Once a piece goes out, the degree of press coverage further confirms traction. If there is little pickup, perhaps another angle is needed, or it may be that the issue simply doesn't resonate. Rather than having endless internal debates about agreeing on the perfect message, Reprieve has been able to move faster and make better decisions by allowing more flexibility to float ideas externally.

One of Reprieve's big successes has been its campaign to stop lethal injections. After a lawyer in the United States called on behalf of a client slated to be executed, a Reprieve volunteer identified the drug provider, a wholesaler operating out of the back of a driving school in London. Reprieve sued the British government for allowing the export of drugs for executions in contradiction to national and European policy that opposed the death penalty. The issue garnered a flurry of press coverage, eventually resulting in a government export control that was subsequently replicated across the European Union. When states turned to new drugs not manufactured in Europe, the team persuaded manufacturers to implement distribution controls to prevent misuse of medicines in executions. In combination, Reprieve's actions have led to an ongoing shortage of execution drugs in the United States.

There is no one-size-fits-all technique. Shifts in attitude might be measured through reported behavior changes, the response to a real or constructed scenario, or the results of a psychometric instrument. By being creative it's possible to find early, measurable indicators even for impact of a more intangible nature.

Multidimensional Problems

Achieving social impact is frequently a multidimensional problem. When we tackle a single factor in isolation, we may make some short-term progress only to see it fade over time. Sustainable change usually requires going beyond satisfying the immediate need – whether it be hunger, lack of skills, or access to services – to also address the underlying motivations, support systems, and incentives, as well as the policies that created and reinforce the status quo. If we consider only the symptoms, we may find ourselves repeatedly applying Band-Aids.

One in three children in the United States are overweight or obese, resulting in health issues that cause them to miss school, learn less, and lose productivity, while also inflicting an enormous cost on society. FoodCorps wants to create a future where all children eat healthy foods so that they are ready to learn and able to reach their full potential. It's doing this by bringing leaders from AmeriCorps, a US national service program, to high-need schools. Service members promote a supportive food culture, work with cafeterias to provide healthier foods, and conduct hands-on lessons to inspire kids to fall in love with vegetables.

FoodCorps measures its impact along two dimensions: changes in students and changes in school environments. To measure changes in student attitudes, they use a vegetable preference survey. In 2017, the survey found that 55% of FoodCorps' students showed improved interest in vegetables. Occasionally FoodCorps also crosschecks student behavior by comparing before and after photos of student lunch trays to confirm the amount and type of foods being consumed. This review has shown that students in FoodCorps schools with more hands-on learning activities are eating triple the amount of fruits and vegetables. In addition, to measure change in schools, the Healthy School progress report tracks the adoption of best practices across the school itself, such as planting and teaching in gardens, promoting healthy foods on the menu, and engaging school leaders and educators.

By holding itself accountable to both of these important elements of impact, FoodCorps is able to create a self-reinforcing environment in schools in which kids make healthy choices and good options are readily available. Founder Curt Ellis says FoodCorps seeks to "measure our program effectiveness obsessively to improve year over year."

The previous sections describe just a few examples of how validating impact can be tiered under different conditions. What is most important is to find opportunities to test and learn in smaller increments, reduce risks along the way, and make early improvements than can lead to greater benefit.

WHAT MATTERS?

San Francisco's Community Housing Partnership (CHP) was founded in 1990 as part of a new wave to provide ongoing supportive housing and services, rather than temporary shelters, for the chronically homeless. Although it won recognition and many awards for its work, by 2012 it had started asking the tough question – What is the endgame? The national standard across hundreds of thousands of housing units throughout the country was simply to keep people housed and off the streets. In conjunction with a forward-looking funder, CHP conducted a study and found that no one was driving towards the real outcome that mattered: self-sufficiency.

CHP decided to try. In 2015 it adopted a new strategic plan with self-sufficiency at its core and a goal of 10% of residents graduating to more independent living by 2020. Colleagues thought that the CHP was crazy and would likely fail, as such an approach was unheard of at the time. Furthermore, all the work had to be done with philanthropic support, as government funding was restricted to traditional interventions. Despite these hurdles, CHP committed to this ambitious vision. If successful, it will be establishing a new standard for the field.

The experience of CHP raises a crucial question regarding social impact – What matters? Is success defined by getting homeless people off the streets or by helping them gain the necessary skills to become independent over time? Clearly the latter is far more impact-ful and sustainable, but sadly the focus is more often along the lines of the former. Understandably – such shorter-term objectives are lower risk, more easily measurable, and deliver quicker wins. Yet if we seek to maximize the benefit to society, it behooves us to stretch ourselves to aim higher, as CHP is doing.

Measuring what matters also requires us to recognize when our work is no longer relevant. Proximity Designs' primary impact goal is to sustainably increase incomes of rural households in Myanmar. In 2012, selling d.light solar lanterns fit the bill. They were brighter, safer, and less expensive over time than burning candles to study or work after dark. The customers who purchased the product reported income increases of up to 50%. Yet only three years later, as Myanmar opened to foreign investment, rural areas were flooded with solar light alternatives. The market was doing its job, and the marginal impact of Proximity's work had been greatly reduced. So it decided to shut down the product line.

It can be hard for an organization to recognize when its incremental value is no longer meaningful. Usually, as long as fund-ing flows, the work continues. By making the tough call, Proximity was able to turn its attention to new frontiers and fill other needs that would otherwise go unmet. Maximizing impact sometimes means knowing when to let go.

RELENTLESS PURSUIT

One of the most impressive and fascinating nonprofits I have encoun-tered is one few people have heard of, despite being among the larg-est in the world. In fact, for the past three years NGO Advisor has rated BRAC the world's top NGO (nongovernmental organization) for its innovation, impact, and sustainability. I became so intrigued that I joined the board of the US affiliate after leaving USAID and spent a couple of weeks visiting its staff and programs in Bangladesh.

Atypical for a global development organization, BRAC was founded and is headquartered in a developing country. Several other characteristics make it unusual: a persistent presence in just about every corner of the country, a cross-sectoral approach to fighting all dimensions of poverty, and associated commercial enterprises that self-fund almost 80% of their activities in Bangladesh. These in combination allow BRAC to take the long view, deeply understand local culture, and constantly pursue innovative ways to fight poverty.

BRAC is particularly known for simple solutions that are massively scalable. Founder Sir Fazle Hasan Abed is often quoted as insisting "Small is beautiful, but big is necessary." Not long after its founding, BRAC embarked on a now-legendary campaign to tackle diarrheal mortality, the primary contributor to the deaths of 252 out of 1000 children under five in 1979.[8] Since the 1960s, evidence had grown that the right mixture of sugar, salts, and water could effectively treat dehydration from diarrhea that might otherwise lead to death. But oral rehydration therapy (ORT) was largely administered by medical personnel and in clinics, and wasn't reaching the rural poor.

Sir Fazle recognized that the recommended protocols for ORT weren't practical given the realities in Bangladesh at the time: an insufficient number of health centers, a lack of trained personnel, and the high cost of purchasing and distributing premixed packets. Instead, despite opposition from the World Health Organization, he decided to teach mothers to prepare the solution.

Through a series of pilots, BRAC tested directions for ORT formulation, educational messages, and the operation of teaching teams. In what may be one of the earliest instances of a rapid feedback loop for social impact, daily and monthly review meetings identified problems and recommended improvements. For example, some mothers reversed the original instructions for using one pinch of salt and two scoops of sugar to instead use two pinches of salt and one scoop of sugar. To avoid confusion, the instructions were simplified

---

[8] Fazle Hasan Abed, "Address at the Hangzhou International Congress" (transcript of the address as delivered, UNESCO International Congress, Hangzhou, China, May 15–17, 2013), http://www.unesco.org/new/fileadmin/MULTIMEDIA/HQ/CLT/images/sir_fazle_abed_transcript_final.pdf.

to use a single pinch of salt and a single fistful of sugar.[9] Over time, through a series of iterations, results dramatically improved from a paltry 6% in the first experiment to a point at which 67–80% of women were properly using ORT. With this success, BRAC embarked on a massive door-to-door campaign in the 1980s to teach over 12 million women to prepare ORT. In part due to this intervention, since 1979 the mortality of children under five years of age in Bangladesh has plummeted from 252 to fewer than 50 out of 1000 today, saving countless lives.[10]

Since then, BRAC has continued to doggedly chase down any barrier that can keep people trapped in poverty. As an early pioneer of microcredit, BRAC noticed that women who used their loans to purchase a dairy cow were selling milk at low and unpredictable prices, severely limiting their income potential. One of the problems was that without refrigeration they couldn't sell into larger urban markets, leaving them at the mercy of the limited demand in their villages. The solution? BRAC started a dairy processor, Aarong Dairy, which established 101 chilling centers to collect milk from small producers. It has become one of BRAC's largest social enterprises, with around 1500 employees processing 250,000 liters of milk a day. Now poor women are able to sell their milk at a good, consistent price, and BRAC has another income stream to support its work.

People generally believe that the degree of innovation tends to be inversely correlated with the size of an entity. Yet relentlessly seeking impact can focus minds even at the largest organizations.

RANDOMIZED CONTROL TRIALS

Over the past two decades, mission-driven organizations have increasingly used RCTs to evaluate social impact. Some call them the gold standard for evidence. However, RCTs can be slow and expen-

---

[9] A. Mushtaque, R. Chowdhury, and Richard A. Cash, *A Simple Solution* (Dhaka, Bangladesh: University Press, 1996).
[10] Abed, "Address."

sive, work only in certain types of situations, and are not reliably predictive of results for other contexts. They are an invaluable tool for understanding impact, but not a silver bullet.

RCTs were originally used to validate the effectiveness of new medications. Candidates are randomly placed into either a treatment group that receives the medicine or a control group that receives a placebo. By measuring the difference in results between the two groups, we can tell if the treatment worked. This same technique has been used to evaluate a wide range of social programs, such as microcredit, distribution of mosquito nets, workforce training, and convict reentry support services.

Evaluations based on RCTs can inform better program choices. In Chapter Four, we saw how effective interventions were designed based on successful trials for diabetes prevention and seasonal work. When such research exists, it can direct investment towards solutions that deliver the most cost-effective results.

The *Abdul Latif Jameel Poverty Action Lab* (*J-PAL*) is a global research center that has been at the forefront of the use of rigorous evaluations to determine which interventions work and are most cost effective. With a network of 161 affiliated professors at universities around the world, J-PAL seeks to answer critical questions in the fight against poverty.

J-PAL curates a library of practical resources for researchers at http://www.povertyactionlab.org/research-resources.

Of course, some interventions – such as influencing policy, working through collaborative partnerships, or driving macroeconomic growth of a country – are difficult or impossible to measure with an RCT. A realistic control group may not exist, or it may be too difficult to manage all the external variables that may affect the results. When RCTs aren't appropriate, we need to find other ways to gauge effectiveness.

It is also important to recognize that research findings may not translate to new contexts. Just because an intervention has been proven successful in one geography, with a particular demographic, or by a single implementer doesn't mean it will work under other conditions. The external validity of an RCT can vary based on the intervention and needs to be confirmed. This could involve tests ranging from a simple MVP up to and including running another full RCT.

My own biggest concern is using RCTs in a way that constrains rather than enhances innovation. If an RCT is performed too soon, needed improvements can come to a premature halt so that the treatment group can be held static to ensure legitimate results. Instead, by running lighter-weight experiments first, we can identify improvements that increase the likelihood of a strongly positive result in a later RCT. With such tiered validation, an RCT becomes complementary to rapid-cycle testing. This same process can be repeated as an intervention reaches new contexts and greater scale.

Another danger is becoming too beholden to historical RCT results. Even the best solutions can be improved. I've seen some truly world-class organizations begin to stagnate due to fear that any changes to their proven methodologies might invalidate their existing evidence bases. Governments can sometimes reinforce this dynamic by instituting rules that require a specific evidence-based program model, effectively reducing competition and innovation.[11] A positive RCT finding should not be an excuse to stop innovating. Rather, it can serve as the basis for the core program, while continuing to test and validate potential improvements that can be integrated once proven. Over time, as your intervention evolves, a subsequent RCT may become valuable.

Many organizations turn to academia to perform RCTs. Yet while universities have been pioneers in the use of RCTs to evaluate social interventions, their interests are not always aligned with the needs of a nonprofit or social enterprise. Yale economics professor Ahmed Mushfiq Mobarak, who works extensively with implementing organizations himself, observes, "When academics design a study,

---

[11] Brian Beachkofski, "Evidence-based, Innovative, and Accountable," Third Sector Capital Partners blog, January 24, 2018, https://www.thirdsectorcap.org/blog/evidence-based-innovative-and-accountable.

it is with the goal of gaining generalizable learning, not only to solve a specific problem for the specific demographic being studied." Academics have an incentive to publish papers and achieve tenure, both of which require the generation of new knowledge with a much higher threshold of rigor, sample size, and experimental purity than is often necessary for practical decision-making.

IDinsight characterizes this distinction as knowledge-focused versus decision-focused evaluations. While both can lead to better outcomes and are frequently blended together, it is important to calibrate the tool for the purpose. When an organization inadvertently deploys a more knowledge-focused evaluation for the purposes of decision-making, it may spend significantly more time and money than necessary.[12] Many of IDinsight's staff have strong academic training but chose to apply their talent to more practical pursuits. They employ similar randomization techniques, but tailor the level of data to the decision at hand, thereby reducing the timeframe, sometimes from years to months.

RESPONSIBLE IMPACT

When organizations consider lean approaches for a social context, many question whether it is inappropriate or irresponsible to experiment on people's lives. Asking vulnerable people to turn from established habits to try something new and risky could have a profoundly negative effect. What if someone loses a job, is harassed, or comes into harm's way? The Silicon Valley adage to "Move fast and break things" encapsulates a bias to action, in which releasing imperfect software is a reasonable tradeoff for rapid learning and progress. Such a notion needs to be far more considered when those "things" might be human beings.

Yet, experimenting is how we learn and improve. We could just as legitimately ask, Aren't we taking a far greater risk if we roll out an

[12] Shah, Wang, Fraker, and Gastfriend, "Evaluations with Impact."

intervention widely without testing with a smaller number of people first? And is it fair to continue to deliver an outdated or marginal solution, when a far better one may exist? After all, if someone did not take the risk to receive the first tetanus vaccine or heart transplant, innumerable lives would not have been subsequently saved.

Being responsible about risk is yet another strong argument for starting small. When we run an experiment with five people, we can take far more care than with 5000. It allows us to be vigilant to any unintended consequences that can arise when intervening in complex ecosystems. We need to recognize that well-meaning efforts may in fact lead to negative, rather than positive, impact. For example, gaining access to a mobile phone may empower women, but what if it triggers domestic abuse due to jealousy or a disruption of power dynamics in the home? Once we have understood and ameliorated any negative effects at small scale, we can more safely move on to test additional dynamics that may only be revealed at larger scale.

Beyond preventing harm, we also have a responsibility to make people whole, or even better off. When Watsi first started testing its crowdfunding site to raise money for people who needed but couldn't afford surgery, it identified its first three patients through a healthcare provider in Nepal with the assistance of a friend of a friend. Cofounder and CEO Chase Adam considered the worst-case scenario, and after hearing the patients' personal stories, didn't want to get their hopes up only to let them down. So he and his cofounder decided that they would set aside their own savings (to the tune of $4500) to cover the surgeries themselves if the experiment failed. Using a simple, hard-coded website, Watsi launched its first campaign to friends and family, and then to Y Combinator's social news website, Hacker News. The latter generated over 10,000 visitors in less than 24 hours, both demonstrating interest and paying for the surgeries. Since then Watsi has funded over 15,000 procedures.

It is our duty to take care of the people we involve in our work. In designing experiments, we have a responsibility to minimize risks and maximize the value gleaned from results. Participants must freely provide informed consent, be treated respectfully, and have their interests carefully considered. Ethical guidelines, such as those contained in the Declaration of Helsinki by the World Medical Association and the *Belmont Report* by the National Commission for the Protection of Human Subjects of Biomedical and Behavioral Research, have been established to protect subjects and prevent abuse.

For medical interventions, well-defined experimental phases have been codified in regulations to take calculated risks based on anticipated benefit. This starts with extensive preclinical studies in labs, using nonhuman subjects, then progresses to testing safety, then efficacy, then therapeutic effect, and then long-term effects. Typically, only about 20–100 volunteers participate in a phase-1 trial, with numbers increasing in subsequent phases. While many social interventions may involve lower degrees of risk and not require such a formalized structure, the same principles involved in understanding and testing for safety and side effects should apply. By staying small, we can carefully monitor for adverse consequences and affordably correct failures.

TAKING IT FORWARD

The value hypothesis asks whether people will participate and engage. The impact hypothesis asks whether something positive will happen when they do. And the growth hypothesis asks whether there is a path to reach all those who could benefit if so. Starting small allows us to answer all of these questions more quickly and cheaply. The resultant lessons will help us improve our solution and lay the groundwork for massive impact.

Of course, new demographics, new geographies, and greater scale will continue to open new questions. But once you have validated all three pillars of social innovation, you know you're headed down a promising path.

Part III
Transform

Lean methodology can help us design and deliver better products and services, as well as boost their scale and impact. But one great solution is not enough. To address the world's toughest challenges we will need to move beyond delivering individual interventions to transforming entire institutions and ecosystems.

Market and policy failures can result in dysfunctional dynamics that impede adoption or, even worse, reverse progress. The rigid funding mechanisms that we depend on can be at odds with the agility and flexibility that is at the core of innovation. Cultural norms within our organization and beyond can produce antibodies to a new way of working. And, at the same time, so much talent, money, and resources are being left on the sidelines. No one said social impact would be easy.

It can be extremely tempting to keep our heads down and focus on what we can control. But if we don't collectively grapple with the broader headwinds, we will all continue to make far slower progress than is possible, and than is needed. While Parts I and II of this

Lean Impact: How to Innovate for Radically Greater Social Good, First Edition. Ann Mei Chang.
© 2019 Ann Mei Chang. Published 2019 by John Wiley & Sons, Inc.

book focused on the *process* of innovation for a particular solution, Part III will turn to the *context* for innovation – how to put the wind at our backs.

Chapter Ten will delve into the all-too-frequent market and policy failures that exist as well as how we can work collaboratively to address them. In Chapters Eleven and Twelve, we will tackle the elephant in the room – funding – head on. How can social entrepreneurs more effectively navigate the contradictions between available funding and what is needed to innovate? And, perhaps more importantly, how can funders of all stripes reinvent their mechanisms to be more dynamic, allow for risk taking, and embrace an increasingly hybrid landscape? Chapter Thirteen looks inside organizations and focuses on building a high-performing culture that embraces change and the possibility of failure. Finally, Chapter Fourteen looks to the future, and how citizens, nonprofits, companies, foundations, investors, and governments can come together more seamlessly to maximize benefit to all.

We are relying on nineteenth-century institutions using twentieth-century tools to address twenty-first-century problems. It's time for us to stop acquiescing to the old rules of the game and create new ones. Transformation is a journey that can only succeed if we come together.

Chapter Ten
Systems Change

Many of our society's greatest challenges cannot be solved sustainably at scale by any single organization or intervention. At some point, even the best solutions can run into a wall of existing policy and market failures – where neither government or business is meeting the needs of certain disadvantaged populations. If we stay true to our goal and the problem we have chosen, in some cases we'll need to change the system itself.

So, where does that leave a social entrepreneur? Innovation is still essential. A nonprofit or social enterprise is in a unique position to demonstrate to governments and the business community the impact and viability of a particular course of action. Once a new approach is de-risked and shown to be feasible, it becomes a far smaller leap for others to take. For example, a new intervention may prove to save government money in the long run, perhaps by preventing health issues, poverty, or crime. Or, businesses might open their eyes to new revenue opportunities they had overlooked, perceived as too risky, or didn't see sufficient upside to explore.

Lean Impact: How to Innovate for Radically Greater Social Good, First Edition. Ann Mei Chang.
© 2019 Ann Mei Chang. Published 2019 by John Wiley & Sons, Inc.

The Skoll Foundation, a longtime advocate for social entrepreneurship, is among the leading thinkers who have made the shift to a systems mindset. It has come to appreciate the inherent limits of scaling individual organizations. As a result, its focus has expanded beyond the enterprise to embrace the so-called systems entrepreneurs who are taking on the challenge of shifting social systems, building coalitions, and influencing policy.

Rather than feed the hungry, can we open up more equitable opportunities for all, backed up by a safety net? Rather than fighting the fallout of discrimination, can we change the attitudes and laws that enable it? Rather than providing access to clean water, electricity, or financial services, can we demonstrate a viable financial model for businesses to serve those needs?

A VISION FOR CHANGE

An estimated 2.5 billion people in the world need, but don't have, the eyeglasses that would help them lead productive and fulfilling lives. To address society's failure to bring a 700-year-old technology to disadvantaged populations, Jordan Kassalow founded the award-winning social enterprise VisionSpring with a mission to ensure that everyone has affordable access to eyeglasses. Its motto: "See to learn, see to work."

From the beginning, Jordan believed that people express their needs and desires through what they buy. Charging an affordable price gives people dignity and puts the onus on VisionSpring to provide a product customers value enough to purchase. In 2003, it started by selling 800 pairs of glasses in India and El Salvador through what it called "vision entrepreneurs" – its own dedicated sales force. After three years, it became clear that the model had limited potential for scale and was too expensive to ever become sustainable on its own. So Jordan pivoted.

VisionSpring switched to a hub-and-spoke model, opening optical shops that offered a wide range of styles and pricing. The income generated from selling these higher-end products cross-subsidized outreach by vision entrepreneurs to poorer customers in remote locations. The enterprise became more financially sustainable, but growing a direct workforce was slow and painstaking and wouldn't allow for rapid growth into new geographies.

When Jordan met BRAC's vice chairperson Dr. Ahmed Mushtaque Raza Chowdhury, the two men became intrigued by the possibility of leveraging BRAC's extensive network of community health workers in Bangladesh to sell eyeglasses. There was the potential of a triple win: a huge distribution channel for VisionSpring, increased value and income potential for BRAC health network, and extended productive working years for older clients whose near vision was failing. After simplifying the exam procedure and running a small pilot, the possibility became a reality. Since 2006, the partnership has scaled to 61 of 63 districts in Bangladesh and amounts to 25% of VisionSpring's sales. In 2017, they celebrated the millionth pair of eyeglasses sold and expanded the partnership to Uganda.

Based on its success with BRAC, VisionSpring has leveraged partnerships with over 300 organizations around the world. Yet even if it reaches its audacious goal of selling 10 million pairs of glasses by 2020, it would still represent only a tiny fraction of the total need. For vast, long-standing societal challenges, even a highly successful organization can usually only make a small dent. And, as such problems typically lie at intersection of market and policy failures, any one sector only holds part of the solution. In the case of eyeglasses, market forces have encouraged companies to focus on more lucrative, affluent customers, leaving the poor and disadvantaged underserved. At the same time, government policies and aid organizations have prioritized more acute and deadly diseases. Thus, this simple and inexpensive intervention, which can increase productivity by 35% and generate $23 of economic impact for every dollar spent, has fallen through the cracks.

As the organization grew, Jordan and his VisionSpring colleague Liz Smith saw an opportunity to address barriers beyond their enterprise, by bringing government, the industry, and nonprofits together to tackle distribution and access problems more systemically. Thus, the EYElliance was born.

To date, 36 active members across the private, public, and nonprofit sectors have come together in the EYElliance to break through the systemic barriers. This includes promoting school programs so that kids have the necessary corrective eyewear to learn. It also uses the demonstrated success of VisionSpring and others to encourage companies in the optical business to move down market. And it seeks to integrate reading glasses into existing last-mile health networks as another element of basic care.

Among EYElliance's early successes in the public sphere is an agreement with the government of Liberia to develop a national plan for school eye health and to integrate basic eye care into the community health-worker system. Such systemic shifts make it possible to imagine a day when the private sector better reaches underserved markets, governments provide a safety net so all citizens have the potential to learn and be productive, and the social sector can turn its attention to new challenges that are as yet unsolved. The evolution of VisionSpring's path to scale is emblematic of the journey from doing some good to fixing a broken system.

COMING TOGETHER

As with the widespread need for eyeglasses, many of the world's problems can't be solved by any one organization or even one sector alone. Existing markets and policies simply may make it difficult to deliver a sustainable and scalable solution. Certainly, if you are able to succeed alone, do so. It's much simpler.

Otherwise, consider bringing together others who have a vested interest and a piece of the puzzle. I ended up doing this while working at the US Department of State. At the time, only about a third of the world's population was online, while everyone else risked being left further and further behind with less access to information, education, jobs, markets, community, and government services. Although many initiatives existed to bring the Internet to far-flung places, my research indicated that most of the people without access had local coverage but weren't using it. One major barrier was that Internet access was simply too expensive.

It turned out that tech companies wanted to see more people online so they would have more potential customers. Telecom providers were interested in new revenue streams from data services. Governments believed increased access would improve productivity and grow their economies. Nonprofits wanted to empower disadvantaged people and give them better choices. Everyone saw a benefit to their work, yet each was operating in separate spheres.

I tracked down everyone I could find from all of these vantage points and convened a roundtable at the State Department. We found 95% alignment around the challenge of affordability and the need to promote better policies and regulations that would encourage healthy market efficiencies and competition. After spending several months building consensus on the remaining 5%, we launched the Alliance for Affordable Internet (A4AI). Today it includes over 80 organizations representing many of the large tech companies, several countries, numerous nonprofits, foreign-aid donors, and academic institutions. Together, these organizations have gained a louder voice to advocate for change. In an early win, A4AI helped influence the government of Ghana to abolish a 20% import duty on smartphones.[1] A simulation by Deloitte estimated that the reduced taxes could lead to a $370 million increase in GDP over five years due to increased mobile penetration and the resulting productivity improvements.[2]

---

[1] Alliance for Affordable Internet, *Ghana drops import tax on smartphones following advocacy by A4AI-Ghana Coalition*, last modified November 20, 2014, http://a4ai. org/ghana-drops-import-tax-on-smartphones-following-advocacy-by-a4ai-ghana-coalition/.

[2] Deloitte, *Digital Inclusion and Mobile Sector Taxation in Ghana*, Deloitte, February 2015, https://www.gsma.com/publicpolicy/wp-content/uploads/2016/09/GSMA 2015_Report_DigitalInclusionAndMobileSectorTaxationInGhana.pdf.

With growing recognition of the complexity and scale of long-standing social problems, multi-stakeholder initiatives such as the EYElliance and A4AI have become increasingly common over the past decade. In order to address root causes, systems change is often required and can only be achieved through coordinated, collective action among stakeholders. National and local governments can create a favorable policy environment and set budget priorities. Commercial companies and social enterprises can build financially sustainable business models to reach underserved populations. Private philanthropy can invest in research and pilots that demonstrate and de-risk viable solutions. Nonprofits can engage communities and advocate for their needs. Academic institutions can provide research and data to deepen understanding of issues and best practices. By coming together with a shared focus, we can deliver more than the sum of our parts.

GOING OUT OF BUSINESS

Going out of business is not an aspiration we are taught to have. However, in the social sector the ultimate measure of success can be finding a way to make our own work obsolete. While achieving your mission may realistically take decades and new challenges will always emerge, a relentless pursuit of impact sometimes requires us to set aside the instinctive urge to perpetuate our own project or organization.

The efforts to eliminate, rather than perpetually treat, infectious diseases embodies this focus on mission achievement. To date, the global eradication of smallpox as of 1979 has been the first and only success. Still, efforts led by the Global Polio Eradication Initiative and the Carter Center's Guinea Worm Eradication Program have worked with countries, international bodies, and nonprofits to whittle these respective diseases down to only a couple dozen isolated cases a year. Renewed efforts seek to eliminate malaria, and the roughly half million children's deaths it causes each year, by 2040.

Assuming these tremendous efforts succeed, continued work would still be required to prevent a disease from reemerging. However, the needs will shift dramatically and allow major programs, initiatives, and even organizations to wind down.

One that has already put itself out of business is Freedom to Marry, a nonprofit dedicated to legalizing same-sex marriage in the United States founded by Evan Wolfson in 2003. Evan's 30-plus-year crusade started with a paper at Harvard Law School and evolved into a coordinated national strategy, the Roadmap to Victory. To implement it, Freedom to Marry nurtured a broad ecosystem of advocacy groups, state and national politicians, donors, and supportive corporations in a campaign to build public support and state-level victories. The laser-sharp focus paid off. In perhaps the most precipitous shift of attitudes in modern America, public support of same-sex marriage skyrocketed from 32% in 2003 to 63% in 2015.[3] This culminated on June 26, 2015 with the US Supreme Court's momentous decision affirming the constitutional right of same-sex couples to marry. On the day of the ruling, Evan announced in a *New York Times* op-ed that Freedom to Marry would close its doors.

Most social missions will never see the sort of dramatic closure that is possible with disease eradication or a policy campaign. Despite this rarity, any mission-oriented initiative should still strive for a day when it will no longer be needed. As USAID's administrator Mark Green promised early in his tenure: "Every one of our development programs should look forward to the day when it can end. And every investment we make, every innovation we apply, must move a country closer to that day when it can be truly self-reliant."[4]

---

[3] Pew Research Center, *Changing Attitudes on Gay Marriage*, last modified June 26, 2017, http://www.pewforum.org/fact-sheet/changing-attitudes-on-gay-marriage.

[4] Mark Green, "USAID Administrator Mark Green Delivers Remarks at the Opening Session of Global Innovation Week," USAID, September 28, 2017, https://www.usaid.gov/news-information/press-releases/sep-28-2017-usaid-administrator-mark-green-delivers-remarks-opening-session.

TOWARDS REAL SOLUTIONS

In a few cases, problems have the potential to be permanently resolved. More often, policy and market failures can be addressed so that the public and private sector take over. Either way, obsolescence may realistically take generations. However, we still have a responsibility to perpetually move towards systemic change. Curt Ellis, cofounder and CEO of FoodCorps, puts it this way: "Lots of non-profits perform small acts of charity. They see a local need and respond with assistance rather than a solution." In contrast, FoodCorps has huge ambitions to reach 100,000 US public schools with healthy food programs. Through its direct programs, it obsessively innovates to improve its impact year after year. But it is under no illusion that it can do this alone. Its strategy is to demonstrate the potential results that can be achieved, then massively scale by advocating for government policies at all levels that make healthy food environments the norm in all schools.

Similarly, nonprofit Health Leads started by embedding staff within clinics to help patients connect to housing, transportation, food, and other social services. Its aim was to help healthcare providers treat the whole person, given the wide understanding that 70% of health outcomes are tied to social and environmental factors. Over time it became clear that Health Leads' direct services were only a Band-Aid for a more systemic problem and that true change needed to come from health systems taking ownership themselves. Thus, Health Leads pivoted to work with healthcare providers to design, test, and implement integrated programs that meet their patients' social needs and strengthen connections with communities. As policy changes take hold that emphasize value-based funding and patient-centered care, such as the Affordable Care Act and Accountable Health Communities, the incentives will continue to increase for this more holistic and equitable approach.

The strong pull to satisfy immediate needs and keep day-to-day operations running can be all consuming. It's easy to lose sight of the big picture. While we can't ignore the problems facing us today, we also want to avoid being trapped in a never-ending cycle of superficial remedies that never solve the problems. Understanding the complex systems at play is essential for social change. We should never forget to ask ourselves, how could we create a world where our work will no longer be needed?

Chapter Eleven
Financing Innovation

Maybe by now you're convinced that Lean Impact is exactly what you need to radically increase your impact and scale, and thereby fulfill your social mission. Then the reality starts to sink in. How is this even possible? Everyone on your team is running flat out either trying to raise more money or deliver on the commitments that were made to secure the funds you already have. You're not alone.

The structure and availability of funding is by far the greatest barrier to social innovation. Donors, governments, and investors all have their own ideas, strategies, and agendas. Whether they are right or wrong, they hold the purse strings, and thus power and influence over what gets done. Their desire for tangible results can be at odds with what is required for long-term growth and impact. And, the divergent interests of trustees or constituents can drive funding priorities that are siloed, splintered, or otherwise misdirected.

Beyond the question of *what* gets funded is *how* initiatives get funded. In the private sector, investors perform due diligence on a company then place a bet in the form of debt or equity with few strings attached. If results are not delivered, any further funding may

Lean Impact: How to Innovate for Radically Greater Social Good, First Edition. Ann Mei Chang.
© 2019 Ann Mei Chang. Published 2019 by John Wiley & Sons, Inc.

be withheld. But companies are otherwise given wide latitude to take risks, modify their products and services, and pivot based on what they learn. In contrast to investments, grants are often micromanaged – detailing activities, deliverables, "overhead" rates, reporting requirements, and spending down to the dollar. As I'm sure we can all agree, keeping teams on a tight leash rarely yields the most innovative outcomes.

Organizational mindsets, skills, and processes naturally reflect the system in which they work. As Kristin Lord, CEO of global development nonprofit IREX, reflects, "International NGOs are like Darwin's finches, whose beaks have evolved to exquisitely match the idiosyncratic contours of the USAID flower. When they try to drink nectar [funding] from a different type of flower [source of funds], their beaks don't easily fit." Even when more flexible funding is available, leaders are not always prepared to capitalize on it. Britt Lake, chief program officer at the crowdfunding platform GlobalGiving, has been surprised that in situations where it has offered unrestricted grants, "Nonprofits can struggle to identify new ideas that have the greatest potential for impact. As they are accustomed to responding to donor requirements, it can be difficult for them to think outside the box and consider options that are not 100% guaranteed to work."

Creating the space for innovation is not easy, but it can be done. If we are serious about social impact, mission-driven organizations need to find ways to take risks, experiment, learn, and iterate. Draw inspiration from those who are already doing so – some of which you've read about in this book. In this chapter, we'll take a deeper look at the barriers to funding innovation along with creative strategies to overcome them.

While entrepreneurial organizations have found many ways to navigate the existing system, true change will need to come from the funders themselves. To realize the full potential for social innovation, funding practices must be transformed to allow for more flexibility, to incentivize meaningful results, and to adopt an appetite for risk – the topic of Chapter Twelve.

CHALLENGES FOR INNOVATION

The relationship between funders and those receiving funds can be fraught in the absence of aligned interests, shared goals, and most importantly, trust. A commonly held perception among grant recipients is that sharing risks, unknowns, or failures with their donors will put funding in jeopardy. As the CEO of one social enterprise told me, "There's a disincentive, to be honest." For funders, the lack of trust can give rise to micromanagement, rigidity, and bureaucracy. No one is a winner in this scenario, least of all the people we all hope to serve.

At one time, I believed this problem could be solved if donors would simply buckle down and change their ways. Alas, from my time at one of the largest, USAID, I became all too aware of my folly. In the case of USAID, we ostensibly wrote the checks, but were still beholden to a bewildering array of earmarks, directives, and reporting requirements stemming from Congress, US government regulations, and agreements with partner governments in the countries where we worked. While most were put in place to ensure taxpayer money was being spent responsibly, the cumulative effect of these myriad restrictions was to stymie creativity. This was further exaggerated by an overarching aversion to risk, as any single failure had the potential to cause a public relations and auditing nightmare. With government budgets tightening and coming under greater scrutiny, the pressure to avoid any semblance of failure will only increase, stifling the innovation that could ultimately make better use of government funds.

Foundations can be similarly beholden to their trustees or living donors, and impact funds have a responsibility to their investors. Each player in the system is doing what seems right and appropriate, yet the result is counterproductive.

Before we start to explore better options, let's first look at seven of the common ways existing funding structures can impede innovation.

Grand Master Plan

Given the complex nature of social challenges, designing the perfect program in advance is highly unlikely. People and external factors simply behave in unexpected ways. As nineteenth-century Prussian army chief of staff Helmuth von Moltke famously observed, "No battle plan ever survives first contact." Yet, grants from foundations, governments, or corporations can employ an *enforced waterfall* model (described in Chapter One), in which activities, budgets, and deliverables are defined in advance and difficult to change. Thus, when our best-laid plans do go awry, we can be left to execute on a suboptimal intervention unless we undertake a slow and painful renegotiation. Even if we by some miracle get most things right, improvements can always yield greater bang for buck. Inflexible funding prevents both pivoting from failures and stretching towards opportunities.

In her first job out of college at a poor public school in Mississippi, Michelle Brown was shocked to discover how hard it was to access quality reading materials for her students. She spent nights and weekends scrambling to find resources to develop her own curriculum. Years later, at a high-performing charter school in Boston, she was handed a quality curriculum her first day on the job. For once, she could think about instruction at a much higher level. This experience led her to start CommonLit, so all teachers and students would have access to free, quality digital instructional materials.

After stringing together small grants for a few years, CommonLit was fortunate to receive an almost $4 million award from the US Department of Education as part of an initiative to support innovative approaches to literacy. This was a huge boon, but it also came with many strings attached. As Michelle describes it, "Grants are not written with agile development in mind. They want to know exactly what you're going to build, the third-party services you will use, and line items down to the penny." However, the design of a good product necessarily evolves based on user feedback. Having to seek approval for any deviation reduces agility and discourages innovation. At worst, it can even mean programs that aren't working continue anyway, as making changes requires too much renegotiation, reputational risk, or fiscal upheaval.

As international health nonprofit PSI has begun to institutionalize design thinking and prototyping techniques across the organization, it has encountered similar challenges. While some donors have started to embrace the value of an iterative design process, many others still require a fully defined plan at the proposal stage that specifies exactly what will be done, with how many people, and by when, along with indicators to measure progress. This severely hinders PSI's ability to develop transformative solutions, since specifics need to be locked down before fully understanding the context of the problem and the target audience.

Innovation doesn't end with the initial design, even a good one. We should relentlessly seek impact through continuous feedback loops, experimentation, and iteration. Yet one CEO of a social enterprise has found that funders can have a "good enough mentality." She has been surprised by "how surprised funders are when told we want to iterate on something that is already on the market." A first version may work, but that doesn't mean it can't be better, perhaps dramatically so. In extreme cases, evidence-based interventions can even become rigidly codified into legislation and impede contextual adaptations as well as further innovation.

Overhead

Both individual donors and grant makers have long focused on the overhead costs of nonprofits as a primary measure of effectiveness. The overhead rate is an easy proxy to latch onto, as it is a single number that can be calculated from standard tax filings and compared among charities. Certainly, we want to guard against waste and the inefficient use of precious resources, but restricting so-called overhead is more often counterproductive.

Nonprofit consulting firm the Bridgespan Group found that among the 300 nonprofits that account for a third of the combined spending of the top 15 US foundations, 53% suffer from frequent or chronic budget deficits, and 40% have fewer than three months of reserves in the bank. This highlights the long-term damage of restricted project grants that don't support the true underlying costs of building strong institutions.[1] When organizations are in constant financial distress they are unable to make the investments that can enhance productivity, such as employee training, technology infrastructure, and R&D. Sometimes *raising* your overhead is the best way to increase your impact. In fact, shareholders generally reward corporations for increasing R&D spending, as it is a leading indicator of better products to come.

Fortunately, there has been a growing recognition that low overhead is a poor indicator of organizational health. Though it has historically featured overhead rates prominently in its ratings, Charity Navigator, the top US nonprofit rating site, has more recently begun to deemphasize it. In fact, in 2013 Charity Navigator joined GuideStar and BBB Wise Giving Alliance to launch the Overhead Myth campaign to shift the conversation away from financial ratios and towards outcomes and impact.

Silos

Both traditional donors and impact investors can place restrictions based on factors such as geography, sector, demographic, use of technology, and stage or size of company. Given that most organizations need to raise funds from multiple sources, the result can resemble an extreme form of social gerrymandering, where interventions are contorted to achieve an awkward mix of requirements. Needless to say, this can lead to a host of inefficiencies.

To fund the operations and expansion of its savings platform for low-income Americans, EARN receives grants from a number of philanthropic sources. It has found that traditional grant makers often require that funding be deployed for narrowly targeted

---

[1] Michael Etzel and Hilary Pennington, "Time to Reboot Grantmaking," *Stanford Social Innovation Review*, June 27, 2017, https://ssir.org/articles/entry/time_to_reboot_grantmaking.

demographics – corporations care about investing in the communities in which they operate, foundations may want to focus on particular constituencies such as women or Spanish-speaking populations, and still others are interested only in savings that will go towards a pre-defined goal or purpose, such as buying a first home. Delivering and reporting on all of these requires detailed tracking, targeting, and marketing, and can conflict with the natural path for growth based on the greatest needs and mission alignment.

Such restrictions lock out many options entirely. In her research at the Center for the Advancement of Social Entrepreneurship (CASE) at Duke University's Fuqua School of Business, Faculty Director Cathy Clark found that for most impact entrepreneurs, only a handful of donors or investors were likely to hit the sweet spot based on stage of growth, amount of funding, type of funding, sector, and expected returns they need at a particular point in time. Approaching the wrong funders is a waste of everyone's time. On the other hand, approaching the right funder with a bad pitch is a waste of a scarce opportunity. As a result, CASE developed a suite of online tools, Smart Impact Capital (www.casesmartimpact.com), to help entrepreneurs navigate the funding landscape to raise the capital they need.

These silos can also make it difficult to raise money for crucial needs that go beyond a single domain. For example, it is easier to fund solar lanterns, clean cookstoves, or maternity kits than the distribution networks to enable them to reach customers. It's easier to fund targeted mobile apps than the shared technology platforms and infrastructure behind them. And it's easier to fund drugs and education for tuberculosis, HIV, and malaria than strengthening the underlying health systems that provide primary care. Thus, rather than building shared resources that can be leveraged for multiple purposes, we often see duplicative efforts and bespoke solutions.

Projects Versus Solutions

Pressure from donors and investors to deliver immediate, measurable results can also stymie an organization's ability to innovate. In Chapter Six, we learned about the importance of starting small to facilitate fast experimentation, allow for pivots, and avoid wasting resources on solutions that won't work. Yet many funders measure success based on reach rather than lessons learned, sustainable growth, and cost effectiveness. One nonprofit I spoke with described being pushed to scale by a donor before it could streamline its operations, only to be crushed under the weight of manual processes as they grew. Another mission-oriented startup found that impact investors prioritized hitting sales numbers over validating unit economics due to their nervousness over an unproven and unfamiliar market. They bled money with each additional sale and eventually had to retrench.

Grants in particular tend to be project rather than solution based. That is, for one to five years the grantee is expected to deliver the agreed activities, then the money runs out. Over the lifetime of the grant a nonprofit is usually fully occupied meeting its commitments, with little time to test and build a sustainable path forward. After the grant is completed, too often programs are shut down entirely or restarted at a new location in which new funding has been secured. In global development, this extremely inefficient cycle of spinning up teams and programs only to wind them down a few years later is the norm.

Rocío Pérez Ochoa, cofounder of Bidhaa Sasa, a lean social enterprise that distributes and finances goods for rural households in Kenya, was shocked that donors kept framing funding discussions in terms of a project rather than her business. They wanted to know what tangible results she could produce during the life of a grant, sometimes within as short a time as 12 months. That model might make sense for a bulk order of a mature product, but it was not what she needed to test and improve her service, build organizational capacity, and validate her business model.

As a nonprofit that provides open-source software for last-mile community health systems, Medic Mobile was hit by this dynamic on two fronts. It initially worked directly with other nonprofits but struggled to sustain its impact when their grants ended and projects wound down. This led it to work with local and national governments, which had a permanent stake in strengthening health systems.

As for funding, Medic Mobile knew it could never build a cohesive, reusable platform by relying on project funding and made the tough call to turn away restricted grants unless they were well aligned with its strategic plan. Luckily, it identified a set of committed donors who could offer the unrestricted funding that allowed it to make the investments necessary to build a robust platform.

When we focus on short-term deliverables to the exclusion of long-term scale and transformation, we can become stuck in an endless cycle, placing Band-Aids on the same problem over and over again.

The Pioneer Gap

In 2012, Monitor Group's groundbreaking report *From Blueprint to Scale: The Case for Philanthropy in Impact Investing* coined the term "pioneer gap" to describe the lack of early-stage capital for inclusive businesses targeting the poor. The report correlates the gap with the first two of four phases of a firm's development: *blueprint* and *validate*.[2]

Today, the proliferation of innovation funds, contests, prizes, hackathons, and impact-oriented accelerators has gone a long way in addressing the *blueprint* stage, when new ideas are generated. Yet a yawning gap remains in the *validate* stage – what I consider the 99% perspiration required to develop a successful solution, the core of Lean Impact.

As Copia Global's former CEO Crispin Murira says, "There's lots of money for new ideas or for scaled solutions, but it's hard to raise money for the work in between." Funding early-stage ideas is easier, as the sums of money are small and fresh ideas attract attention. The crucial work of validation is less sexy and requires patience. Many organizations struggle in this gulf. Donors tend to be reluctant

[2] Harvey Koh, Ashish Karamchandani, and Robert Katz, *From Blueprint to Scale: The Case for Philanthropy in Impact Investing*, Monitor Group, April 2012, https://acumen.org/wp-content/uploads/2017/09/From-Blueprint-to-Scale-Case-for-Philanthropy-in-Impact-Investing_Full-report.pdf.

to pick up initiatives they didn't initiate. And there can even be an inverse correlation between success and funding, with donor attention drifting to the next shiny thing once a pilot has given them a good story to tell. In the meantime, the real work is just beginning.

Timing

Simply making a decision on a grant can be a long, slow process – possibly a year or even more – for foundations, corporations, and government agencies. Approvals can become bogged down in strategy shifts, internal politics, procurement mechanisms, and board approvals.

This is particularly challenging for early-stage organizations seeking small grants. Imagine applying for an innovation grant to test your promising new idea and receiving a $20,000 award a year later. By then, you've probably either identified other funding or gone out of business. And even if you've managed to cling on, changes in technology or other circumstances may have rendered your proposal obsolete in its original form. This is a sad, all-too-common story.

I have to confess that, despite our best efforts, the Lab's DIV fund at USAID was caught in this trap. Though grantees praised us for our flexibility in supporting innovation, turnaround time was another matter. Our rock-star team worked valiantly to move quickly, but was stymied by budget cycles, internal bureaucracy, and procurement requirements. One of the many benefits of spinning out the Global Innovation Fund (GIF) as an independent nonprofit to do similar work – which had been established based on the successes of DIV – was the ability to move faster outside the confines of a government bureaucracy.

Reporting and Compliance

A final impediment to innovation is the administrative burden associated with many forms of funding. Accepting a government grant can necessitate hiring a new staff person simply to manage the compliance and reporting requirements. For example, a USAID grant has 84 pages of standard compliance provisions – everything from vetting suppliers for terrorist connections to meeting exacting branding standards. To add insult to injury, each funder typically has its own unique requirements for content, format, and frequency of reports. The prodigious time and attention needed to fulfill all these obligations takes away from the real work.

The hardship doesn't end there. For federal government grants, the negotiated indirect cost rate agreement required to reimburse costs such as facilities and general administration imposes rigid accounting procedures that put a straightjacket on an organization's ability to strategically price its products and services for different clients. Managing grants from both public and private funders can become a nightmare. The challenges are significant enough that FHI 360, a global development nonprofit that receives significant funding from the federal government, decided to spin out a subsidiary to allow for more flexibility in working with foundations, corporate partners, and state and local governments that each have their own policies and restrictions.

STAYING ON MISSION

If the existing funding mechanisms make innovation so difficult, what can you do? Be willing to push back, and if necessary walk away. I know, this sounds crazy when a grant might be the difference between staying in business and considering layoffs. I'm not suggesting it's an easy choice or that grants always have to be 100% aligned with your mission. But if the alternative is accepting restrictions that take you off mission and trap you in a grant starvation cycle, negotiating for more flexibility may be worth the risk. Sometimes the funder may even admire your chutzpah!

Because of their commitment to radical listening, Health In Harmony writes in its grant proposals that its first step will be to ask communities what they want. Then, it plans to do just that. Certainly not all donors will be so flexible, but Health In Harmony has been pleasantly surprised at how many do agree. Some donors are even relieved by this fresh approach. Over time, Health In Harmony has earned respect by taking a stand and refusing to implement programs that are not wanted by a community.

Many organizations have come to regret changing their plans to satisfy funders because they can see how it has impeded their ability to fulfill their mission. As they've gained more financial breathing room, they start to wean themselves from grants that aren't either strongly aligned or altogether unrestricted. Some of the most impressive organizations I've profiled in this book have increasingly shifted to accepting funding only when it is flexible or fits with their strategy, including Health Leads, Medic Mobile, Living Goods, the One Acre Fund, CareMessage, d.light, and VisionSpring. I, for one, see a correlation. If enough organizations balk at inappropriate restrictions, maybe funders will get the hint and change their tune.

Remember, bigger is not always better. Too often, in the absence of profits as a benchmark we measure success in terms of more programs, more staff, and more money raised. A smaller, more effective, financially sustainable organization that brings a clearly differentiated value proposition can sometimes do more good.

INNOVATION WINDOWS

When Eric Ries came to speak with my team at Mercy Corps about applying principles from *The Lean Startup*, he was asked how to make room for innovation in the context of preplanned grants. He suggested the idea of carving out an innovation window, as part of a standard grant proposal, to build in room to experiment with better solutions. This might only represent a small percentage of a larger grant. But if that, say 5%, leads to identifying an alternative that is even 10% more cost effective, impactful, or scalable, it will have more than paid for itself.

It turned out that Mercy Corps already had a program in Ethiopia called PRIME (Pastoralist Areas Resilience Improvement through Market Expansion), which included elements of this thinking. Within the five-year, $62 million USAID-funded program, most of the work was targeted towards direct interventions. However, a $5 million innovation and investment fund was set aside to make investments that could catalyze sustainable growth through new approaches or business ventures.

Of course, most grants are a tiny fraction of this size. However, if we stick to the Lean Impact principle of starting small, experimentation doesn't need to be expensive. It only requires a commitment to be scrappy, stay curious, and relentlessly seek impact. When Summit Public Schools decided it needed to disrupt its entire classroom model, it had little money and no idea how to iterate. Rather than spending a lot of money on consultants, the team read *The Lean Startup*. They also tapped into pro bono coaching from Google staff, and eventually partnered with Facebook engineers to build a technology platform to capture the data needed to drive their feedback loop.

mPower Social Enterprises, founded out of Harvard and MIT, was able to successfully negotiate with USAID to incorporate a phased-innovation window. The USAID Agricultural Extension Support Activity sought to improve farmers' access to inputs, best practices, and finance using digital technology in 12 districts of Bangladesh. Given that mPower wasn't sure what would work, it negotiated the freedom to fail. In the first year, it deployed and tested 14 prototypes through a series of rapid experiments, then selected 5 or 6 to take forward. While USAID is not normally a particularly flexible funder, mPower was fortunate to work with a supportive agreement officer who helped to convince other parts of the agency to take this more flexible approach.

When writing a grant proposal or negotiating a grant agreement, consider ways to introduce an innovation window, either as a small ongoing percentage of work or as an initial experimental period to determine the best path forward. Realistically, some donors will be delighted, while others will balk. But you'll be more likely to come away with the flexibility you need to maximize your impact and scale.

FLEXIBLE SOURCES

Even with an innovation window and the best of circumstances, restricted grants are still, well, restricted. In an ideal world, social sector funding would be entirely unrestricted with accountability coming through performance targets or tiered follow-on funding. This would free organizations to experiment, learn, and double down on the best solutions. But, we're not there yet.

Flexible funding sources can complement more traditional grants by opening space to both generate new ideas and experiment in existing programs. Sometimes you can find progressive donors who directly support innovation, such as the Draper Richards Kaplan Foundation, Echoing Green, the Omidyar Network, the Emerson Collective, the Skoll Foundation, the Mulago Foundation, and GIF. Other times, philanthropists, individual giving, crowdfunding, or earned revenue can be used to create your own flexible pool.

A common strategy is to seek donations from high–net worth individuals who appreciate the importance of innovation for achieving long-term impact. Given the wealth being generated in Silicon Valley, tech philanthropists have become a favored target. Living in San Francisco, some days I can feel like a tour guide, given the number of international nonprofits coming to town looking to tap into tech wealth and know-how. My advice? Don't pitch the same activity-based programs you would to a traditional foundation or government. Tech philanthropists are typically more interested in disruptive innovation with the potential for massive scale and transformational impact. *The Giving Code*, a report published by Open Impact, includes valuable insights into the Silicon Valley donor mindset.[3]

In Chapter Eight, I described how Code for America funds the ongoing operations of its California food stamp enrollment service

---

[3] Alexa Cortés Culwell and Heather McLeod Grant, *The Giving Code*, Open Impact, 2016, https://www.openimpact.io/giving-code.

through various government sources. But government won't pay for activities such as customer discovery, testing prototypes, and building the website. So for R&D it turns to philanthropists from its deep network in the tech community, exemplified by Reid Hoffman, cofounder and executive chairman of LinkedIn.

Faith-based nonprofits such as Catholic Relief Services (CRS) that have a large base of unrestricted funding through individual donors have a unique opportunity to leverage these resources to invest in innovation. Each year, CRS sets aside a $4 million internal innovation pool. As it believes that innovation will start closest to the problem, any staff member can submit a simple proposal for a programmatic, business, or operational idea. The fund supports them to test if the solution works, measure the results, and determine if it can go to scale.

FINANCING ROUNDS

Chasing all these sources of funding can be exhausting. Many CEOs and executive directors report spending more than half their time fundraising, rather than working towards their core mission. Is there another way?

Crisis Text Line runs a 24/7 texting service to connect people who are suffering to a trained crisis counselor, anywhere in the United States. While Crisis Text Line is a nonprofit, the team thinks of themselves as a tech company first. As such, they eschewed the high burden and restrictions of traditional funding sources. Director of Communications Liz Eddy explains, "They expect that in five years you are doing exactly the same thing you were five years ago. What we are doing now is different from six months ago, based on data for what works and doesn't work."

Constantly working the circuit to raise money would be a huge distraction from its mission. Instead, Crisis Text Line took a page out of the tech startup book and concentrated its fundraising in discrete rounds. Once the big push is over, team members have the breathing room to put their heads down for a year or more and just do the work. For its second round, Crisis Text Line put together a simple four-page prospectus outlining the opportunity to do good through tech and data, projections for growth and costs, the amount of money needed, and the minimum donation level. It sought to be as transparent as possible by including a three-year budget. Based on a $20-million goal, it was oversubscribed and walked away with $23.8 million, all in unrestricted funds from a combination of individual donors and forward-leaning foundations.

The notion of funding rounds isn't limited to the tech world. After fundraising for both a for-profit company and the nonprofit he founded, VisionSpring's Jordan Kassalow was struck by the contrast between his experiences. With the for-profit organization, funders cared about the founding team, market size, and the value proposition. They wouldn't have thought of asking him to perform specifically defined activities. In contrast, on the nonprofit side, funders kept insisting on different geographies or demographics that would take VisionSpring off mission. After a few years he focused his energy on attracting unrestricted capital, with limited exceptions. Similarly to Crisis Text Line, he put together a prospectus of what was needed to build the team and systems that would bring the organization to the next level, raising $5 million.

HYBRID STRUCTURES

Over its more than 30 years of identifying and nurturing emerging leaders, Echoing Green has had a bird's-eye view of the landscape of social change. Its flagship program, the Echoing Green Fellowship, provides unrestricted seed-stage funding and leadership development to aspiring social entrepreneurs, now numbering nearly 800. Among them are the founders of Teach For America, City Year, and the One Acre Fund.

In its first two decades, almost all of Echoing Green's fellows proposed nonprofit organizations to tackle social problems. But over time there has been a gradual shift in the diversity of models being used. While in 2006 only 15% of its applicants proposed social businesses with for-profit elements, those numbers have risen steadily to nearly 50% as of 2018. Its experience reflects mine – a landscape in which more and more, the most interesting social ventures are some sort of hybrid and the lines between legal structures have become blurred. This poses both challenges and opportunities.

The phenomenon of for-profit social enterprises using grant funding to validate and de-risk a business model, then subsequently tap into private investment, is on the rise. We made a number of grants in this vein through USAID's DIV program, including with Off Grid Electric and other pay-as-you-go solar companies.

Some organizations have established multiple entities in order to straddle the available funding streams. This might involve pairing a nonprofit in the United States to receive philanthropic dollars with a for-profit company in the operating country to build a sustainable business. Others have created both for-profit and nonprofit sister organizations side-by-side, to raise investment capital to grow the core business while using charitable funding sources to address market and policy failures through advocacy, capacity building, and outreach to the most disadvantaged customers.

Clearly, there is no one-size-fits-all solution for funding. The existing systems and mechanisms were established in a day and age when legal structures were more binary and innovation rarely intersected with social good. Leading social entrepreneurs and their funders are pioneering ways to navigate the grey spaces in between, but a more fundamental shift will be needed to fully unleash the potential for social innovation.

Chapter Twelve
A Message to Funders

Much of this book has served as a guide for social entrepreneurs, whether at nonprofits, social enterprises, hybrid companies, or corporations. Yet its lessons are equally, if not more, important for the foundations, philanthropists, government agencies, impact investors, corporate social responsibility (CSR) departments, and individual donors who fund them. As described in the first part of Chapter Eleven, perverse funding incentives and restrictions represent the single greatest barrier to the adoption of lean approaches to innovation. Our means are impeding our ends.

We need nothing short of a revolution in how social good is funded. Nicola Galombik, an executive director at investment group Yellowwoods, describes a puzzling disassociation in which the same people are "chasing elephants in the private sector and chasing mice in the social sector." Rather than adopting an investor's mindset to take calculated risks in pursuit of growth and impact, philanthropic investments tend to be risk averse and prefer to deploy well-known interventions over and over again. Alas, most are subscale and do not fully address root causes.

Lean Impact: How to Innovate for Radically Greater Social Good, First Edition. Ann Mei Chang.
© 2019 Ann Mei Chang. Published 2019 by John Wiley & Sons, Inc.

Funders can help achieve radically greater social good by empowering entrepreneurs, nurturing ambition, and approaching their work with a dose of humility. Empowerment requires shifting the frame from implementing a predefined plan to betting on a team and outcome. Ambition engenders a restless will to seek better solutions that can reach further and do more. And, humility entails a recognition that we don't have all the answers and need to experiment and learn to achieve better results.

This message doesn't only apply to grant-making institutions. Philanthropists, and even modest individual donors, also contribute to the dysfunctional incentives. Are you asking a social venture about its overhead rates rather than its trajectory for learning and improvement? Are you restricting donations based on your interests rather than trusting a team to make the best choices to achieve its mission? Are you measuring success in terms of activities and compelling stories rather than sustainable outcomes? Are you basing decisions on personal relationships rather than cost-effective impact? If any of these might be true, this chapter is also for you.

A NEW RELATIONSHIP

We need to start by fundamentally reimagining the relationship between funders and recipients, from one of suspicion and micromanagement to one of trust and reward. This will require change on all sides. Donors will need to establish clear goals, then let go of some control and select teams and organizations to empower as true partners. Nonprofits and social enterprises will need to accept more risk, become responsible for results, and develop the skills and judgment needed to accelerate learning rather than execute a plan.

As a successful businessman, private equity investor, and social entrepreneur, Chuck Slaughter has lived this dynamic from multiple standpoints. He observes that, "Foundations tend to base funding decisions 90% on strategy and 10% on people, whereas venture capitalists consider these more as an even 50–50 split." I would go further to suggest that in many cases the "strategies" foundations fund could be more accurately described as tactical interventions that reflect the foundation's own theory of change.

When the spotlight is so heavily focused on a predefined plan, agreements naturally focus on execution and tend to slavishly specify the expected activities, budget, staffing, and overhead. In contrast, when teams are empowered to pursue a shared goal, the conversation shifts to providing guidance, building capacity, and learning together. We've all seen this story before in commonly accepted leadership principles – micromanagement doesn't work. The most effective and creative teams are the ones that feel empowered.

In Rockefeller Philanthropy Advisors' 2017 report, *Scaling Solutions Toward Shifting Systems*, the first of five recommendations is to empower grantees by consciously shifting the power dynamics through trust, respect, and openness. This creates an environment in which organizations can make mistakes, pivot, learn, and focus on the work of scaling and long-term systems change.[1]

Such a relationship should ideally involve not only greater flexibility in the structure of grants, but also a more collaborative approach to direction and design. At USAID, we expanded the use of the bureaucratic-sounding Broad Agency Announcement (BAA) as an alternative procurement mechanism that allows for co-creation among a diverse array of public and private partners when the ideal solution is unclear. With a BAA, interested parties submit a relatively lightweight statement of interest. Those selected to participate collaborate to develop one or more concept notes that are then evaluated by a review panel. Rather than USAID dictating the design in a grant solicitation and organizations responding with formal proposals, this more open format allows for an exchange of ideas and the opportunity to build strategic partnerships.

---

[1] Rockefeller Philanthropy Advisors, *Scaling Solutions Toward Shifting Systems*, September 2017, http://www.rockpa.org/scaling-solutions.

UNRESTRICTED FUNDING

Making grants less restrictive and less prescriptive is an important first step towards building trust. With unrestricted funding, also known as general operating support, an organization's leaders are able to balance between the tactical needs of their operations today and the strategic investments required to achieve their mission tomorrow. R&D can lead to transformative breakthroughs, IT infrastructure can increase productivity and accelerate feedback loops, and training staff can build new skills and capacity.

Of course, relaxing restrictions requires funders to trust and be willing to cede control to their grantees. But, more and more foundations are recognizing that healthy, empowered institutions will be more likely to deliver greater social impact in the long run. The Edna McConnell Clark Foundation (EMCF) has been a leader in this regard in its mission to help economically disadvantaged youth. Around the turn of the millennium, its strategy shifted from seeking nonprofits that would execute on EMCF's vision and theories for systems change to supporting the best organizations in building the capacity to execute on their own visions for greater impact. Rather than requiring predefined programming, EMCF provides flexible capital that allows for innovation and pivots. And by making an upfront commitment, its investment frees grantees to focus on execution of their own business plans rather than being constantly distracted by fundraising and donor demands.

More recently, in 2015 the Ford Foundation made a deliberate shift in its funding strategy after feedback from grantees led President Darren Walker to believe Ford was "project-supporting nonprofits to death."[2] He recognized that general operating support was crucial for organizations to invest and plan for the long term. To do so, Ford doubled its overhead rate on project grants and made a big splash by announcing a $1 billion commitment for the Building Institutions

[2] Alex Daniels, "Ford Shifts Grant Making to Focus Entirely on Inequality," *Chronicle of Philanthropy*, June 11, 2015, https://www.philanthropy.com/article/ Ford-Shifts-Grant-Making-to/230839.

and Networks (BUILD) initiative. BUILD will invest in the capacity and sustainability of social justice organizations through five-year unrestricted operating grants, plus additional support for institutional strengthening. In an article in the *Stanford Social Innovation Review*, EVP for Programs Hilary Pennington asked the all-important question: "How do we break our own addiction – let alone that of our grantees – to funding activities, rather than impact?"[3]

The good news is there is a growing recognition of the importance of unrestricted funding. According to the Foundation Center's 2014 edition of *Key Facts on U.S. Foundations*, general operating support now represents 23% of foundation grants.[4] While it is still far from the norm, the proportion has inched up from only 19% of foundation grants in 2006.[5] Newer foundations and philanthropists, particularly those focused on innovation and entrepreneurship, have continued to expand on this trend.

While I believe that funding should be unrestricted in almost all cases to empower teams and allow for the agility that fuels innovation, this does not equate to a lack of accountability. But, organizations should be held to results, rather than how they get there. This can be done through constructive incentives such as milestones, tiered funding, and outcomes-based payments.

TIERED FUNDING

One of the tried-and-true mechanisms to encourage innovation in the private sector is the use of tiered funding, perhaps best exemplified by VCs in Silicon Valley. Tech startups typically receive multiple

[3] Hilary Pennington, "Focus on Building Strong Organizations," *Stanford Social Innovation Review*, Summer 2016, https://ssir.org/up_for_debate/pay_what_it_takes_philanthropy/hilary_pennington.

[4] Foundation Center, *Key Facts on U.S. Foundations: 2014 Edition*, 2014, http://foundationcenter.org/gainknowledge/research/keyfacts2014/grant-focus-priorities.html.

[5] Foundation Center, *Highlights of Foundation Giving Trends: 2008 Edition*, 2008, https://www.issuelab.org/resources/13515/13515.pdf.

tranches of financing, starting with a seed round from friends and family or an accelerator, followed by an angel round from high-net-worth individuals, and finally progressing to multiple rounds from VCs known as Series A, Series B, etc. The earlier the round, the higher the risk and the smaller the size of the investment. As a startup proves technical feasibility and market demand, the risk comes down and the dollar amounts go up. And if it doesn't? The startup simply can't raise more money and goes bust.

No one micromanages these startups along the way. They are set off to succeed or fail on their own, albeit with various support systems. Nevertheless, the companies are motivated because their survival is at stake. They know what questions need answers and what traction must be demonstrated to make a compelling case for the next round. This system has arguably led to a pace of innovation that is the envy of the world, giving rise to some of the most transformational and successful companies of the modern era.

While there are many differences between the private and the social sector, elements of this model have been successfully adapted for purpose rather than profit. At USAID, our DIV program was inspired by this VC style of funding. It incorporated three stages, at levels of around $100,000, $1 million, and $5 million, each based on successively higher levels of maturity and evidence of impact. Although government is notoriously risk adverse, by starting with relatively small awards at Stage 1 we were able to place more and far riskier bets than would have been possible with larger grants. Based on our successes, we later established GIF as an independent entity based on a similar tiered model, along with other donor partners and additional financing tools, such as debt and equity.

Both DIV and GIF take an open innovation approach, accepting applications across a wide range of sectors, geographies, and problem areas. Their goal is to identify and support the development of the most cost-effective solutions for social impact. Other funders of open innovation can specialize in particular stages of development. For example, the Draper Richards Kaplan Foundation and Echoing Green support early-stage social entrepreneurs, while the Skoll Foundation focuses on more mature social enterprises that have achieved some scale. Silicon Valley–style startup accelerators are also getting into the game, providing early-stage social enterprises with seed funding along with mentorship, networking, and skill building. Among these, Fast Forward focuses exclusively on technology-driven nonprofits, 1776 tackles government-dominated markets, and the renowned tech accelerator Y Combinator now includes nonprofits in every cohort.

In contrast to open innovation, directed innovation seeks to draw talent, attention, and engagement to targeted problems where existing solutions are insufficient. One prominent cluster of such initiatives are the Global Grand Challenges, initially started as the Grand Challenges for Global Health by the Bill and Melinda Gates Foundation, and later expanded as an umbrella for a collection of challenges undertaken by Gates, USAID, Grand Challenges Canada, and a number of regional partners. Most employ some form of tiered funding, initially seeking a broad range of new ideas with small grants, then doubling down to scale those that prove to be most promising. At USAID our Grand Challenges spanned a wide range of areas, including literacy for children, humanitarian crises, maternal and child mortality, clean energy for farmers, scaling off-grid solar systems, and the response to the Zika and Ebola crises.

During the early stages of development, follow-on funding decisions should consider innovation and learning metrics, rather than vanity metrics such as reach. These measure progress towards the success criteria for value, growth, and impact. Experiments and pilots can improve on key drivers such as customer satisfaction, cost basis, and adoption rate. If the necessary thresholds are not reached, but the pace of learning is high and a new pivot looks promising, another round of funding at the same stage might be worth consideration.

Tiered funding is particularly valuable in the early stages. As risks can be high and expected financial returns can be low, organizations can have difficulty accessing traditional forms of private financing. With tiered grants, donors take on calculated risk, but only at levels commensurate with the stage of development. Grantees then have the runway to experiment, though they must demonstrate traction in order to access the next tranche of funds. As these are high-risk bets, the expectation is that only a small fraction will succeed.

For many donors, the overhead associated with issuing numerous small grants can become a barrier. One way to reduce transaction costs is to encapsulate tiers as milestones in a single overarching grant. We did this in USAID's Securing Water for Food Grand Challenge by defining rigorous criteria for subsequent disbursements, with the expectation that only a fraction of grantees would succeed and with only sufficient budget to cover those. Thus, we eliminated the need for a new costly and time-consuming procurement cycle for each tranche, while maintaining selectivity and rewarding results. Other tiered funds, in the face of limited staff bandwidth, have contracted out the selection and disbursement process to a third party altogether.

If you want to manage risk while promoting innovation, tiering funding in some form is one of the best tools available to do so. Another is paying for outcomes.

PAY FOR OUTCOMES

As opposed to tiered funding, which is granted in advance of work being performed, outcomes funding is usually disbursed after the fact, on the basis of success. In both cases, the focus shifts from prescribing activities to rewarding actual results, either through follow-on funding or outcomes-based payments. In the outcomes scenario, the risk of failure is borne by either the grantee or the financier, rather than the donor.

On one end of the spectrum, a prize competition can inspire new inventions by providing an award for a singular accomplishment, such as the $10 million Ansari X Prize won by SpaceShipOne for being the first nongovernmental organization to launch a reusable manned spacecraft into space twice within two weeks. On the other end of the spectrum, various forms of pay-for-results contracts can provide ongoing compensation for each instance a specified outcome is achieved, analogous to a commission-based compensation structure for sales.

I consider paying for outcomes to be the holy grail because the interests of grant makers, recipients, and beneficiaries become fully aligned. Grantees gain far the flexibility and motivation to experiment with more cost-effective and scalable solutions. Funders deploy dollars far more efficiently, only paying when the desired outcomes are achieved. And, the incentives focus all parties on maximizing the positive impact for beneficiaries. In a sense, an open, competitive market is established for social good.

Of course, huge hurdles exist to achieving this ideal state. Certainly, many desirable benefits to society are not so discretely measurable and thus not conducive to performance-based financing. Even when clear outcomes can be defined, the cost and burden of reliable monitoring can be high. Existing entities may not have the skills, experience, and processes to handle such a structural shift. And mechanisms to finance the required up-front investment and absorb risk are not widely available, particularly for nonprofits.

Still, while recognizing that a complete shift to a pay-for-outcomes world may be in the distant future, there are enough compelling benefits to warrant a strong and continued push towards this ideal. Given the real challenges, we would be best served by not being purists. In many cases, a blend of traditional grants, tiered funding, and outcomes payments may be the most practical.

Let's explore the most common tools used to pay for outcomes – prizes, advanced market commitments (AMCs), and impact bonds – along with other types of outcomes-based incentives.

Prizes

Although incentive prizes have existed in some form for centuries, the X Prize Foundation has perhaps done the most in modern times to draw attention to them as a tool to push the technological boundaries of existing solutions. With a prize, the performance characteristics for a desired invention are specified in advance and the sponsor issues a cash award when a team is deemed to have met them. For social good, the desired outcome can be a breakthrough in capability or cost that will expand the realm of potential impact. The associated award and publicity can attract both fresh talent and increased investment to a needed advancement.

Of course, most prizes are of a far more modest scope and scale than an X Prize, though they retain many similar characteristics. The US government even got in the game with the America COMPETES Reauthorization Act of 2010, meant "to invest in innovation through research and development, and to improve the competitiveness of the United States." Among other provisions, the act allows government agencies to sponsor prize contests with awards of up to $50 million, though most are far smaller. Today, the Challenge.gov website lists over 800 such government challenges, with a goal of tapping into the innovative ideas of citizens.

In the social sector, the distinction between challenges and prizes can become somewhat blurred. Challenges typically identify a problem and allow for a range of potential solutions, whereas a prize specifies quantifiable performance criteria that the winner must achieve. In theory, the former are structured as tiered-funding tranches while the latter are paid only upon success. However, given that most mission-driven organizations don't have the resources to fully self-finance the upfront costs to compete for a prize, oftentimes prize competitions include some amount of funding for R&D.

One prize we fielded at USAID was the Desal Prize – an award for innovations in desalinating brackish water for drinking and agricultural use in the many water-stressed environments around the world. The goal was to produce a minimum of 85% recovery of freshwater, powered only by renewable energy – twice the industry standard for existing reverse osmosis systems. Out of 68 applicants from 29 countries, a panel of judges selected five semi-finalists who each received seed money to test and develop their devices. They competed head-to-head at the US Bureau of Reclamation's Brackish Groundwater National Desalination Research Facility in New Mexico. A photovoltaic-powered electro-dialysis reversal system by a joint team from MIT and Jain Irrigation won the $140,000 grand prize. In addition, the winners became eligible for $400,000 in grants to implement pilot projects with smallholder farmers.

Tom Kalil, former deputy director for technology and innovation at the White House Office of Science and Technology Policy, observes that the US government has made more than $4 trillion in financial commitments that are contingent on failure. For example, the United States guarantees loans and agrees to assume the debt obligation of borrowers if they default. Shouldn't we balance those with more investments that are contingent on success, such as prizes? In other words, rather than taking a loss when something bad happens, let's be willing to *spend* money when a breakthrough becomes possible.

Advanced Market Commitments

AMCs are a less common, but interesting, funding tool that combines the open competition of prizes with the ongoing delivery terms of pay for outcomes. Here, the funder issues a contractual guarantee to purchase a large quantity of a product once it is developed, thereby creating a viable, outcomes-based market. AMCs are typically used by governments or large donors who want to encourage companies to invest in products that require a large upfront investment and have an unclear payoff.

The first and best-known use of an AMC was in 2007, when five countries and the Bill and Melinda Gates Foundation pledged to purchase millions of doses of a safe and effective vaccine for pneumococcal disease, a major cause of pneumonia and meningitis that kills 1.6 million people every year. An independent assessment committee was set up to select eligible manufacturers based on meeting minimum product specifications, including efficacy, safety, and cost per dose. As of December 2016, 164 million doses had been procured from two suppliers, GlaxoSmithKline and Pfizer, with an additional 160 million doses expected in 2017.

Using an AMC to address a market failure for the broader public good was possible in this scenario, as GlaxoSmithKline and Pfizer are large corporations with sufficient financial resources to make the investment in research, development, and manufacturing in advance of receiving any payment. Realistically, most cash-constrained non-profits and social enterprises would be challenged to do the same. In such situations, milestone payments for interim progress can help enable them to pursue such ambitious goals.

While the global health community has been at the forefront of performance-based financing mechanisms for innovations with a high social return and an uncertain financial return, these techniques are well worth considering to open competition and fuel social progress in other sectors as well.

Impact Bonds

Social impact bonds (SIBs) are perhaps the mechanism most closely associated with outcomes funding and have been applied for a range of purposes, including reducing recidivism, the number of children in foster care, youth unemployment, and the need for special education. SIBs hold the promise of outcomes funding at its purest: the government only pays the provider for agreed-upon social outcomes when they are delivered. Because the typically nonprofit providers aren't able to finance activities or shoulder risk, private investors supply the upfront capital in the form of a bond. These investors are promised a rate of return but are only paid if the expected outcomes are achieved and thus assume the risk of failure. An independent evaluator measures outcomes and determines payments. Finally an intermediary or project sponsor often coordinates all these entities, processes, and relationships (see Figure 12.1).

The first SIB was deployed in the United Kingdom by Social Finance in 2010, with the aim of reducing the prison population in Peterborough by lowering the rate of reoffending for first-time con-victed criminals. Rather selecting a single rehabilitation program that might or might not work, the government agreed to pay the project sponsor, One Service, based on the actual reduction of recidivism and the savings accrued from fewer people in jail. One Service in

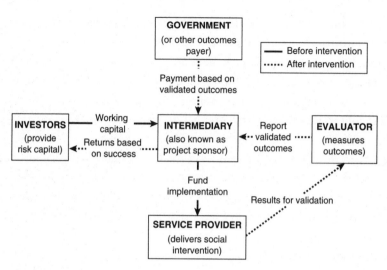

Figure 12.1   Impact bond structure.

turn coordinated among multiple service providers to support ex-offender needs such as housing and employment. Private investors assumed the risk by purchasing SIBs on the promise of a healthy return if the expected outcomes were achieved. In the final accounting, recidivism was reduced by 9% and the investors were repaid in full.

Much attention and excitement has been generated by the potential of SIBs to harness private investment capital for social benefit. Alas, the reality hasn't quite lived up to the hype. As of the start of 2018, only 108 SIBs had been contracted globally.[6] And, private financing largely serves to buffer risk, with existing donors or government still paying for the interventions as well as much of the design and transaction costs. The complexity and multiple parties required to establish and run a SIB have made them expensive, slow, and thus not easily scalable.

[6] Emily Gustafsson-Wright and Izzy Boggild-Jones, "Paying for Social Outcomes: A Review of the Global Impact Bond Market in 2017," Brookings Institution, January 17, 2018, https://www.brookings.edu/blog/education-plus-development/2018/01/17/paying-for-social-outcomes-a-review-of-the-global-impact-bond-market-in-2017.

While SIBs are no panacea, they have galvanized efforts to better measure outcomes, raise attention to cost effectiveness, and adopt a results-oriented mindset in funding. These important building blocks can serve as the foundation for evolving simpler pay-for-results mechanisms. A number of more recent initiatives have already sought to simplify the process.

A close sibling to SIBs, development impact bonds (DIBs) largely differ from SIBs by virtue of their use in developing countries with a donor agency or foundation as the outcome payer, rather than government. One of the newest is the Village Enterprise DIB, which seeks to alleviate poverty in East Africa by helping communities start microenterprises. With a total budget of over $5 million, it's one of the largest DIBs to date.

What's particularly interesting are some structural adaptations to make the Village Enterprise DIB simpler, less expensive, and more flexible than its predecessors. In fact, you could argue that it isn't actually an impact bond at all, as no bonds were issued to private investors as part of the deal. Instead, the implementing nonprofit, Village Enterprise, is on the hook to shoulder the risk and obtain its own financing. This removes the complexity of brokering a multiparty arrangement between payers, investors, and the provider simultaneously. In addition, an outcomes fund has been established to allow new donors and providers to join over time without having to renegotiate the entire structure. Project sponsor Instiglio sees the arrangement as a step towards an outcomes-based challenge fund – a far more streamlined market for outcomes with lower transaction costs.

Outcomes-based Incentives

While the purity of funding entirely based on outcomes is theoretically appealing, it can also be impractical. What if you don't have the latitude to do something so experimental, but still want to move towards aligning incentives with outcomes? Taking an outcomes mindset doesn't have to be an all-or-nothing choice. There are many degrees to which funding can be outcomes oriented, with prizes, AMCs, and SIBs at the far extreme.

The key question to ask is what can create the incentive for improved outcomes. If it's not realistic for a grant to be 100% outcomes based, can it be 10%? Or even 1%? Though 1% may sound paltry, if it comes in the form of an unrestricted bonus, it can be quite valuable to a nonprofit with limited general operating funds. And simply sending the clear signal that outcomes matter tends to focus minds. Many nonprofits are unable to shoulder the financial risk or working capital for a contract that is 100% outcomes based but can accept a smaller variable payment as part of a grant where direct expenses are covered.

Beyond the existing funding agreement, the potential for future funding can also be a strong incentive. Oftentimes, the association is implied, but vague. Publishing explicit performance criteria for subsequent awards can shift the risk-reward calculation for investing in improvements. Again, there can be a spectrum as to whether meeting the bar means guaranteed funding, likely funding, or eligibility for funding. In a sense, you could consider this a variation of tiered funding.

Third Sector Capital Partners, a nonprofit advisory firm focused on outcomes-oriented funding strategies, applied both of these techniques in its work with King County, Washington to improve timely access to outpatient mental health and substance abuse treatment. Working with 23 of its providers, the county set tailored performance benchmarks for timely intake and transition to routine care, then amended the existing contracts to offer a 2% bonus for meeting improvement targets. That's the carrot. The stick comes by 2020, when a greater portion of payments will become linked to outcomes and providers that are not meeting performance goals may no longer be competitive. By taking this staged approach to incorporating outcomes payments, Third Sector was able to cut its time to launch in half relative to other comparable projects.

These and other innovations in pay for outcomes will hopefully continue to simplify structures and lead to far broader application. The more we can move towards funding outcomes rather than activities, the better we can incentivize innovation and impact.

BLENDED FINANCE

In blended finance, public or philanthropic dollars can leverage greater amounts of private investment through mechanisms such as loan guarantees, subordinate debt or equity, risk insurance, currency hedging, and technical assistance. Historically, the predominant use has been in public–private partnerships for infrastructure projects such as energy, water, and transportation. Yet the same tools are becoming increasingly applicable, and needed, to fund social innovation.

As the business models for social ventures become increasingly hybrid, so must sources of financing. The Omidyar Network's *Across the Returns Continuum* report describes this graduated spectrum between fully commercial and purely philanthropic endeavors.[7] Today, many mission-oriented organizations are able to generate some amount of revenue. For them, relying solely on grants would dramatically limit how much they can raise, and thus grow. Yet to rely purely on service fees or private investment would push them towards less risky and more profitable markets, forgoing opportunities for deeper impact. There is a huge gap between the expected –100% return for grants and the expected risk-adjusted market-rate returns of +5% or more for most investments (see Figure 14.1). Financing mechanisms that can blend the two are the best option to support social enterprises that straddle both worlds.

When the perceived risk of an unproven model or market is too high to offset the anticipated returns, early-stage concessionary funding is invaluable. This was the case with USAID DIV's funding of Off Grid Electric that I described in Chapter Eight, in which grant funding helped validate a novel business model for selling to poor, rural households. Such innovations for seemingly less lucrative markets can be difficult to finance, even for impact investors seeking to

---

[7] Matt Bannick, Paula Goldman, Michael Kubzansky, and Yaesmin Saltuk, *Across the Returns Continuum*, Omidyar Network, November 15, 2016, http://omidyar.com/sites/default/files/file_archive/Across%20the%20Returns%20Continuum.pdf.

preserve capital. However, once the market opportunity has been demonstrated, private investors will follow suit.

Grants can also encourage larger corporations to enter markets they would otherwise overlook. In 2002, the UK Department for International Development (DFID) offered a £1 million matching grant to the telecom company Vodafone to develop a system for repaying microfinance loans via SMS. The resulting service, M-Pesa, has blossomed into Kenya's most important financial service and is used by over three-quarters of the adult population of Kenya, with transaction volumes now amounting to over 50% of GDP.

Even when a social venture can successfully raise private capital, incentives may be needed to ensure the most challenging markets – such as those that are poor and remote – are served. Unabated, market pressures will inevitably steer capital towards more lucrative opportunities. In Tanzania, DFID incentivized household solar distributors to invest in the underserved Lake Zone with performance payments for incremental sales that tapered off by 25% a year as the market became more developed. For Off Grid Electric and other vendors, the subsidy was the encouragement they needed to enter a market that had not previously been economically viable.

DONOR COLLABORATION

As with blended finance, when donors can combine their efforts towards shared goals, the results can be far greater than the sum of the parts. For recipients, coordinated funding can reduce the number of proposals, reports, divergent priorities, and ongoing touch points, freeing resources for more productive work. For funders, efficiencies can be gained through shared diligence, coordinated strategies, and greater leverage. A win-win for social good, but one that requires letting go of some control.

For the campaign to achieve marriage equality in the United States, I was fortunate to participate in one of the most successful donor consortiums, the Civil Marriage Collaborative (CMC). The

CMC was founded by a handful of foundations in 2004 to pool resources and strategically align grant making to advance marriage equality. Over 11 years, the CMC deployed $20 million in public education and advocacy grants at both the state and national level, magnified by an additional $133 million from many other aligned partners, ultimately supporting the work of thousands in achieving the freedom to marry in 2015.

If the donor partners had directed their grants independently, they would have likely made divergent decisions without the benefit of in-depth analysis on the quality of organizations, strategic importance, and potential for results. In contrast, by pooling those dollars with others, they were invested based on CMC's 10/10/10/20 strategy. The aim was to reach a tipping point nationally by funding effective organizations to achieve marriage equality in 10 states, civil unions in another 10 states, limited civil protections in yet another 10, and some degree of organizing in the remaining 20. Individual state selections were determined through a rigorous benchmarking process based on the baseline of public support, the capacity of state-level organizations, and the legislative landscape.

Sometimes donors, like those in the CMC, come together on their own. Other times, a compelling grantee can force the issue. As it grew, Bangladesh-based nonprofit BRAC became frustrated with the high transaction costs required to satisfy different, onerous requirements for reports, reviews, and meetings from each of its donors. After politely articulating its concerns in multiple forums, BRAC was able to bring together the funders for some of its largest programs into donor consortia – the first in 1989 for its Rural Development Programme. Each consortium committed to long-term funding under a single budget and standardized reports, reviews, and evaluations, sacrificing a degree of independent control and ownership for the greater good.[8] The resultant flexibility, agility, and long-term planning have contributed significantly to BRAC's success.

[8] Dirk-Jan Koch, "A Paris Declaration for NGOs?" *Financing Development 2008: Whose Ownership?* ed. OECD Development Centre (Paris: OECD Publishing, 2008), 62–63, http://dx.doi.org/10.1787/9789264045590-en.

Happily, given their immense benefits, donor collaborations seem to be on the rise. In Chapter Eight, we learned about two of the most powerful ones: Gavi, to increase access to immunization, and Blue Meridian Partners, to scale solutions for American youth living in poverty. In addition, Co-Impact was recently launched as a global collaborative to bring together philanthropists seeking to solve social issues at scale. Participants include the Rockefeller Foundation and a number of signatories of the Giving Pledge, including Bill and Melinda Gates, who are investing together in high-potential system change efforts for underserved populations in low-income countries.[9] I hope we will continue to see donors increasing their efforts to collaborate in the future.

A CALL TO ACTION

In their 2018 annual letter, Bill and Melinda Gates describe using their philanthropy "to test out promising innovations, collect and analyze the data, and let businesses and governments scale up and sustain what works. We're like an incubator in that way. We aim to improve the quality of the ideas that go into public policies and to steer funding toward those ideas that have the most impact." They go on to say, "If we don't try some ideas that fail, we're not doing our jobs."[10]

Even the largest foundation in the world recognizes that it is tiny relative to the spending of business and government. Foundations, philanthropists, and foreign aid will never be sufficient in themselves to address the world's needs. But, they have an outsized role to play in fueling transformative innovations when returns may be too low for markets and risks may be too high for governments.

[9] Olivia Leland, "A New Model of Collaborative Philanthropy," *Stanford Social Innovation Review*, November 15, 2017, https://ssir.org/articles/entry/a_new_model_of_collaborative_philanthropy.

[10] Bill Gates and Melinda Gates, "Our 2018 Annual Letter," *gatesnotes*, February 13, 2018, https://www.gatesnotes.com/2018-Annual-Letter.

To do so will require a new mindset and new tools. First, we need to recognize that our current interventions are insufficient to reach our goals and aspire to devise far better solutions that will bend the curve of progress. Second, innovation can only thrive if funders empower teams with light-touch incentives. This requires a radical rearchitecture of funding, in order to shift from supporting a linear model of plan–execute to a continuous cycle of test–iterate. Finally, foundations, philanthropy, and foreign aid can play an increasingly catalytic role by intentionally leveraging the larger pools of funding that are necessary to reach the size of the need.

As donors, you hold the keys to unleashing radical social change.

Chapter Thirteen
Making It Stick

If you're reading this book, you are clearly motivated to maximize your impact and scale. But what happens a day, a week, a month, or a year from now? Before the norms, habits, and culture of your organization reassert themselves, how do you move from theory into practice?

Adopting an entrepreneurial mindset is an important first step. Consistently applying it requires both a clear purpose and aligned incentives. Imagine you want to have a healthier diet. Knowledge of the basic tenets of nutrition is certainly necessary. Yet for most people, knowing what to do is not enough. Life interferes. However, maybe you have your annual physical and the doctor reports that your cholesterol is high or you're prediabetic. You better make changes, or you'll have serious problems. Now you have a compelling purpose and incentive – to lower your cholesterol or blood sugar and avoid a serious chronic health condition. Still, the day-to-day choices can be hard. Maybe your family and friends offer to cook healthy meals together and stop bringing cookies. Continual reinforcement can help you to build new habits and keep from slipping back into your unhealthy ways.

Lean Impact: How to Innovate for Radically Greater Social Good, First Edition. Ann Mei Chang.
© 2019 Ann Mei Chang. Published 2019 by John Wiley & Sons, Inc.

When organizations embark on a quest to become more innovative, they typically start by bringing in new skills, talent, and tools. This might include running an innovation workshop, hiring a new innovation team, or engaging experts on disruptive technologies. The basic tools and techniques can be taught or hired relatively quickly. But, then what? If staff is evaluated and rewarded based on their success in winning large grants or faithfully delivering on pre-planned commitments, then what is the message we are really sending? Without a more systemic transformation, those new teams and efforts can become marginalized and frustrated – while for the rest, it's business as usual.

A culture of innovation arises from measurable stretch *goals* that inspire, ongoing *incentives* that reward experimentation and learning, and entrepreneurial *people* who are willing to take risks. It's a rearchitecture of an organization, starting from its core. This may sound daunting, but this chapter will give you the practical tools to start this transformation.

CULTURAL BARRIERS TO INNOVATION

How to transform a traditional organization into a more nimble one is an age-old challenge. In the social sector, the muscle memory that develops from writing grant proposals and executing grant agreements can become deeply ingrained and permeate the culture. These habits continue to propagate as individuals join new teams. Even when more flexible funding is available, the familiar rhythms of grant cycles can still dominate.

With the enforced waterfall model of most grants, a comprehensive program design must be submitted in a proposal before work can begin. Everything must be thought through in advance and convincingly pitched as the best option. Thus, organizations become accustomed to creating detailed designs within resource constraints, then executing to that plan. Deep faith is placed in "experts" and solutions, which are in turn sold to donors as competitive advantages.

As we now know well, this is the polar opposite of lean thinking. At the end of a two-day workshop I led with one nonprofit, a number of the staff self-identified the biggest barrier as their own perfectionism. Whether identifying a problem, interviewing a customer, or deploying an MVP, they would hesitate to take the next step forward until they were confident they were on the right path. But, unlike a grant application, you don't only have one shot with Lean Impact. Experimentation and failure are natural parts of the learning process. Peter Murray, president of social enterprise incubator Accelerate Change has found that "Rapid experimentation can be jarring for organizations that are used to running proven models. Nonprofits don't like failing, even if they are failing fast and iterating."

In addition, given that many nonprofits are perpetually strapped for both time and money, particularly due to a lack of unrestricted funds, a scarcity mentality can easily take hold. There is always too much to do and not enough to do it with. Naturally, such an environment encourages a focus on juggling short-term needs rather than seeking long-term opportunities. As Doniece Sandoval, founder and CEO of Lava Mae, puts it, "Nonprofits generally lack a growth mentality, as they need to fight for every penny. This stifles their ability to be creative and constrains their willingness to take risks."

When I moved from the tech sector to the social sector, I admit that the most difficult adjustment for me was finding it no longer acceptable to question experts. Now I don't mean me questioning others, but rather others questioning me. In Silicon Valley, the ethos was to question everyone and everything with the belief that the best ideas arise when they are poked and prodded from all sides. Now, somehow I was considered an "expert" and very few people were willing to tell me when I was wrong. How would my ideas get better?

When global development nonprofit Pact started its innovation journey, it launched an online internal marketplace in which anyone could share innovative ideas. To determine the best ones to take forward, all staff was given the ability to vote proposals up or down. It quickly became apparent that given the collegial organizational norms, very few people were comfortable voting down ideas. Asking tough questions or critiquing peers was not part of the culture. Eventually, the crowdsourcing approach had to be abandoned, and the marketplace evolved into an online resource for sharing best practices.

Cultures are deeply embedded and don't change overnight. Superficial initiatives will quickly become subsumed by unstated norms. But when the core drivers themselves change, a culture will begin to shift and adapt in response.

CULTURAL TRANSFORMATION

Culture forms over time as a natural reflection of the incentives at play, along with the norms and systems that shape individual and group behavior. We can't shift a culture simply by putting up motivational posters or declaring a new set of organizational values. Rather, culture flows from the formal and informal reward systems that encourage or discourage particular practices.

To transform an organization, we need to rearchitect it from the ground up to reflect a new set of values and priorities (see Figure 13.1). This starts with reorienting *goals* to stretch us beyond our comfort zones and require a shift from business as usual. Then, *incentives* need to be aligned up and down the organization to embrace risk taking, experimentation, and data-driven decision-making. Finally, we must create a team of *people* with diverse talents who are willing to embrace change. The behavior of people is shaped by their incentives, which in turn reinforce the goals. We'll explore each of these layers in detail next.

To successfully instill a culture of innovation, change must occur at all three levels. If we attempt to induce a shift by introducing a few "innovative" people, without modifying the goals and incentives around which the current culture was formed, behavior will quickly revert to form. The results can be ephemeral or take hold only in pockets.

If changing an entire organization at once isn't feasible or desirable, the same approach can also be applied at the team or department

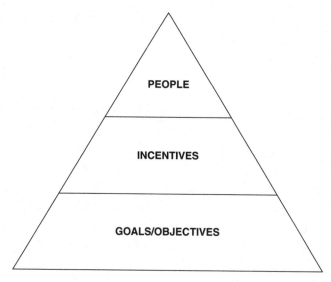

Figure 13.1   Drivers of cultural transformation.

level by instituting a different set of rules and rewards. Consider the formation of Defense Advanced Research Projects Agency (DARPA) as an agency under the US Department of Defense. In 1957, the Soviet launch of the world's first satellite, Sputnik 1, forced the military to recognize that its existing institutions were ill suited to advanced research. A new agency that could take risks on leap-frog technologies had to be built from the ground up, with an anticipated high rate of failure as part of its DNA. To do so, DARPA instituted a new playbook that included hiring program managers on fixed two-year terms to bring in fresh talent to take on ambitious endeavors with a relatively short fuse.

There are many ways to start your journey to establishing a culture of innovation. Summit Public Schools and Copia Global shared *The Lean Startup* book with their teams to establish a common framework and vocabulary. Watsi and New Story participated in the Y Combinator accelerator. The San Diego Food Bank was sponsored by the San Diego Foundation to participate in a workshop led by Moves the Needle. PSI brought in IDEO.org as a consultant. Many others have taken online courses from +Acumen. Each path brings slightly different emphases and tools, but all tap into an innovation mindset. What's important is making it stick.

Goals

There are the rare occasions (such as with the discovery of penicillin due to the accidental contamination of a petri dish) when innovation arises from a serendipitous discovery. Far more often, innovation is the result of a painstaking process of experimentation in pursuit of a clear goal. The story of Thomas Edison's development of the light-bulb is emblematic – over a thousand failed attempts before he succeeded. While others had produced incandescent lights, Edison had his sights set on identifying a filament that would burn longer and cost less. His goal wasn't to invent a lightbulb; it was to create a *commercially viable* lighting system.

Chapter Two covered the importance of a measurable, audacious goal. Whether it is to send a man to the moon or eradicate polio, a stretch goal motivates teams. The stretch part is critical. If you can come even close to reaching your goal with business as usual, there's not a compelling reason to take the risk of trying something new. I like to challenge my teams by asking, What would you do to be 10 or 100 times more effective or scalable? It's a good way to shift the discussion out of an incremental mindset.

Your audacious goal is the foundation upon which an innovative culture is built. It is the compelling need that makes innovation an essential, rather than discretionary, activity. Clear goals are important at every level – for the entire organization, each division, right down to the individual. These goals should cascade so that individual goals articulate how each person will contribute to the division's goal, and the division's goal articulates how it will help achieve the overall organization goal. The larger goals serve to keep the big-picture mission in mind, while the individual ones guide direct activities and trade-offs.

Be careful not to allow your goal to devolve into a vanity metric. I've talked with too many organizations that have inspiring and audacious missions, but the day-to-day focus predominantly revolves around how many people were reached and how much money was raised, without a clear connection to how those add up to transformational change. Particularly at the team and individual level, goals should center on innovation metrics – the unit level targets that are needed to achieve the overall objective, such as adoption rate, net promoter score, or unit economics.

At Google, we tracked goals using a system called OKRs (Objectives and Key Results) for every level of the company, with both a quarterly and annual review. "Objectives" defined the overall goal, while "key results" broke down the measurable progress for that time period. Typically, only three to five objectives were included to ensure focus on the most important priorities. At the end of each quarter and year, OKRs were self-graded with a score between 0 and 1. Unlike many other management-by-objectives systems, the expectation wasn't to score all 1s. In fact, those who met their goals regularly were encouraged to be more ambitious. Of course, a 0 wasn't a great showing either. On average, a score of 0.7 was considered ideal – indicating substantial progress towards a challenging goal. As the company recognized that the more you stretch, the more often you are likely to fail, OKRs were not used for performance ratings directly. Instead, they served as a tool for clarifying priorities and building alignment around shared goals. John Doerr's 2018 book, *Measure What Matters: How Google, Bono, and the Gates Foundation Rock the World with OKRs*, chronicles how OKRs have led to explosive growth at a wide range of organizations.

Incentives

Incentives are the substrate out of which culture emerges and takes hold over time. If you're not happy with the culture, look beneath the surface at what formal and informal signals are being sent. You'll find that most people behave quite rationally based on the incentives they encounter.

Some incentives are formally institutionalized through objectives, performance reviews, bonuses, promotions, recognition awards, and criteria for hiring and firing. As these have concrete repercussions, they tend to disproportionately drive behavior. Other incentives are subtler and are telegraphed through what leadership and colleagues highlight, discuss, and encourage. When the various incentives are inconsistent or in conflict, people can respond unpredictably, by being less than forthright or even passive aggressive.

To build an innovative culture, incentives need to shift from rewarding expertise, execution on predefined tasks, and hitting vanity metrics to rewarding learning, risk taking, and performance improvement. For change to take hold, this message must be consistently reinforced at all levels, both formally and informally. Many organizations give mixed messages without realizing it. Leaders may stand on stage, espouse the importance of innovation, and highlight some flashy examples. But what actually matters, as reflected in objectives, metrics, promotions, and informal cues, still revolves around raising money and executing plans.

I recently ran a two-day Lean Impact workshop with staff from Independent Sector, an association of nonprofits, foundations, and corporate-giving programs. Everyone was energized by the new, dynamic tools, but by the second day people started to wonder how they could keep the momentum, as all the normal workplace pressures resurfaced when they went back to work. Not only were participants concerned about their own time, but they also weren't sure their colleagues would be supportive of unfamiliar activities such as conducting interviews and running experiments. To reinforce the support of leadership, COO Victor Reinoso offered each team a reward if they met certain learning targets by continuing their interviews and experiments. Brilliantly, he also offered the entire organization a day off if all three teams succeeded, incentivizing everyone to pull together to establish a new way of working.

The traditional measures of success that are celebrated and rewarded tend to be *vanity metrics* along the lines of grants submitted, dollars raised, beneficiaries reached, and deliverables and compliance requirements met. But none of these give a meaningful indication of whether progress is being made towards the overall social mission. In contrast, *innovation metrics* track the unit-level characteristics, such as satisfaction, costs, or yields, which will shift the trajectory so that a stretch goal becomes achievable.

These innovation metrics may be one and the same as your value, growth, and impact success criteria (see Table 6.1 for an example). An improved net-promoter score reflects customer satisfaction that is likely to increase both ongoing engagement and word-of-mouth viral growth. Better unit economics, with lower costs and higher revenues, will enable an intervention to reach more people. And greater yields – whether in the form of income increased, test scores improved, or lives saved – indicate a path to mission fulfillment. Those metrics that matter should be tracked and measured in organization, division, and team objectives and reinforced on an ongoing basis.

Improvement on innovation metrics doesn't always proceed linearly, so shorter-term progress might measure the pace of learning for both teams and individuals. Are interviews being conducted, experiments run, and data collected? How quickly are hypotheses being proven or disproven? Are sufficient risks being taken so that we are seeing both successes and failures? Do we pivot quickly when the data indicates a particular path is unlikely to produce the results needed? These can also be set as objectives, reinforced in performance reviews, and celebrated in meetings to reorient the culture.

As a new culture takes hold, decisions will be driven more and more by hard data – from interviews with beneficiaries and stakeholders, results of experiments, or ongoing usage and feedback – rather than expert opinions. What is valued will shift from who you are and what you know to how eager you are to learn. The cofounders of Bridge International Academies believe that nobody's opinion matters, including their own. They didn't select the location of their first school on emotion or preference, but rather ranked two dozen countries based on five factors for success. Kenya came out on top.

Leaders must reinforce the values that underpin a culture of innovation visibly and consistently. They use data to make decisions, share information transparently, engage the best people irrespective of rank, encourage constructive risk taking, celebrate learning from both successes and failures, drive for continuous improvement, and adopt a bias towards action. Over time, these attributes will seep into an organization's norms, and a new culture will emerge.

People

Christy Chin, managing partner at the Draper Richards Kaplan Foundation, describes the characteristics of the most promising social entrepreneurs as data driven, curious, deeply respectful of beneficiaries, and driven by a sense of urgency to solve a problem. More so than in the private sector, humility stands out as an essential quality for tackling complex dynamics in communities that are not our own.

A culture based on the principles of Lean Impact is not for everyone. For those accustomed to the more consistent rhythms of the social sector, the pace of constant change may be too unsettling. Bridge International Academies has recognized the importance of hiring staff comfortable with change and iteration, given the ongoing experiments and improvements constantly being made in their schools. Yet finding such people can be difficult given the hierarchical business culture in Africa, where they work.

Transforming an existing culture can be far more difficult than creating a new one from the ground up. When CEO Mike Quinn introduced rapid prototyping at Zoona, a company in southern Africa that provides financial services to underserved communities, he met with some resistance. Many staff quickly embraced this new approach, but others reverted to their comfort zones. Over time, as more staff adapted and new staff was purposefully hired with a learning mindset, a new culture began to take hold. Mike recognized that in order to make Zoona a top place to work and accelerate the pace of progress, he had to raise the bar on performance and accountability. This included finding a compassionate way to make some tough choices and move poor performers out of the organization.

Any major change is disruptive, and not everyone will make the transition. I've heard similar stories from many entrepreneurial leaders who have been brought in to lead established nonprofits, one over a hundred years old. One way or another, a large portion of the existing leadership team turned over. Some weren't happy with the changes and opted out, while others couldn't keep up. The challenge comes not only from adjusting to a new way of working, but also the high standards of performance that are essential to delivering disruptive solutions. Those who may have coasted before suddenly need to step up or step out.

Beyond an entrepreneurial mindset, adding new and diverse perspectives to a team can expand the potential landscape of ideas, perspectives, and approaches. The increasingly hybrid composition of the social sector can be well served by bringing together the understanding of people and problems from nonprofits with the business models and fast-paced delivery of the corporate world. Other domain and functional expertise can further expand the range of tools a team can draw from, whether it be digital technology, behavioral science, marketing, scientific research, anthropology, or beyond.

In fact, Launchpad Central, an online platform created by Steve Blank and Jim Hornthal to support lean innovation, has found that across its database of more than 16,000 teams, the highest performing teams are also the most diverse. This includes dimensions of gender and ethnicity as well as subject expertise, such as bringing together engineers and MBAs. Jim believes a mix of different experiences improves the crucial ability for a team to recognize patterns from interviews, data, and findings. He likens it to a game of Boggle. If you turn the tray by 90 degrees, you're likely to see a completely different set of words that you missed before. Perspective matters. And, as projects rarely end where they begin, a team with perfectly tailored expertise at the start may not realize when a pivot outside their domain is required.

A WORD ON FAILURE

Innovation cannot exist without failure. And yet, failure is taboo in the social sector. During the time I was leading the USAID Lab, I asked my teams for an example or two of failures from their portfolio to use in an upcoming speech to aspiring social entrepreneurs at MIT. My hope was to highlight the role of failure in the innovation process, along with common pitfalls to avoid. At first, I received no responses. I asked again, but still no response. Only after some cajoling, badgering, and reassurance was I able to elicit a few stories. And, still there was wariness in sharing them at a public forum. Don't forget, this was the bureau created as a hub for innovation at the agency. Risk taking and celebrating failure was part of our charter. Yet, exposing our own failures, and those of our grantees, was still a bridge too far.

Again, it's the funding dynamic that fuels this dysfunction. The concern is that if an organization is perceived as producing anything other than a pure, unadulterated success funders will balk. As a result, the easiest path is to avoid failure if possible and obscure failure when it occurs. This risk aversion and lack of transparency frequently interfere with the experiments, learning, and pivots needed for Lean Impact.

Many organizations have sought to shift this cultural dynamic by celebrating failure. MoveOn, a grassroots progressive advocacy group, created the concept of a "joyful funeral" to honor risk taking, effort, and creativity, even when the outcome wasn't successful. Rather than bemoaning a failure, the staff would declare, "Yay, joyful funeral" and share the resultant lessons with the rest of the team. At one point, they even engraved the project name on a digital gravestone for the internal website. MoveOn considers killing projects essential to staying nimble and relevant, making space for even better ideas to emerge.

The fail faire, or fail fest, is a growing tradition that has also proven to be a popular outlet to laugh, learn, and celebrate what we learn from our failures. Some are standalone events, such as Wayan Vota's annual Fail Festival DC for global development, that bring together practitioners across organizations for fun, commiseration, and a shared mission to reposition failure as a badge of honor rather than a source of shame. Many more are entirely internal affairs, held regularly to surface lessons learned and build cultural acceptability.

We ran our own at USAID's annual internal conference on science, technology, innovation, and partnerships. While participants were often initially reticent, it was frequently the most popular session of the week. Having some well-known executives start by sharing their own failures set the tone and helped get the juices flowing. After hearing from leaders they respected and admired, everyone else felt it a sign of hubris not to share their own failures.

It is important to distinguish between a good failure (to be celebrated) and a bad failure (to be avoided). The good kind of failure is expected when we take a calculated risk to test our assumptions. When an MVP produces different results than we expected, it helps us learn, improve, and ultimately deliver greater social impact. If we always succeed, we're likely not taking enough risk or thinking out of the box. Good failures help us avoid bad failures (such as Tenofovir's trial or One Acre Fund's passion fruit rollout from Chapter Six), when we fail big and waste far more resources than necessary to learn a lesson. For both types of failure, sharing the experience openly is an essential part of learning.

Perhaps one of the most difficult times to take risks is in the heat of a humanitarian crisis. Yet, the International Rescue Committee (IRC), one of the largest humanitarian aid nonprofits, is seeking to do just that through its Airbel Center for innovation. As a recent article in the tech magazine *Fast Company* described: "In Silicon Valley, failure is worn as a CEO's badge of honor – proof that he or she has simply dreamed too big. In the arena of humanitarian aid, that notion is a luxury. Failure for an organization like the IRC can mean starvation, sickness, lives lost. But if the IRC can succeed in finding innovative solutions during this time of unprecedented crisis, it will demonstrate how important it is to take risks, even when – or especially when – so much hangs in the balance."[1]

---

[1] Matthew Shaer, "Inside the IRC: How A Visionary Aid Organization Is Using Technology to Help Refugees," *Fast Company*, November 21, 2016, https://www.fastcompany.com/3065447/how-a-visionary-aid-organization-is-using-technology-to-help-refugees.

If even talking about small failures is hard, acting on large ones is even harder. Recognizing that a program or organization is no longer delivering differentiated value and winding it down is an exceedingly rare occurrence. Instead, mediocre work tends to continue as long as funding is available. This serves to redirect precious resources to inferior solutions and undermine better options. Knowing when to let go or pivot, particularly in the face of strong personal attachment, is one of the hardest decisions for leaders to accept.

Embracing risk taking and failure can be a difficult, but essential cultural shift. In the words of Winston Churchill, "Success is stumbling from failure to failure with no loss of enthusiasm." For social innovation to deliver impact at scale, a new mindset must take hold. This means moving beyond quick wins to the deeper work of culture change. We need to architect our organizations from the ground up to move fast, take risks, be audacious, and relentlessly seek impact.

Chapter Fourteen
A World of Impact

We are at an extraordinary moment in the evolution of our society, a point at which charitable entities are increasingly embracing business-oriented approaches to expand their scale and impact, while companies are increasingly recognizing the need to balance profits with their benefit to society. As the two ends of this spectrum creep towards each other, new hybrid entities and financing have emerged from social enterprises to benefit corporations and from venture philanthropy to impact investing. Only by harnessing the best of both our hearts and minds can we create an ethical, inclusive, and prosperous world.

Research by Cone Communications has found that 89% of Americans would be more likely to purchase from companies that are associated with a good cause and 60% weigh social and environmental commitments in their investment decisions.[1] The millennial generation has particularly embodied this spirit, with a more integrated view of profit and purpose. Social values influence where

---

[1] Cone Communications, *2013 Cone Communications Social Impact Study*, 2013, http://www.conecomm.com/research-blog/2013-cone-communications-social-impact-study.

Lean Impact: How to Innovate for Radically Greater Social Good, First Edition. Ann Mei Chang. © 2019 Ann Mei Chang. Published 2019 by John Wiley & Sons, Inc.

they work, what they buy, and how they invest. Cone also found that 75% of millennials (versus 55% of the overall population) would accept a lower salary to work at a socially responsible company.[2] As the appetite for social responsibility has grown more sophisticated, simply associating with a cause is no longer enough. More and more consumers, employees, and investors are looking beyond corporate social responsibility (CSR) activities and expecting meaningful social impact as part of core business activities.[3]

All this interest has stoked demand for more organizations, financing, and solutions that meld profit and purpose. Yet despite some impressive outliers that have shined a light on the potential at the intersection of "doing well by doing good," the vast majority of institutions and funding remains trapped on one side or another of the historical dichotomy. As a result, the growing number of hybrid organizations struggle to obtain funding that matches their dual objectives. High-impact social enterprises can't raise sufficient capital to reach massive scale, while businesses that are able to access capital and grow quickly often only deliver modest social impact.

The reality is that our existing legal structures and funding streams were designed with either profit or purpose at the fore. Efforts to retrofit them for dual intent have cracked open the window for blending between the two, but still leave a wide gulf – the *hybrid gap* (see Figure 14.1). To fully realize our potential to improve the world in which we live, we will need better tools, entities, and financial structures so that *all* of our available resources can be harnessed for good. Corporations and investors should see making a contribution to society as a nonnegotiable requirement. Nonprofits and donors should see sustainable business models as essential for scaled impact. But beyond the natural evolution, we will also need revolution in the form of new hybrid mechanisms intrinsically designed to bring the best of both worlds together.

---

[2] Cone Communications, *2016 Cone Communications Millennial Employee Engagement Study*, 2016, http://www.conecomm.com/research-blog/2016-millennial-employee-engagement-study.

[3] Cone Communications, *2013 Cone Communications Social Impact Study*.

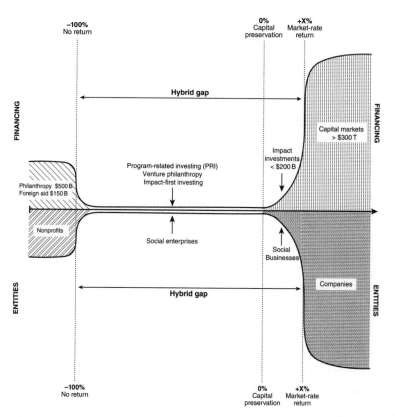

Figure 14.1   The hybrid gap.

TRIPLE BOTTOM LINE

As 2018 kicked into gear, Larry Fink, CEO of BlackRock, penned a bombshell letter to the CEOs of the world's largest companies. "Society is demanding that companies, both public and private, serve a social purpose," he wrote. "To prosper over time, every company must not only deliver financial performance, but also show how it makes a positive contribution to society."[4] Coming

---

[4] Larry Fink, "A Sense of Purpose," BlackRock, accessed April 22, 2018, https://www.blackrock.com/corporate/en-us/investor-relations/larry-fink-ceo-letter.

from the head of the world's largest global investment firm with over $6 trillion in assets under management, this could be seen as throwing down the gauntlet. The implicit implication was that BlackRock would back up this expectation with its prodigious dollars and shareholder votes.

Over the past few decades, more and more investors, customers, and employees have demanded that the companies they invest in, buy from, and work for reach beyond pure business goals to broadly benefit society as a whole. As a consequence, the notion of CSR has evolved dramatically, from brand-burnishing philanthropy that amounted to not much more than window dressing to an increasingly integrated and essential aspect of core business strategy. At the forefront are companies such as Starbucks, which has leveraged the heft of its purchasing and employment power to promote ethical and sustainable sourcing of coffee beans, hire from disadvantaged populations such as refugees and veterans, and minimize the company's environmental footprint.

This more holistic approach to doing business is referred to as the triple bottom line – creating value across profits, people, and planet. Although vast room for improvement still exists, we are already starting to reach the limits of the traditional corporate construct. Even the most progressive proponents must couch their social responsibility initiatives primarily in the language of profit, spurning short-term wins for long-term growth and sustainability by protecting workers, stakeholders, and the environment. When financial results appear to be compromised in any way, the backlash can be quick, as Unilever's CEO and long-time poster child for responsible capitalism, Paul Polman, discovered when he was publicly attacked for his good works when profits stalled.[5]

We must ask our companies to do more. Yet, today's corporate legal structures ultimately hold them accountable for maximizing

[5] Tom Borelli, "Unilever and the Failure of Corporate Social Responsibility," *Forbes*, March 15, 2017, https://www.forbes.com/sites/econostats/2017/03/15/unilever-and-the-failure-of-corporate-social-responsibility.

profits. Sourcing coffee beans from smallholder farmers living in extreme poverty works when it generates enough customer loyalty to offset higher costs. But what about those farmers living in even harder-to-reach geographies, lacking infrastructure, or requiring more extensive training? There is a limit to how far pure businesses can reach towards social impact. Later in this chapter, we'll explore how new structures could help push farther into the hybrid gap.

IMPACT INVESTING

Similar shifts in social consciousness are gaining influence on the investment front. On the lighter end of the spectrum are the now $22.9 trillion of *responsible investment* funds incorporating environmental, social, and governance (ESG) factors in their strategies, that have grown 25% in just two years to account for a total of 26% of all assets under management.[6] They typically take a "do no harm" approach by applying a negative screen to avoid companies that do not meet their stated criteria. On the more proactive end are *impact investment* funds, which incorporate a positive intent to generate social and environmental impact alongside a financial return. The Global Impact Investing Network's (GIIN) 2017 *Annual Impact Investor Survey* quantified at least $114 billion in impact investment assets.[7] In October 2017 the Rise Fund, an impact investment fund at private equity firm TPG Capital, raised a record $2 billion, bringing increased prominence and celebrity attention to the space. While there is no canonically agreed definition and the differences are a matter of gradation, in general responsible investing screens out

---

[6] Global Sustainable Investment Alliance, *2016 Global Sustainable Investment Review*, 2016, http://www.gsi-alliance.org/wp-content/uploads/2017/03/GSIR_Review2016.F.pdf.

[7] Abhilash Mudaliar, Hannah Schiff, Rachel Bass, and Hannah Dithrich, *Annual Impact Investor Survey 2017*, Global Impact Investing Network, May 17, 2017, https://thegiin.org/research/publication/annualsurvey2017.

companies that don't meet thresholds of good citizenship and impact investing affirmatively screens in companies that can deliver on desired social benefits. Both aim to encourage better corporate behavior by voting with their dollars.

These efforts should be lauded and expanded as they create incentives from the financing side for businesses to consider all dimensions of their triple bottom line. At the same time, they do little to close the hybrid gap. According to the 2017 GIIN survey, a full 84% of impact investors seek risk-adjusted returns at or close to market rate.[8] Almost all of the remainder target capital preservation at a minimum, leaving limited financial room to maneuver to maximize social and environmental impact.

The result is more and more dollars chasing the limited number of high-quality deals that can deliver both strong returns and meaningful impact. In its annual survey of the industry, GIIN has found that the top challenges identified have consistently been "lack of appropriate capital across the risk/return spectrum" and "shortage of high-quality investment opportunities with track records."[9] Impact funds too often compete for the same small pool of good investments while leaving businesses with submarket returns struggling.

Without any financial sacrifice, what additionality can impact investment contribute beyond what markets would do on their own? Former dean of Stanford Law School Paul Brest, who teaches courses on impact investing at the Stanford Graduate School of Business, is skeptical about whether the bulk of capital directed to impact investment truly achieves "investment impact." By his definition, "Having impact implies causation, and therefore depends on the idea of the counterfactual – on what would have happened if a particular investment or activity had not occurred." Concessionary investments can meet this bar by accepting lower financial returns or taking on higher risk. But non-concessionary investments, which are seeking

---

[8] Mudaliar et al., *Annual Impact Investor Survey 2017*, 46.

[9] Abhilash Mudaliar, Aliana Pineiro, and Rachel Bass, *Impact Investing Trends: Evidence of a Growing Industry*, Global Impact Investing Network, December 7, 2016, https://thegiin.org/research/publication/impact-investing-trends.

risk-adjusted market-rate returns, can only do so if they address market frictions that prevent ordinary investors from participating.[10]

Negative and positive investment screens can discourage bad behavior and encourage good behavior, within the confines of a profit-seeking envelope. But they don't go far enough to bring companies into underserved communities and markets in which risks are higher and returns are lower. So how can we better harness the growing interest and enthusiasm for investing as a tool for social good? We need to start by envisioning new, hybrid mechanisms for investments and entities that can move beyond the traditional split between nonprofit and for-profit endeavors.

CLOSING THE HYBRID FINANCE GAP

With the Rise Fund doubling down on the long list of impact investment funds promising market-rate returns, I've become skeptical that traditional financing can ever evolve to serve the full spectrum of the growing hybrid financing need. In reality, most existing funds accepting returns below capital preservation come from otherwise philanthropic sources – program-related investments (PRI) that are drawn from the same pool as grant funding at foundations or venture philanthropy and impact-first investments by wealthy individuals that amount to a more progressive form of philanthropy. Ashoka, a global nonprofit leader in social entrepreneurship, observes, "The current financial gap is at the stage when money required is too big for foundations & philanthropists, and too small and too risky for institutional social investors."[11]

---

[10] Brest and Kelly Born, "Unpacking the Impact in Impact Investing," *Stanford Social Innovation Review*, August 14, 2013, https://ssir.org/articles/entry/unpacking_the_impact_in_impact_investing.

[11] Caroline Le Viet-Clarke, "Unlocking Blended Finance for Social Entrepreneurs," Ashoka, September 28, 2016, https://www.ashoka.org/en/story/unlocking-blended-finance-social-entrepreneurs.

This schism is not surprising when I consider my personal finances. I have a pool of money set aside for my retirement, for which I'm trying to maximize financial returns to avoid going broke if I live to a ripe old age. On the other hand, I have another pool I've committed to charitable contributions, for which I'm seeking maximum impact and no returns. As much as I believe that the highest leverage opportunities for impact fall in the hybrid gap, I'm still reluctant to compromise the returns in my core retirement account by making investments at below risk-adjusted market-rate returns, even if they can deliver strong social benefit. I expect this is a simplified microcosm of the financial world at large.

So if it's unrealistic to attract significant investment further down the returns spectrum, how can we tap into these huge pools of private capital for social good, beyond the limits of screens to select companies that already have an investable profile? I believe the greatest expansion will come not from shifting expectations for returns, but rather from increasingly sophisticated forms of blending between investment and philanthropic pools. We are already seeing many such bespoke deals, some of which were described in Chapter Twelve. These are beginning to bridge the financing gap for everything from social enterprises to vaccinations to infrastructure in low-income countries.

Market-based funds seek opportunities that are deemed to offer a financial return commensurate to the risk of failure. When the degree of risk is considered too high or the anticipated reward too low, blended finance can bring in philanthropic capital and other submarket instruments to reduce the risk or enhance the reward, thus turning an uninvestable deal into an investable one (see Figure 14.2). Some common mechanisms include loan guarantees, technical assistance, risk underwriting, currency hedges, and first-loss or other subordinated debt or equity positions.

But, one-off deals will not scale. Transaction costs are high, deployment is slow, and recruiting and coordinating diverse players with different goals and timelines is incredibly complex. According to Cathy Clark, faculty director at the Center for the Advancement

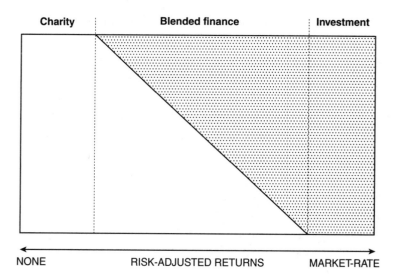

Figure 14.2 Blended finance.

of Social Entrepreneurship at Duke's Fuqua School of Business, "There has been a tremendous amount of experimentation around investment vehicles at the deal level, but less so at the fund level. In our 2017 scan of social enterprise financing deal structures, for example, we found 13 different investment vehicles in use to finance social enterprises around the world. Helping these vehicles roll up into robust investments at the fund level is one of the significant challenges for the impact investing sector over the next 5–10 years."

The time has come to learn from one-off successes and systematize mechanisms to pre-blend philanthropic and investment capital in a variety of gradations to scalably fill the growing hybrid gap. The result will be better leveraged donor dollars and expanded opportunities to deploy private capital in ways that can achieve substantial impact.

Blended Funds

One promising opportunity to bridge the hybrid investment gap is to blend across multiple types and sources of funds towards a common goal. Convergence was established in 2016 as a global network for blended finance with a deal marketplace, assistance in designing blended mechanisms, and extensive data and intelligence. It believes that by leveraging public and philanthropic funding, as much as ten times the private sector dollars could be unlocked. CEO Joan Larrea describes four archetypes for blended financing:

1. *Phased.* A spectrum of funding types are deployed over time based on risk and maturity, typically starting with the most concessionary options, such as grants, and moving on to increasingly market-based instruments.
2. *Technical assistance.* Grants or other risk-absorbing capital are used as a sidecar to offset higher transaction costs in a frontier market.
3. *Concessional capital.* Tiered financing tools, such as first-loss capital, junior equity, or debt, are included *within* a funding stack to offset risk in a more challenging market.
4. *Risk absorption.* Concessionary instruments such as loan guarantees, risk insurance, or currency hedges are deployed alongside a financing structure to offset risk in underserved markets or to demonstrate viability of newer markets.

For social entrepreneurs, navigating the disparate relationships, financial structures, objectives, and requirements for multiple funding instruments can be incredibly complex and time consuming. Each financing stack needs to be crafted to create a suitable vehicle based on the enterprise characteristics and available sources. This involves a degree of financial engineering that can distract from the core mission. Thus, blending finance at the investment fund, rather than the enterprise, level would be a more scalable and sustainable way to bridge market gaps.

One of the organizations Convergence has supported is Alina Vision, which aims to raise $300 million in grants, equity, and debt for a holding company that will build and scale a network of surgical eye-care centers. Employing a phased approach, the vehicle will deploy grants to explore potential markets, equity to establish new hospitals, and debt to scale ongoing operations. Having the full suite of financial tools available gives it the flexibility needed to effectively serve its social mission.

At USAID's Lab, the Partnering to Accelerate Entrepreneurship (PACE) initiative has sought to catalyze early-stage private investment by partnering with more than 40 incubators, accelerators, and seed-stage impact investors. For early-stage accelerator and seed fund Village Capital, a PACE grant served to offset the relative high cost of due diligence when making small investments, allowing management fees to be kept at a standard 2% and a resultant $15 million in private capital to be raised.[12] Another PACE grant supported Investisseurs & Partenaires to expand access to financing through three West African impact investing funds by preparing local entrepreneurs to become investment ready through skill building and hands-on support.[13] In both of these cases, grant funds served as technical assistance to unlock investment capital for markets that would not have otherwise been served.

The Global Health Investment Fund, a social impact investment fund for financing the development of vaccines and other medical interventions, is one of the larger examples of a blended fund that incorporates concessional capital. This $108-million fund, structured by JPMorgan Chase and the Bill and Melinda Gates Foundation, intends to deliver a return of 5–7% to its investors. To offset risk, Gates and the Swedish International Development Cooperation Agency have committed to covering the first 20% of any loss.

As a more generalized tool, GIF, partially funded by the Lab, invests donor dollars flexibly across the hybrid spectrum based on the unique needs of an organization. For example, Babban Gona is a

[12] USAID, "Village Capital: Democratizing Investments," USAID Partnering to Accelerate Entrepreneurship, accessed April 22, 2018, https://www.usaid.gov/sites/default/files/documents/15396/2017_PACE_Village_Capital_final.pdf.

[13] USAID, "I&P: Expanding Impact Investing in West Africa," USAID Partnering to Accelerate Entrepreneurship, accessed April 22, 2018, https://www.usaid.gov/sites/default/files/documents/15396/2017_PACE_IP_final.pdf.

for-profit company that sells end-to-end services to small-holder farmers in Nigeria through an agriculture franchise model. Emblematic of the increasingly hybrid nature of social ventures, it seeks to address many of the same challenges as the nonprofit One Acre Fund. To offset perceived risk, GIF provided concessional capital to Babban Gona in the form of $2.5 million of subordinated debt, which has served to catalyze over $18 million in additional loans.

While such investments enable GIF to test and build valuable best practices in hybrid financing, it also recognizes that far larger pools of funding would be available if it can also engage partners who seek capital preservation or a modest financial return. To meet this market demand, GIF is exploring the potential of raising private capital for a new investment vehicle to complement its grant fund.

Exciting progress has also come from a growing number of high–net worth individuals, particularly in Silicon Valley, who have established their philanthropic giving through a limited liability company (LLC) business structure rather than traditional foundations, including the Omidyar Network, the Emerson Collective, and more recently, the Chan Zuckerberg Initiative. While an LLC does not offer a tax write-off, it can deploy funds far more flexibly through a combination of grants, debt, equity, and other instruments. For example, Omidyar allocates both philanthropic and investment budgets for each of its initiative areas, enabling it to work with the most innovative and impactful organizations, regardless of whether they are nonprofits, for-profits, or somewhere in between. My hope is that these pioneers will become the new normal, and such hybrid quasi foundations will be recognized as the preferred means to maximize philanthropic impact. New legal structures that allow flexibility while preserving some of the tax incentives associated with foundations could further fuel their use.

Traditional financing mechanisms continue to fall behind the creativity of social entrepreneurs and new business models, leaving potential impact on the table. If donor collaboration and pooling can achieve outsized results, going further by leveraging the resources of private investment holds the promise for even greater benefit.

Outcomes Credits

Blended funds are one way to reduce the friction of financial engineering so hybrid investment deals can be done more efficiently, cheaply, and scalably. *Outcomes credits* could be a way to do the same at the transaction level when funding outcomes. Imagine a more flexible cross between an advanced market commitment and a social impact bond. A government or donor sets aside funds for the desired outcome, such as reducing teen pregnancies or school dropouts, rather than pre-designating an approach or entity that may or may not succeed. Any organization can be certified, if it meets the stated criteria, and receive payments once outcomes are validated.

Outcomes credits offer a financial "pull" incentive for nonprofits and businesses to achieve a range of desired social outcomes, such as improved health, education, income, and housing, based on the promise of a reliable revenue stream. Governments or other donors can set the price point for outcomes below their existing costs or anticipated benefits as a way to deliver more bang for buck. In contrast to a traditional grant, providers have the freedom and incentive to innovate, as improving value would win them more customers and reducing costs would benefit their own bottom line.

The pay-for-success experts at Social Finance have started to explore what appears to be a subsidy form of outcomes credit, which they call an outcomes rate card. In their scheme, the government sets predetermined prices for a menu of outcomes, then uses this rate card to contract with service providers. By standardizing the financial terms, deals can be put together far more quickly, cheaply, and transparently.[14]

Another related funding instrument comes from Roots of Impact in the form of social impact incentives (SIINCs). SIINCs use outcomes-based premiums paid directly to an enterprise to incentivize impact while keeping the overall business attractive on a risk-adjusted

---

[14] "Outcomes Rate Cards," Social Finance, accessed April 22, 2018, http://socialfinance.org/how-pay-for-success-works/outcomes-rate-card.

return basis. In one of the first transactions, SIINC payments were used to bring diabetes treatment and prevention services to the lowest income populations in Mexico.[15] Without the supplemental revenue stream, such demographics can easily be neglected by for-profit enterprises that, despite best intentions, need to show an appropriate degree of profitability to attract capital.

When the desired outcome can be directly associated with the provision of a product or service, outcomes credits could potentially be disbursed as vouchers directly to the target beneficiaries rather than the provider. This would empower the recipients with selection, preference, and dignity. As an example, if you are trying to expand access to electricity, you could give a voucher to rural households that offsets the cost of any certified home solar system, minigrid access, or electrical grid connection. In many ways, these vouchers are similar to food stamps, school vouchers, and Medicare accountable care organizations, all of which provide a form of government paid voucher to qualified individuals who can in turn choose among available providers.

NEW ENTITIES

Not only are existing investment tools ill suited for an increasingly hybrid landscape, but our institutional structures hold us back as well. I know many social entrepreneurs who have struggled to decide whether to incorporate as a nonprofit or a for-profit, sometimes even deciding to do both. For a nonprofit, the social purpose is institutionally enforced with the benefit of contributions being tax deductible. However, equity investments, lobbying activities, and the use of any profits are curtailed. On the other hand, for-profit businesses have full flexibility in their activities and investors, including in some cases accepting grants. But, the pursuit of profits has primacy over purpose, particularly when external financing is involved.

---

[15] "Social Impact Incentives (SIINC)," Roots of Impact, accessed April 22, 2018, http://www.roots-of-impact.org/siinc.

Into this void have risen the low-profit limited liability company (L3C) and the benefit corporation. L3Cs, based on the framework for LLCs, were first adopted by Vermont in 2008 and are now recognized in 10 states. More recently, the benefit corporation, based on the C-corporation framework, was introduced in Maryland in 2010 and has since expanded to 33 states. Both hybrid structures enshrine a company's intended public benefit alongside financial goals in its charter. As of April 2018, there were approximately 1600 L3Cs[16] and 5400 benefit corporations in the United States.[17] As a traditional C corporation is legally bound to maximize financial performance for its shareholders, any tradeoff of purpose over profits may be problematic. However, with a benefit corporation, executives and boards must balance between social, environmental, and financial factors.

Benefit corporations represent an important step in the right direction. Yet, while directors and executives are required to consider the social mission in decision-making, the benchmarks for profits are far more concrete and thus still tend to dominate. The B Corp certification, administered by B Lab, takes one step further in bolstering the mission side of the equation with rigorous standards and an independent validation of social and environmental performance. This sends a clear, positive signal to investors, employees, and customers who wish to see their social values reflected in their choices. Still, there is opportunity to raise the bar even more by moving from a requirement for generating some impact to one of maximizing impact, and put impact on par with the traditional imperative to maximize profits. An alternate approach is the UK community interest company (CIC), which requires any profits to be reinvested for social benefit.

Somewhat analogous to the use of LLCs for philanthropy, private investment companies have the flexibility to pioneer

---

[16] "What Is an L3C" and "Latest L3C Tally," interSector Partners, April 1, 2018, https://www.intersectorl3c.com/l3c.

[17] "Find a Benefit Corp," B Lab, accessed May 1, 2018, http://benefitcorp.net/businesses/find-a-benefit-corp.

new structures that further break away from the nonprofit and for-profit dichotomy. Yellowwoods, a global private investment group with a strong South African heritage, has in recent years incubated a number of social enterprises, including Harambee Youth Employment Accelerator, alongside more traditional companies that include the Nando's restaurant chain and the Hollard Insurance Group. Across its portfolio, all entities are required to seek both revenues and impact, running across the full spectrum from impact-first nonprofit social enterprises to profit-seeking businesses. This mix opens intriguing possibilities of beneficial synergies. For example, Nando's has been an early employer of Harambee's youth and Hollard is an investor in Harambee's first pay-for-performance impact bond.

We are only beginning to scratch the surface of entities that can operate effectively in the hybrid gap. More experiments are needed. Ultimately these will require new legal structures and tax incentives that can reduce friction for the new breed of social entrepreneurs who draw freely across nonprofit and for-profit funders, business models, and success metrics to maximize their scale and impact.

SMARTER GIVING

Whether or not you work professionally in the social sector, you are likely giving some of your time and money to organizations that are working to create a better world for all of us. Through each of these touch points, you can influence and demand paths to greater impact at scale.

Alas, in its 2015 *Money for Good* report philanthropic advisors Camber Collective found that while the average American family donates 3.6% of its income to charitable causes, only 9% compare nonprofits before giving. And, most make their choices based on name recognition rather than impact.[18] It should come as no surprise

---

[18] "Money for Good 2015," Camber Collective, 2015, http://www.cambercollective.com/moneyforgood.

that nonprofits respond to these signals by burnishing their brands and keeping overheads low rather than competing vigorously on the degree to which they can deliver cost effective impact.

The good news is that there are signs that these trends are starting to shift. New research from the UK Charity Commission found that over half of young people in the United Kingdom are making more informed choices by performing checks on charities before making a donation, compared to only 29% of people over 75.[19]

When you consider making a donation, do you ask the organization the simple question, Does it work? What experiments have been run to further increase social impact? Do the beneficiaries love and demand what is being offered? How will you reach the size of the need? What is in the research pipeline? How has cost effectiveness improved since last year?

In the same way that investors ask tough questions and demand strong financial results from companies, donors should ask tough questions and demand strong social impact from nonprofits. If enough of us direct our gifts to organizations that strive towards Lean Impact, our voices will reverberate and spark change.

IN CONCLUSION

We hold a shared responsibility to fight injustice, alleviate suffering, open opportunity, and nurture our planet so that we engender a world we can be proud to call home. Lean Impact starts with an audacious goal and then brings a Silicon Valley appetite for innovation together with scientific rigor and a business-like focus.

Radical social change rarely happens in isolation. It requires us to work across sectors and institutions to address the market and

---

[19] Charity Commission for England and Wales, "Young People Are Savvier and More Generous When Giving to Charity at Christmas," December 18, 2017, https://www.gov.uk/government/news/young-people-are-savvier-and-more-generous-when-giving-to-charity-at-christmas.

policy failures that keep us trapped in the status quo. It requires us to bridge the traditional paradigms of profit and purpose to embrace new hybrid mechanisms that bend towards social good. And it requires us to look at our own lives holistically and acknowledge the influence we have through our choices in work, purchases, investments, and donations.

There is no one right path to Lean Impact. What matters is setting our sights high, learning as fast as we can, and finding every possible way to maximize value, growth, and impact. In other words...

Think big. Start small. Relentlessly seek impact.

Disclosures

The organizations mentioned in *Lean Impact* have been selected based on their relevance to the topic, and I have not received any compensation for their inclusion. The quotes and stories I share are taken from my own interviews and experiences, aside from those with external citations. While I endeavored to confirm factual accuracy of all content, I maintained final editorial decisions over the presentation and framing.

I have in the past or present received financial compensation from the following entities mentioned in this book, either as an employee or consultant.

Google
Mercy Corps
USAID
US Department of State
Rockefeller Foundation
Independent Sector
UK Department for International Development (DFID)
Lean Startup Company
UNICEF
Bridgespan Group

I have relationships not involving any financial interest or compensation with many organizations in the book. Among these,

Lean Impact: How to Innovate for Radically Greater Social Good, First Edition. Ann Mei Chang.
© 2019 Ann Mei Chang. Published 2019 by John Wiley & Sons, Inc.

I have listed my more formal board, advisory, and volunteer affiliations below.

BRAC USA
IREX
PATH
Brookings Institution

Acknowledgments

This book is the culmination of a journey that began eight years ago as I started to contemplate a transition from my long-time career in the tech industry to dedicating the second half of my career to the pursuit of social good. There are innumerable people who have inspired me, taught me, supported me, invested in me, and encouraged me along the way.

First and foremost, I am deeply grateful to Eric Ries for his visionary book, *The Lean Startup*, which was the direct inspiration for *Lean Impact*. His ability to capture these important principles in accessible, compelling terms has established a new model for twenty-first-century entrepreneurship. I am humbled by the opportunity to bring these concepts to mission-driven organizations of all shapes and sizes. As I was contemplating my next steps after USAID, Eric's enthusiasm and unwavering support gave me the impetus to walk away from some exciting job opportunities to pursue this project. He has been incredibly generous in extending his brand, agent, networks, conferences, platform, infrastructure, and professional services for this new purpose. I had the pleasure of working with Eric at a startup 15 years ago, and am delighted that our paths have intersected again through this new endeavor.

I also want to extend my thanks to the Lean Startup Company, for welcoming me as part of the team and embracing Lean Impact throughout their work. Special thanks to Heather McGough, who has been a wonderful champion, along with Hugh Molotsi, Andy

Lean Impact: How to Innovate for Radically Greater Social Good, First Edition. Ann Mei Chang.
© 2019 Ann Mei Chang. Published 2019 by John Wiley & Sons, Inc.

Archer, CJ Legare, Julianne Wotasik, and Amber Hinds. And special thanks to Adam Berk, who has been my partner in designing and piloting workshops that combine his background in Lean Startup with new concepts from Lean Impact. In the social sector, we have a tendency to create too many siloed institutions, brands, and initiatives with minor variations that are inefficient, confusing, and can even work at cross-purposes. I've been delighted to have the opportunity to collaborate and build together towards this common vision.

I am also deeply indebted to Steve Blank, upon whose shoulders the Lean Startup approach stands. Many of the theories contained within *Lean Impact* can be traced back to his original insights and theories. I was also incredibly fortunate to build on the curriculum of his groundbreaking Lean LaunchPad class, as part of the teaching team (along with Amy Herr, Steve Weinstein, and Pete Dailey) for Hacking for Impact at the University of California, Berkeley in the fall of 2017.

The *Lean Impact* book also stands on the shoulders of Leanne Pittsford and Leah Neaderthal, who along with Christie George pioneered the Lean Impact movement and community in 2012. Their early recognition of this need led to conferences, minisummits, a blog series, and an online guide. Lean Impact was acquired by the Lean Startup Company in 2016.

I am so grateful to Christy Fletcher and Fletcher and Company for taking a chance on me, based on barely a paragraph describing the concept for this book, and representing me throughout the publishing process. I especially want to thank Sylvie Greenberg, who has so patiently and wisely coached me, as a first-time author, on everything from writing my book proposal to finding the right publisher to navigating all the vagaries of the often perplexing book industry.

At John Wiley & Sons, Brian Neill has been absolutely instrumental in taking my ideas and making them into the book you see today. He has been incredibly responsive to all my naive questions and helped me navigate all the big and small things needed to publish a book today. I also want to thank my editor at Wiley, Vicki Adang, for her invaluable guidance, feedback, and encouragement that helped shape the manuscript. Outside Wiley, I want to thank Adrienne Schultz for her assistance in line editing the manuscript on short notice and making it far more readable as a result.

I owe a debt of gratitude to Marcus Gosling, who designed the trademark ink swooshes for *The Lean Startup* and *The Startup Way*, and contributed the beautiful cover art for *Lean Impact*. I also want to thank the folks at Anagraph, including Rachel Gepner, Indhi Rojas, and Alma Alvila, for creating the figures you see throughout the book.

Of course, many people have been at the vanguard of bringing lean and related innovation approaches to the social sector for some time. Among the best, with whom I have had the privilege to learn from and collaborate with, are Tom Kalil, Kevin Starr, Sonal Shah, Jocelyn Wyatt, Buddy Harlan, Caroline Whistler, Sasha Dichter, Christy Chin, Dennis Whittle, Thane Kleiner, and Cathy Clark. So many of their brilliant ideas and insights are woven throughout this book.

At the heart of this book are the inspiring stories of social entrepreneurs, nonprofits, companies, foundations, investors, and their advisors who have blazed the path for the rest of us to follow. I am awestruck by the over 200 organizations and over 300 individuals who so generously volunteered their time, experiences, and lessons learned in interviews for this book. They are unfortunately too numerous to list here, but I want to extend my truly heartfelt thanks to each and every one of them. Choosing which stories to include was a painful task, and know that those who do not show up directly on these pages were still essential in shaping the ideas and framing for this book. I especially want to thank everyone at Harambee Youth Accelerator and BRAC for hosting me for extended visits.

I have learned that writing a book involves its own write–measure–learn feedback cycle. I am so grateful for all the people who generously volunteered their time to struggle through early versions of the manuscript and provide honest feedback that has dramatically informed and improved the book, from conceptual framing to typos. A huge thank-you to Chris Kirschkoff, Anna Chilchuk, Graham

Gottlieb, Anne Healy, Steve Weinstein, Sarah Revi Sterling, Caroline Whistler, Alicia Philips-Mandaville, David DeFerrenti, Kristin Lord, Cindy Huang, Lona Stoll, Cathy Clark, Sheila Herrling, Sonal Shah, Cynthia Martin, Stephanie Krmpotic, Andrea Kress, Fang Yuan, Elliot Susel, Marilyn Gorman, Adam Berk, Eric Ries, and Heather McGough. Despite running a half-billion dollar nonprofit as his day job, Patrick Fine takes the prize for the most detailed and comprehensive editorial feedback. I was lucky to have his unparalleled eye for bringing clarity to concepts.

Thank you to George Ingram at the Brookings Institution for being my champion and hosting two expert roundtables to discuss key elements of the book. I also want to thank all the esteemed participants who read advance chapters, offered their expertise, and engaged in lively discussions that made all the hard work seem worthwhile.

In addition to feedback on the book itself, a number of hands-on workshops played a significant role in shaping the content and framing. Thanks to TEDGlobal, Skoll World Forum, CCIC, Independent Sector, DFID, the Rockefeller Foundation, and InterAction for the opportunity to pilot test workshops of varying formats.

On a personal level, finding a path to connect my career in Silicon Valley to my desire to contribute in some meaningful way to ending global poverty was not at all straightforward. I can't thank Anne-Marie Slaughter, Melanne Verveer, and Neal Keny-Guyer enough for making an early bet on me, seeing the potential, and giving me amazing opportunities to learn and contribute. I would not be here without their unflinching sponsorship and support.

I am particularly grateful for having had the chance to serve in my dream job at USAID. Special thanks to Jennifer Anastasoff for recognizing the opportunity, Jim Watson for making it happen, Raj Shah for his audacious vision for the Lab, Gayle Smith for being a champion and advocate, Michele Sumilas for removing obstacles and keeping me on the right path, and the entire, awe-inspiring team at the Lab who are working tirelessly to transform global development. I will forever be grateful to Lona Stoll, who taught me how government works, told me when I screwed up, and has an encyclopedic knowledge of everything Lab, USAID, management, and innovation. While she was ostensibly my deputy, things always turned out better when I did what she told me rather than the other way around.

A final heartfelt thank you to my mom and my good friends who have unwaveringly supported and encouraged me throughout my life and the writing of this book. An extra shout-out to Barb Voss and Jan Zivic, who shared some invaluable tips and tools that made the process far more manageable than it might have been otherwise.

About the Author

Ann Mei Chang is a leading advocate for social innovation who brings together unique insights from her extensive work across the tech industry, nonprofits, and the US government.

As chief innovation officer at USAID, Ann Mei served as the first executive director of the US Global Development Lab, engaging the best practices for innovation from Silicon Valley to accelerate the impact and scale of solutions to the world's most intractable challenges. She was previously the chief innovation officer at Mercy Corps and served the US Department of State as senior advisor for women and technology in the Office of Global Women's Issues. Prior to her pivot to the public and social sector, Ann Mei was a seasoned technology executive, with more than 20 years' experience at such leading companies as Google, Apple, and Intuit, as well as at a range of startups. Ann Mei earned a bachelor of science degree in computer science from Stanford University.

Lean Impact: How to Innovate for Radically Greater Social Good, First Edition. Ann Mei Chang.
© 2019 Ann Mei Chang. Published 2019 by John Wiley & Sons, Inc.

Index

Page references followed by *fig* indicate an illustrated figure; followed by *t* indicate a table.